JOHNNY BOB

THE LIFE AND TIMES OF JOHN R. HARRELL OF LOUISVILLE, ILLINOIS

CARY O'DELL

AMERICA
THROUGH TIME®
ADDING COLOR TO AMERICAN HISTORY

America Through Time is an imprint of Fonthill Media LLC
www.through-time.com
office@through-time.com

Published by Arcadia Publishing by arrangement with Fonthill Media LLC
For all general information, please contact Arcadia Publishing:
Telephone: 843-853-2070
Fax: 843-853-0044
E-mail: sales@arcadiapublishing.com
For customer service and orders:
Toll-Free 1-888-313-2665

www.arcadiapublishing.com

First published 2022

ISBN 978-1- 63499-400-2

Typeset in 10.5pt on 13.5pt Sabon
Printed and bound in England

Acknowledgments

This book could not have been completed without the extraordinary candor (and courage) of the following people: John R. Harrell, Dion Davis, Angelyn Comer Garcia, Tod Harrell, Jeb Harrell, and Xon Harrell, as well as Lester Kellums, Mark Kellums, Johnny Leib, Codean Baker, Harold Leib, and Priscilla Laughton Hutton.

I would also like to thank all of the following for their invaluable assistance: Marceline Ambuehl, Dolores Ford Mobley, Tom Denton, Jean Bailey, Vicki Thompson, John Bayler, Evelyn Ford, and Kent and Rena O'Dell.

My personal thanks to Karmon Runquist and Mike Heintz.

Contents

Introduction:
Mansion on the Hill

The past is never dead. It's not even the past.

William Faulkner

Although I grew up in the northern part of the state of Illinois (Galesburg, to be exact), I spent a lot of my childhood and teens in Sothern Illinois, the part of the state often referred to as "Little Egypt." Both sets of my grandparents lived there, in the small town of Kinmundy, Illinois (pop. 900), and after my dad retired from his job in 1997, he and my mom returned to live in Kinmundy permanently.

Still, unlike most of the natives from that area, for all the time I spent there and all the people I knew or had heard of, I had never heard any mention of a man named Johnny Bob Harrell until one day, around 2013, when a friend of my mother's made a passing mention of him and this overgrown, Mt. Vernon-style home in the nearby town of Louisville, about 18 miles east of Kinmundy.

As I was at that time already writing a book on the onetime dome home of architect/designer/thinker Buckminster Fuller located in Carbondale, Illinois, I decided that another short article on this other unexpected small-town architecture might make an interesting addition. So, at first, that was how I began.

Originally, I thought I was just going to write about this house, this giant replica of George Washington's famed mansion, built for god knows what reason and that was now, somehow, still standing all this time later.

Yet once I began research into this house and the man who built it, a far bigger and far more interesting story soon unspooled. It was a story about a local man named John Robert (a.k.a. "Johnny Bob") Harrell who, in the early 1960s, along with building a giant architectural folly, once founded a religious "cult" and sheltered on his property almost 100 people including a military deserter. It was also the story of his property being stormed early one morning by a fleet of over 100 armed military and police officials who had come to reclaim that AWOL marine. It was also the story of this small-town eccentric who then fled from the law and was on the run with his family for eighteen months, who ended up in jail for four years only to later, after his release, reconstitute his home and his Louisville property into a para-military training facility to cater to doomsday-focused survivalists.

It was a story that unfurled like a novel.

Yet in the very beginning, there was one thing about his story that I could not find. I could find no mention of when Harrell died—no obituary or public document. For help, I turned to my cousin, Dolores Ford Mobley, who is an expert on genealogy, having explored and traced back every branch and twig of our family tree. I figured she, with her amazing research prowess, could unearth the info I was looking for. I called her and gave her all the information I had about this Johnny Bob Harrell. She said she would look into it. About a week later, Dolores called me. "Cary," she said, "I think he's still alive." Surprisingly, he was—alive and well and still living in Louisville.

So, in early 2015, I reached out to Mr. Harrell. We spoke. Later, we met. In time, I would talk extensively with Mr. Harrell, in person and over the phone. Then I would speak with some of his children, then with some of his one-time "cult" members, then some of the townspeople who lived through those chaotic days in the early 1960s. I even tracked down and talked to Dion Davis, the young, one-time AWOL marine whose presence on the property turned the Harrell saga into a national news story.

Nothing prepared me for the stories they would each tell, and nothing prepared me for how much I would come to like them.

1

Hallelujah

whatever
returns from oblivion
returns to find a voice

"The Wild Iris" by Louise Gluck

In keeping with an odd Southern Illinois tradition, where town names are often pronounced differently that they are spelled (for example, the town of Cairo is pronounced "Keh-ro," not "Ki-ro"), the town of Louisville is pronounced "Lewis-ville."

Louisville is located about 25 miles south of Effingham, Illinois, and about 100 miles east of St. Louis. The Little Wabash River flows along its east side. The town is the county seat of Clay County and has a population, today, of about 1,100—the highest it has ever been.

Louisville proudly claims a couple of famous former residents in its history, including baseball player Tom Richardson, who would go on to play in the Major Leagues in 1917, and John Riley Tanner, who served as the Governor of Illinois from 1897 to 1901.[1] However, the city's most infamous citizen is John Robert Harrell.

Depending on who you ask, Johnny Bob (as Harrell is often referred to) is either a great patriot and religious visionary or the disturbed former leader of a frightening religious cult; he is either a harmless eccentric or a very charismatic and dangerous man with a long history of exploiting people and breaking the law.

Harrell was born, at home, in Xenia, Illinois, on January 16, 1922. At a young age, he and his parents moved to Louisville into a still-standing house on the town's Garden Street.[2]

Although not born in Louisville (founded in 1838), his family had long staked a claim to the town. Johnny Bob was at least the third generation of his locally-prominent family to reside in Louisville.[3] His grandmother ran the town's general store in the late 1890s. His mother was Natalia E. Moore. She was a onetime school teacher in town, then the city clerk, then a US postal employee, and then a tax tabulator for the State of Illinois. She married Johnny Bob's father, Jerome Harrell, in 1921.[4] She gave birth to John Robert the following year, on January 16, 1922, and another son, Eugene, a year or so after that. Sadly, Eugene would not survive childhood, passing away at the age of two and a half.[5]

Johnny Bob's father, Jerome, worked in a variety of jobs, including auto sales, before he passed away in 1939.[6]

From an early age, Johnny Bob was seen as the town's "fair-haired boy" (and was later described in the press as just that) and as a major go-getter.[7] His first job was at the movie theater in the nearby town of Farina.[8] By his late teens, he was managing the local roller rink, and would purchase that business himself only a few years later.[9] "That Johnny Bob's going to be the first millionaire in Clay County," or so supposedly said the town's one-time real estate broker A. C. Thompson.[10]

Along with being hard-working and rather ambitious, Harrell was also quite devout. He came from a religious family and once boasted of his perfect attendance at Sunday school. Yet he said he was only truly "saved" when he was in eighth grade at which time he was baptized by the local minister in the nearby Wabash River.[11]

After graduating local high school (where Johnny Bob was captain of the basketball team), Harrell was able to go off to college.[12] First, he attended a junior college in Illinois' capital city of Springfield, then the University of Arkansas and, finally, he attended Indiana Tech in Fort Wayne. His major was the field of engineering.[13] Yet despite his attendance, he never graduated from any of the schools.[14]

Like most men of his generation, Harrell was pulled into the service during World War II. He served with great honor, eventually achieving the rank of lieutenant and becoming both a bomber pilot and an army flying instructor.[15]

During his military stint, Johnny Bob was extremely frugal with his monthly salary. Every check he got, he sent back to his mother in Louisville. By the end of the war, Harrell had amassed a nice nest egg for himself, and it was these monies which he later used for his first business deals.[16] Harrell was discharged from the military in 1945.[17]

That same year, in March, Harrell married his wife, Betty.[18] Auburn-haired Betty Lou Harrell, *née* Clark, was born in Flora, the seventh of nine children.[19] She was supposedly a decedent of Revolutionary War hero George Rogers Clark.[20] At one time, she was employed at the Flora Shoe Factory.[21] The Harrells were married on March 24, 1945, in Enid, Oklahoma, where Lt. Harrell was stationed at the time.[22]

After leaving the armed forces, Mr. and Mrs. Harrell returned to Louisville. He began his career in the junk business.[23] He also began a family. Mrs. Harrell gave birth to the couple's first child, a son, Tod Eugene, in 1947, the same year that the couple formally "rededicated" themselves to Christ.[24]

Along with Tod, the Harrells would soon have other children: Xon (often misidentified as "Don" in later newspaper articles) was born in 1951; the couple's first daughter, Cathy, was born in 1956.[25, 26]

In the late 1940s, Harrell made the acquaintance of a man named J. S. Kibler from nearby Olney, Illinois. Kibler had been tinkering with a new type of mausoleum construction.[27] This new tomb type provided non-underground internment but was far more affordable than more traditional mausoleums; in fact, it was even supposedly $300 cheaper than a "normal" below-ground burial.[28] Intrigued by the man's idea, Harrell purchased the concept and quickly patented it with the U.S. government.[29] After the mausoleum style caught on in southern Illinois, Harrell began to franchise the blueprints nationally. His patent was rumored to have earned him millions.[30] A mausoleum based on Harrell's patent is located in a Louisville cemetery. Another is present down the road a bit in a cemetery in Kinmundy.

For Harrell, business was so good that, eventually, he had to construct a brick building on a very large tract of land he owned just north and east of the Louisville's town square. This building, once emblazoned with a large sign that stated "Harrell & Company," is still standing and is still owned by the Harrells. It has served a variety of purposes over the years. First, though, it was the headquarters of his mausoleum business and was staffed by his mother and various "office girls."[31]

With his mausoleum money, Harrell began to buy up local land and property.[32] He also founded his own construction firm. One of his most enduring buildings is located on Chestnut Street (formerly Sailor Spring Road) in Louisville. This building, constructed around 1954, is a rather large structure, with seven rooms inside, nine front-facing windows, and a large, over-hanging porch with the porch roof supported by four thick, square, white pillars. After this building was built, it was rented to a federal agricultural agency. It would later become the office building for Harrell's construction company and eventually Harrell's personal home.[33]

In time, Johnny Bob Harrell would turn himself into a major property and land baron within southern Illinois. Along with the roller rink and a local motel on nearby Highway 45 which he built, he also either built new or bought apartment buildings and other structures in Louisville or in neighboring towns. In Kinmundy, Harrell owned several buildings as well as for many years the Kinmundy Bank building.[34] In Farina, he owned the town's movie theater for a time.[35] At the height of his career, Harrell was said to have owned over 2,000 acres of land throughout various Midwest states.[36]

Along with his real estate holdings, Harrell diversified into other businesses including automobile sales.[37] Harrell also became the owner of some very profitable oil wells over in Indiana.[38] In regard to the "luck" he had in finding oil, Harrell said it was the Lord Himself who guided him, saying, "The Lord has told us where to drill for oil and we have never had one dry hole yet."[39] With his mother, Harrell also ran a busy sporting goods company, selling, among other things, rifles through the mail.[40] He was also, at one time, the owner of a plant for the manufacture of cement blocks.[41]

By the 1950s, Johnny Bob Harrell was Louisville's largest employer, with over 100 people on his payroll.[42] He was also, easily, the town's wealthiest person. He was also a respected community leader with membership in the town's Chamber of Commerce and in the local Rotary Club.[43] Additionally, he was the director for the local district of the Boy Scouts and was also a member of the city's school board having been elected to the post in 1958.[44] For a time in the late 1940s and early 1950s, Harrell even wrote a weekly column, titled "You Are What You Think," for the local newspaper; written anonymously, its themes were usually faith and patriotism.[45]

Despite the Harrell Family's relative wealth, though, Tod, Harrell's eldest son, says that though "We lived better than most others," the family was far from "high society" due to his father's very frugal nature. The family also moved frequently—often inhabiting various properties of their father's until he sold them or rented them right out from under the family.[46]

The family's modest living was no doubt an outgrowth of Harrell's profound faith. Since being "saved" in the eighth grade, Harrell's religious fervor had steadily been growing more and more intense. In 1947, he claimed to have experienced his first direct encounter with the Holy Spirit.[47] The Spirit, he said, visited him and his wife for three hours one evening in their home; it was a profound experience that forever deepened his belief.[48]

At times, Harrell's religious zeal was so strong that it intersected with his business interests. None of his businesses were allowed to be open on Sunday, not even his motel.[49] Those ideals, and his growing concerns about communism, even began to seep into his addresses at the weekly Thursday meetings of the local Rotary.[50] At one 1959 Rotary speech, Harrell alarmed many when he suddenly went off on a tangent:

> This town is overrun with Communists. There are Communists right here in this assembly that on a given day will overrun and take over this county. US currency will be of no value. A woman cannot walk

down the street of the square in Louisville without being insulted by whoremongers wearing ties.[51]

As can be surmised, Harrell and his family were very active in their local church. Of the town's four churches, the family attended Louisville's Methodist Church. Still standing today, the Louisville Methodist is located at 435 Chestnut Street, not far from the town's main square. At the time, the Methodist Church possessed the largest congregation of any church in town, often attracting as many as 250 worshippers every Sunday.[52]

Along with serving as a lay leader, Harrell was also the church's Sunday school superintendent, taught Sunday school, was a member of the church's financial committee, was the head of its "Pastoral Relations" committee, was a song leader, and was also on its Board of Trustees.[53] Harrell also personally footed the bill for many of the church's activities; when a new two-story educational expansion building was to be built for the church in the 1950s, he provided both the funds and the necessary labor.[54]

Harrell was a major mover and shaker within the church—sometimes, it seems, to the consternation of others. He had a forceful personality with more than a bit of braggadocio. In his powerful position, Harrell frequently took to the pulpit himself, augmenting or extending the sermon given by the church's pastor. It was in these sessions that Johnny Bob began to perfect his skills of oratory, skills that were impressive and persuasive to many. After Harrell spoke to a congregation in Kinmundy, he proved so impressive that his appearance was even written up in the local newspaper:

> At the first Johnny Bob said that he was no speaker but before he had finished, his listeners were of the opinion that he was a very able speaker.... We are of the opinion that few will forget his message very soon.[55]

A later reporter who witnessed a Harrell "performance" described it too:

> The tall, handsome [Harrell] had "stage presence" and was platform-wise. He gave the audience a sly smile and stood without moving on the podium. His voice was soft and caressing and he had the knack of seeming to look straight into the eyes of each woman in the room. His voice was clear and warm. Deep down inside, every female in the audience was sure he was talking, with his terrible sincerity, directly to her.[56]

Yet it was not just women who became enraptured.

Reverend A. Vance Comer was a very smart and accomplished man. Born in 1918, Comer was a native of Oklahoma. He had earned two bachelor's degrees (in music and American history) and a master's degree (in music), all *magna cum laude*, before obtaining his divinity degree from Asbury Theological Seminary in Asbury, Kentucky.[57] He was also fluent in several foreign languages.[58]

Comer would become a well-known and beloved part of the Methodist community in southern Illinois. He served for many years as the minister for the Methodist Church in Kinmundy, Illinois, beginning in 1952. He was also a regular fixture at the annual Southern Conference of Methodist Churches.[59] One year, at the conference held in Granite City, Illinois, Comer met John R. Harrell.[60] The men struck up a quick friendship. Their friendship would endure for all the years Comer was preaching in Kinmundy.

Also in Kinmundy at that time was Lewis J. T. O'Dell (the author's grandfather). He served for many years as superintendent of schools in Marion County, the county that borders Clay County to the west. Along with living in Kinmundy, he worshiped at Kinmundy Methodist where, for many years, his pastor was Rev. Comer. At times, after Comer met Johnny Bob, Comer would borrow chairs from the Kinmundy High School for the upcoming annual conferences. The elder O'Dell would also often volunteer both his youngest son, Kent (this author's uncle), and the family truck to help transport the chairs to Louisville. Kent O'Dell recalls, "The entire way over, all Vance would talk about was Johnny Bob."[61]

After departing the Kinmundy church in 1956, Comer was transferred to a church in Lebanon, Illinois.[62] The Comer family, which included his wife, Avelyn, and young daughter, Angelyn, would reside in Lebanon for a year before Comer was transferred to Louisville's Methodist Church.[63]

Comer's transfer to Louisville, in 1960, may have been influenced by the power wielded in the area by Johnny Bob. Later, in print, Johnny Bob would boast that Comer's reassignment to the church in Louisville was very much of his doing, but done "under the guidance of the Lord."[64]

Successful, wealthy, and locally renowned, it made perfect sense that John R. Harrell would be the one asked to give the commencement address to the graduating class of Louisville High School on May 29, 1958.[65] Yet even that was not Harrell's highlight for May. Just a week or so earlier before his high school speech, Mrs. Harrell gave birth to the couple's fourth child. A boy, he was named John Lance and, so as not to be confused with his father, was usually called "Lance."[66]

Yet for all those occurrences, it is what would happen next to Johnny Bob, only a few days later, that would change him and Louisville for decades to come.[67]

Johnny Bob and his eldest son, Tod, had just returned from a trip to D.C. (father and son flew there in one of Harrell's personal planes; Harrell owned two by this time), when, over the next few weeks, Harrell began to rapidly lose weight. Then, later that same month, Harrell noticed a lump on the side of his neck. At first, he was unconcerned; it was no more than the size of a kernel, but in time, it began to grow larger. That, combined with recent feelings of unending tiredness and his sudden, unexpected weight loss, made Johnny Bob pause.[68]

As his wife and two of the Harrells's young children had just faced their own medical issues, Johnny Bob was no stranger to going to the doctor. Growing concerned about the growth on his throat, Harrell went off to see his physician, Dr. Wattlesworth, located in the nearby town of Olney.[69]

Wattlesworth quickly referred Harrell to a throat specialist at the Carle Clinic located in Champaign, Illinois.[70] At the clinic, according to Harrell, he was examined by two Mayo-trained doctors, a Dr. Lore and a Dr. Cooley.[71] The two physicians advised Harrell to immediately have the mass from his neck excised. Harrell would relate later:

> It took about an hour and a half. They started down here by the Adam's apple and ended up close to the left ear. As we were talking if it was cancerous, they said they didn't hardly think it was but some of these things you don't know about...[72]

By the time Harrell returned to the clinic a week or so later to get the stitches from his neck taken out, the biopsy of the mass—"about the size of a walnut" now—had been completed. It was not good news. It was cancer of the lymph system (which Johnny Bob would later call "the most dreaded of all cancers"). The clinic's diagnosis was, again according to Harrell, later confirmed by the Mayo Clinic in Rochester, Minnesota, and by the Armed Forces School of Pathology ("wherever that is," Harrell later joked), where Mayo also sent their lab results.[73]

In his fight against his cancer, Harrell seemed open to just about any approach. He wrote later, "First of all, I was ready to do whatever medical science said," but also added, "I asked the Church to pray for me" and he also went to see two locals who specialized in faith healing.[74]

The first faith healer was Mag O'Dell (no relation to the author), a woman out of Flora, Illinois. According to Harrell, "Aunt Mag," as she was called by all, was "little, short, black-haired" and "a woman of God." She was known for her religiously-based healing powers. She anointed Harrell's head with an oil and prayed for him after he came to her with his cancer diagnosis.[75]

On the recommendation of Rev. Comer, Harrell also went to see a man by the name of Brother Evans.[76] "Brother Evans" was J. O. Evans of

Mason, Illinois. A onetime prosperous farmer, Evans quit farming after answering a call from God and turning, instead, to faith healing. In his new "practice," Evans saw "patients" at his home or at his office in Iuka, Illinois. He also traveled extensively, performing healings.[77]

On the verge of starting radiation therapy, however, Harrell decided to follow some of the actual medical advice he was given and journey to the famed Mayo Clinic located in Rochester, Minnesota.[78]

Choosing not to fly, Johnny Bob and his wife, Betty, departed by car from Louisville for Rochester on Monday, January 11, 1959. Harrell reported to the Mayo Clinic on Tuesday morning for his first meeting with his consulting MD, Dr. R. S. Fontana. Harrell also began a battery of tests and X-rays to discover the extent of his cancer and its "parent" source. Harrell related that the exams went on for two days; "It seemed like to me they were going to punch a hole right through me," he later said.[79] Finally, Harrell completed the necessary tests and waited out the days until the results could be analyzed.

On the following Friday, Johnny Bob and Betty returned to meet with Dr. Fontana at the hospital. Dr. Fontana said, "We've found some trouble in the left kidney area. This must come out and come out immediately."

Harrell responded, "Do I have any other choice?"

The doctor replied, "You have no choice at all. It is very urgent. It should be done immediately."

But even with the surgery being performed imminently, the Mayo doctor still had other devastating news. Even with the removal of the cancer, Johnny Bob still did not have much time to live—precious little time, in fact. At most, the doctor said that Harrell might have only sixty days of life left.[80] This exchanged occurred on January 16, 1959, Johnny Bob's thirty-seventh birthday.

For their indefinite stay in Minnesota, Johnny Bob and his wife had procured a room at one of the motels near the clinic that specifically catered to Mayo patients and their families. Later, they changed hotels to be closer to the area's Catholic hospital where Johnny Bob's surgery was to be performed.[81]

After they received their horrible news, Mr. and Mrs. Harrell retreated to their motel. As was the couple's custom, after dinner—their room came equipped with a kitchenette—the Harrells sat down at the dinner table and began to read the scriptures.[82] That evening Johnny Bob drew particular comfort from Psalms 91:4: "Under His wings He shall protect you...." Yet Harrell said later, "I couldn't read it. I just choked up and finally closed the book."[83]

Later that night, Harrell made a phone call to Rev. Comer advising him of his upcoming surgery and asking for both his prayers and the prayers of the church. "Preacher," Harrell said, "Be sure and pray, for unless the Lord steps in, they are going to cut me open Monday morning." Shortly after hanging up, Harrell and his wife began to prepare for bed. But first, as was also their custom, the Harrells knelt by their bed to pray aloud.[84]

> We started praying. I prayed awhile and the longer I prayed the better I felt and the worse I felt.... That's just the way I felt. I got smaller as I knelt by that bed. It just seemed that I shrank.... I became like a lone blade of grass and whichever way the wind blew, I swayed with the wind, which was the Spirit. Then all became calm.[85]
>
> ... All at once, when I got into that condition, God's Spirit fell from the celling of that room! He enveloped my whole body! It was like somebody took a barrel that had one end out of it and shoved the whole barrel over me, and the bottom of the barrel hit the top of my head. The single impact was so strong it seemed to recess my head down into my shoulders. It was so rough, rugged and powerful![86]

Harrell went on and exclaimed later, "God's spirit walked through the door, just walked in! ... The whole room was dynamically electrified and seemed to shout the power of His Presence!"[87]

As Johnny Bob continued to pray, he felt the power of the Lord's great healing being dumped upon him again and again by the "bucketful"! Later, the Presence became so profound that it tussled the bodies of both him and Betty.[88] Harrell later shared:

> [It was] a rushing force that pushed us, just shoved us! My wife fell into me, I fell into a table stand and I knocked the stand, with the table lamp, into the wall! The lamp almost fell off the top of the stand. We lay sprawled on the floor. ...
>
> I grabbed my throat, and before I choked out, I told my wife, "The Spirit is in my throat!"
>
> ...all at once, it exploded, like a bomb, and it ran out all through the flesh, electrifying the whole neck area. Then I could breathe again.[89]

Harrell would go on to tell of other details of that night:

> "His Being has an unseen glow as white as driven snow."
> "The prison bars had fallen! I was free!"
> "I knew now how Jacob felt when he wrestled with the Lord!"
> "[He had] the combined force of a million Niagara Falls."
> "He is grandeur, honor, glory, nobility, splendor, pomp, circumstance, preeminence, joy unspeakable, and love sublime."[90]

Later, Harrell would find himself sitting on the bed, the toes on each of his feet "burning."[91] Harrell then noticed the clock in the room. Last he had recalled, it was 9:30 p.m. but now, the time was 12:30 in the morning.[92] Exhausted by the experience, the Harrells fell into a dead sleep only to be awoken three hours later—the Spirit had returned.[93]

Once again, Harrell and his wife were devastated by the Presence of the Lord! Harrell conveyed later, "This went on and on; this was at three-thirty, and at four-thirty, still the same thing."[94]

Harrell would go on to explain that the experience might have been so intense because not only was the Lord in visitation that night, so was the Devil. These two forces seemed to be fighting over Harrell's cancer with Johnny Bob nothing more than helpless flesh being pulled between the two of them.[95]

By morning, after a long and unforgettable night, though, it was the Lord that was the victor.[96] That next morning—Saturday the 17th—Johnny Bob awoke to find his face horribly swollen. He said, "My eyes looked like little pin points in a couple of big mud holes."[97] His visage was so swollen, in fact, that he spent the first hour of the day with ice compresses pressed to his skin.[98]

It had been a long night. Still, the couple tried to center themselves in normalcy; they were due back at the clinic at 9 a.m.[99] Johnny Bob met with Dr. Fontana again. At the appointment, Harrell began calmly, "Doctor, have you time for a story?"[100] Johnny Bob related his experiences of the night before, but despite Harrell's riveting account of what he had gone through, Dr. Fontana attempted to press forward.

"Your condition is still serious," the doctor said. Fontana wanted to schedule the surgery but Harrell told him that he was going back home to Illinois.[101] Although Harrell promised to be back in touch, Johnny Bob said, deep down, he knew he would never return to Minnesota and that he would never need to.[102]

Harrell had been healed. He said, "God burned from me all disease as though He were a raging Celestial fire!"[103] To date, there is no record of any cancer surgery of any kind ever being performed on John Harrell.

Johnny Bob knew that what had happened was special, remarkable. He said later that he believed it was also for a reason. Harrell came to believe that he was meant to be a messenger for the Lord unto, among others, Dr. Fontana. Harrell wrote, "There was some purpose for me being at Mayo's when this happened, else the Lord would have healed me earlier."[104]

Later that Saturday, John and Betty left for the long drive back to Louisville. Harrell wrote later, "We drove into Illinois, stayed all night at a motel." Once again, the Lord made his presence felt. Harrell wrote, "The Lord graced that room practically all night, just sweeping back and forth as a giant dove. The closer we got [to] home, the better it was—the closer, the better."[105]

According to Johnny Bob, he never had to see another doctor of any kind regarding his cancer (of the lymph system or anything else) ever again. In fact, evermore, the Lord continued to heal him. He said, "When I was going up there [to Mayo's], I had another lump coming on the other side of my throat.... That one is gone! My blood pressure is down to normal, the pain has left, and everything is all right."[106] Later, Harrell would say that that evening the Lord even cured his wife's allergies.[107]

Only one week after his healing and his return to southern Illinois, Harrell began to speak publicly of his miraculous healing experience. He began each of his talks with a simple, powerful declaration: "Until a few weeks ago, I had cancer in the lymph system."[108] The story that Johnny Bob told, and the passionate way in which he told it (e.g. the Lord "like a tornado!"), was, of course, a crowd-pleaser and soon Johnny Bob was in demand to retell it often.[109]

After making his first "appearance" at the Methodist church in Louisville on February 23, 1959, at the request of its pastor, Joseph Evers, Harrell soon fanned out to other churches— "tiny roadside chapels that dot the cornfields," as one person put it—as well as clubs and community groups in other areas.[110] For example, in July 1959, he spoke in the nearby town of Mt. Vernon.[111] Before the end of the year, there would be over 150 other speaking engagements which Harrell traveled to by way of car, train, or plane.[112]

No matter how far he had to travel, Harrell always refused to be compensated by any of the churches or reimbursed for any of this travel expenses, a fact that was also often noted in newspaper accounts about his appearances.[113] He believed the message he was delivering was too important, and to the standing room only crowds that often came to see him, it was.[114]

Harrell's story, according to one later journalist, "Made Harrell a virtual messiah in this Bible Belt Country."[115] His story was too important not to share with as many people as possible. Hence, in October 1959, a full written account of Johnny Bob's healing was "published" by the Herald Press of Louisville, Kentucky.[116] The finished, softback monographic was titled *The Manifestation of God in the Healing of John R. Harrell*. It was forty-three pages long. The brown-colored paper cover featured the illustration of an eagle in flight. The inside front cover, meanwhile, featured a photo of a handsome, suited, and distinguished-looking Harrell.[117]

Though the text was written by Rev. A Vance Comer, who also provides a short introduction to the book and who calls Harrell's story "most remarkable," the content within the booklet is a straightforward transcript of the oral testimony or sermon that Harrell delivered many times from the pulpit and the podium. This particular address was from a February 1959 meeting of the Methodist Men organization of the Clay City Methodist Church.[118]

When *The Manifestation* is read today, it is easy to see why Harrell, both the man and his message, were a hit with so many. Harrell's speaking manner is quite approachable and he even becomes downright folksy. Relating a story about Aung Mag, Harrell adds, "[She always] ties her hair up in a knot (I don't know whether she glues it, wires it or how she holds it up there)."[119] Later, talking about the Mayo Clinic, he says, "They tell me they have eight hundred doctors; I didn't count them."[120] He even reutilizes the old joke of a mortician "burying his mistakes."[121]

Later, after recounting the full experience of him and his wife that night in Minnesota, Johnny Bob brings his story to a powerful climax and concludes it all as a bit of a rabble-rouser: "Won't you let Him have His way in your heart? You've been nice to talk to: I appreciate it! Remember, Christ is the answer!"[122]

Interestingly, sometimes the things that Johnny Bob says in *The Manifestation* seemed to predict things in his own future. He says at one point, "I'm not against big houses, big automobiles nor anything else."[123] As mentioned, the cover of the booklet bears the illustration of a soaring bald eagle, prefiguring Harrell's later incarnation as an avowed "America First"-type patriot.

Harrell's powerful testimony and the publicity that he got around his story seemed to begin to greatly influence others. In 1962, he said that, after his healing and his holy visions, many others in the church and those he preached to also began to have visions and be healed, miraculously, from various ailments even though Johnny Bob did say at the time, "I am not here to put doctors out of business."[124]

Unfortunately, some people seemed to take those visions of theirs too far, yielding a tragic byproduct. Inspired by what Harrell experienced and preached, at least two others in the Louisville area decided that they too would let God heal them as opposed to traditional medicine. One was an older man with a heart condition who decided to forgo his prescribed medication. The other was a young woman, an epileptic, who stopped taking her insulin. Both later died.[125]

Even though Johnny Bob never advocated their actions, many locals still blamed him for their deaths. It would be one of many things that Harrell would eventually stand accused of.

Sin City

I navigate according to no star
I strike a match and watch it burn…

"Elegy for My Mother" by Richard Katrovas

In his miraculous healing, Johnny Bob Harrell had been given far more than just a second chance at life and a second career as a mesmerizing public speaker. For surely if Johnny Bob had been saved, he had been saved for a very special and important reason. Later, Harrell would say, "This case was not a normal experience, but one which is termed as a Bible experience which happens only to those who have a work of considerable magnitude cut out for them."[1]

After his alleged healing, Johnny Bob claimed that he was now receiving instructions and visions from the Lord on a near daily basis.[2] Also, the most urgent prophecies he was receiving were about the imminent threat that the nation was under from both heathenism and, especially, communism.[3]

In his weekly sermons to his own church and to the churches he traveled to and to various local groups, Harrell began to regularly give impassioned sermons about the evils of the encroaching Red Menace. His infamous Rotary club speech was delivered in May 1959.[4]

The threat of communism weighed heavily on many people's minds at this time, and had for many years. Though by 1959–1960, full-bore McCarthyism had faded and been denounced by both high-ranking politicians (like former President Harry Truman) and the press, the Cold War was still raging and the House Committee on Un-American Activities was still in existence. It had only been a few years since the execution of Julius and Ethel Rosenberg for domestic spying. It was in 1960 that the U.S. convicted KGB spy Rudolf

Abel (the subject of the film *Bridge of Spies*). A fear of communism's insidious spread helped along by U.S. "pinko" sympathizers was still strong and its flames were fanned by all sorts of American-born propaganda. The so-called. "Red Scare" certainly convinced John R. Harrell, who became determined to draw out and cast out any sign of communism. He grew to believe that certified communists were rife in both the state and federal governments and were even thick among the citizenry of Louisville.[5]

Though Harrell had the full support of his church's new pastor, A. Vance Comer, the platform that Johnny Bob now had, and how he was choosing to us it, did not sit well with the church leaders of his state. When news of Harrell's holy crusade against the Reds reached them in Chicago, their headquarters up north, the Methodist organization continually asked Harrell and Comer to dial back their anti-communists tirades.[6]

Harrell, though, took those requests as a complete affront and as evidence of yet another insidious communist plot.[7] He then proceeded to denounce the church's national council for their liberal stance and activities. According to Harrell, not only were certain high-ranking officials corrupt, so, too, were many individuals in his very own church.[8]

In time, Harrell began to call out the sins of many of his own church's parishioners—accusing them of everything from communism to adultery.[9] Those accused though struck back, soon appealing to the church's governing body to remove Harrell and Comer.[10]

Later, Johnny Bob said that that, too, was a tactic. He claimed:

> Since I was Chairman of the Pastoral Relations Committee, in charge and representing the church on matters relating to its pastor, they by-passed me and went to the District superintendent, unofficially carrying stories, tales and sowing dissertation with the church claiming the congregation desired the pastor to leave and by far the majority were in favor of it—so they said. At the same time, they agitated for my removal from Sunday School Superintendent, which I had been for many years. The Communistic tactics of fear, rumor, apprehension and consternation were promised to the fullest.[11]

Obviously not everyone in the local Methodist congregation was in agreement with this new direction that their church was taking, but for everyone that spoke out against Harrell, just as many stayed true to Johnny Bob whose speaking skills, distinguished physical presence, and great sincerity gave him an extraordinary charisma. Even a one-time Illinois states attorney once said of Johnny Bob, "He's so darn intelligent, and has such a gift of gab, I used to tell myself, 'Better not listen, or he'll have you believing those crazy ideas of his.'"[12]

However, plenty of others did listen to him. Johnny Bob's fervor against communism convinced many that the Red Threat was very real and very close. Johnny Bob was able to convince so many, in fact, that it eventually created a divisive divide among his church's congregation. As Priscilla Laughton Hutton, then a teenager and member of the Methodist church remembers, "You were either for him or against him, no one was in between."[13]

Louisville, of course, had only 900 people in it and Harrell was the town's largest employer—as well as its most outspoken citizen. Everything he did made news and made news fast. Soon, Johnny Bob's campaign and powers of persuasion not only divided the town's largest church, they began to divide the entire the city of Louisville.

Though he had precious little concrete evidence behind him, Harrell nevertheless vehemently continued lecturing every Sunday about a communist–Louisville connection. In time, his pronouncements became far more grave, accusatory, and alarming. According to Johnny Bob, there were at least 100 fully fledged communists, organized in six communist cells, alive and living in Louisville—a steep percentage in a town of only 900 people. Moreover, these communists were not just anybody in town. According to Harrell, a local banker, a dentist, and an area chiropractor were all secret communists.[14]

Along with lurking in town and infiltrating the local schools and government, these communistic individuals were all—again, according to Harrell—indulging in all sorts of other untoward behavior. Some nights, according to him, they were even meeting, after midnight, on a Louisville street corner, to swap wives.[15] They were also spotted, or so someone said, haunting the streets late at night dressed in long capes and turbans.[16]

For every rumor that Johnny Bob created, though, just as many were started about him. A case in point is the often-repeated story that Harrell once bought and closed down the Louisville movie theater and boarded it up because he objected to the morality of the film it was showing.[17] Actually, that local theater was barely active already and was probably going to close when Harrell decided to purchase it. Further, he bought it not to show films but to have a prime piece of downtown Louisville real estate; he had hoped to turn it into apartments.[18] Still that rumor got started, and it stuck. That rumor was soon joined by others. Gossip—about both sides—flew over back fences and sprung up on the school playgrounds with stunning speed.

Without question, Harrell was a divisive individual, a lightning rod for controversy. Increasingly, everything bad and outlandish that ever happened in town (like the closing of the movie theater) was soon labeled the fault of Johnny Bob. However, for everyone who doubted Harrell and his claims, others believed, which started to create a stunning chasm among the citizenry. For example, the local states attorney was a great critic of Johnny Bob, but his office secretary was a supporter of his.[19] It is even said that differing opinions about Johnny Bob created friction in some local marriages.[20]

Eventually, neighbors grew suspicious of neighbors, and those who labeled Johnny Bob a crank were sometimes themselves discredited as just part of the problem Harrell was rallying against.

Meanwhile, nothing, it seems, could dissuade Harrell and his believers from their views about local communists, not even States Attorney H. Carroll Baylor, thirteen years on the job, who, ultimately issued a statement to try to calm the situation: "The FBI has check and so has state authorities. They found no communists here and none have ever been here."[21]

However, Johnny Bob Harrell was not backing down, and soon, he would have a platform beyond the church to share his views. He was about to enter politics. Politically speaking, Johnny Bob came from a distinctly conservative and Republican background.[22] As a young man, Harrell though leaned liberal and his stance on many issues got him labeled briefly as the "black sheep" of the family.[23] As he got older though, earned more money and had children, he began to move towards the right. It would be a drift he would never diverge from.

In September 1959, the then thirty-seven-year-old Harrell announced his candidacy for the Republican nomination for the U.S. Senate.[24] If he won the primary, he would take on incumbent Democrat Paul Douglas for the state senate seat.[25] Harrell would label characterize Douglas as "the most dangerous senator in America. He is a rank socialist to say the very least."[26]

Shortly after Harrell's announcement, Illinois newspapers began to introduce their readers to the successful down-state businessman who they described as a married father of four, WWII veteran, a commissioned officer, and aircraft pilot as well as the head of a business firm who was "engaged in several business endeavors including construction."[27] Most of the articles about his candidacy also recounted Harrell's miraculous Mayo Clinic healing story.[28]

From the start of his campaign, Harrell made his reasons for running perfectly clear. He stated that God had told him to enter the race and added:

> Our people have been deceived, defrauded, hoodwinked, cheated, robbed, pillaged and deluded by some of her so-called leaders into believing they can vote themselves rich with their own money when actually we stand at this moment on the brink of economic and Communistic disaster.[29]

Harrell's campaign slogan, printed on his campaign business cards and emblazoned on various giant highway billboards, was straight-forward: "Put God Back in Government."[30]

Such heavy religious rhetoric in a political race attracted many of similar beliefs but it also greatly antagonized those wishing to maintain a firm division between church and state. One local was quoted in the newspapers as saying, "Folk's [are] losing faith in religion what with the way religion is being used."[31]

In his 1970 thesis on Harrell, author Ronald A. Kramme notes that except for some locations downstate, Harrell's candidacy for political office was not treated that seriously throughout the rest of Illinois.[32] It got little financial support (Harrell footed the entire cost of the campaign himself) and he got no notable political party assistance.[33] The majority of Harrell's campaign took place in churches, largely steering clear of other sites of political discussion though he did take part in at least one debate which took place in Park Ridge, Illinois, in February 1960.[34] At that event, Harrell openly accused his fellow candidate, Warren Wright, of rampant dishonesty.[35]

As tends to happen in political situations, mud began to be thrown and tactics soon turned ugly. Harrell, himself, quickly became the target of crank telephones calls when strangers called up him or his family and stated such vile messages as "You have 24 hours to live!"[36] Meanwhile, every trip to the mailbox at their Louisville home brought with it a new set of threats sent to or left for the Harrell family.[37] Harrell labeled those and anything else done against him and his campaign as a "smear campaign" engineered by the local "Conspiracy Party."[38]

While some of these alleged "attacks" and smears against Johnny Bob might have been non-existent or exaggerated, others though were quite real. On December 7, 1959, someone called the Louisville grade school and said that a bomb had been placed in the school.[39] The unknown caller said it was the work of Johnny Bob Harrell.[40]

At the school, panic ensued as all the children were rushed out of the building. Meanwhile, parents, police and firefighters all rushed to the school grounds the moment word spread. People yelled "Johnny Bob is going to bomb the school!" as they ran door to door alerting others or ran to the school to rescue their children.[41]

Though ultimately nothing was found in the school building, the gossip had begun and the damage to Harrell's reputation was done. Retaliatory threats against Harrell and his family only increased as the day wore on. The threats became so great that eventually Harrell and his family had to barricade themselves inside their Louisville home for the remainder of the day.[42]

The next morning, Harrell (who was a member of the local school board) went to the school and met with its principal in an attempt to diffuse mounting tensions and repair the situation.[43] Later, Harrell said the bomb threat was "a carefully laid Communist trick."[44]

As always, the rumor mill kicked into high gear in the days after the bomb scare. One rumor had it that Harrell's own children were the ones who had warned their school mates about the alleged bomb.[45] Another rumor had Harrell allegedly withholding his children from attending school that same morning, a rumor that gave credence to Harrell being responsible for the bomb or at least the threat of it.[46]

Later, on the day of the 8th, Harrell was met at his home by the local sheriff. The sheriff was not alone. Accompanying the lawman was a psychiatrist who was introduced to Harrell as "Dr. Smith."[47] Harrell immediately doubted that "Smith" was who he said he was; some years later, Harrell would recount of that meeting:

> Then he asked me, "You are speaking out against Communism[,] aren't you?" I informed him, I most certainly was, after which the so-called Dr. Smith laughed and informed me that he had been all over the State of Illinois and that he had never seen a Communist. He desired me to explain to him what one was whereby I called to his attention and explained of the low, vile and most Godless creed of slavery the world has ever known. At this explanation, the so-called Dr. Smith's face became flushed and red. He jumped to his feet immediately stating he had to leave. He was called to declare me insane, but he was caught off guard by my vivid explanation of a Communist. Perhaps it fit too well.[48]

Long after Smith's departure, Johnny Bob would continue to question the man's identity and his credentials. Harrell said, "Having gone through much vigorous training as a pilot in World War II and having known psychiatrists and psychiatric procedure, I quickly stated this man was not a bona fide psychiatrist but a fake!"[49]

Meanwhile, a new batch of rumors started to spread that said Harrell had been found "insane" by the doctor. However, it was not just that doctor that was questioning Johnny Bob's mental state. Also publicly calling into question Johnny Bob's mental well-being was prominent local Louisville businessman James Morgan. Jim and his wife, June, had once been very close friends with the Harrells (and Mr. Morgan was once even in Johnny Bob's employ), but Johnny Bob's recent fire-and-brimstone campaign had firmly placed them at odds.[50]

Mr. Morgan himself had suffered from depression and other mental health issues some years before and he believed he recognized in Harrell some of those same tell-tale symptoms.[51] The Morgans then began to circulate a petition, eventually signed by twenty-eight local citizens, asking for authorities to evaluate Harrell's mental state.[52] One of those who signed was, allegedly, Harrell's own uncle.[53]

Though outraged by the suggestion that he was not of sound mind, in response Johnny Bob nevertheless decided to address the issue head on and put it to rest. On his own and at his own expense, Harrell traveled to the Chicago area (specifically Niles, Illinois) where he allowed himself to be examined by a psychiatrist, Dr. David Busby.[54] Harrell stated at the time that he would reveal and abide by whatever findings Dr. Busby reported.[55]

According to Harrell, once he arrived at Dr. Busby's office, he subjected himself, for the next four days, to constant observation and "every test known to psychiatry."[56]

In the end, Dr. Busby concluded that Harrell was mentally sound. Busby even drafted a letter that stated his diagnosis. His letter read in part:

> It is my conclusion and professional opinion that at the present time Mr. Harrell shows no evidence of mental illness, there being specifically no psychosis or significant neurosis manifest. It is my further considered impression that he seems to be a man of high caliber and personal integrity.[57]

Hence, with that evidence in hand, in February 1960, Harrell, in Clay County Court, filed a libel suit against the twenty-eight signatories of the original petition, charging them each with libel. Harrell had, apparently, obtained a copy of the document as, in his suit, he named each of the twenty-eight. Those sued by him were Ray Summers, Vaughn Brown, Roy Dawkins, Jr., Ralph Taylor, Scott Moore, Loretta Garrett, Glen Harper, Jack Daugherty, Gilbert Lampe, Edna Mae Griggs, James Morgan, Ella Hastings, Aleen Headlee, James Dawkins, Jerry Tant, Dale Batemen, Larry Joe Burke, M. G. Green, Herman Garrett, Leland Bryant, Lois Harper, Royal Erwin, James Griggs, June Morgan, Ralph Hastings, Burhman Headlee, William H. Beare, and Berlin Bateman.[58]

In the suit, Harrell sought a total of $225,000 in damages.[59] A motion to dismiss the case was filed seven days after the original suit was filed.[60] Though the case was eventually dismissed, in November 1961, many of those originally named in Harrell's suit did have to go out and hire attorneys, something most of them could hardly afford.[61]

Even after the case was jettisoned, many of the signatories of the petition still lived in fear of retribution from Johnny Bob or his followers for years afterward. In his excellent master's thesis on Johnny Bob, written in 2004, the late Dain Garrett tells the story of how, years later, when the grandchildren of one of those signers cleaned out their grandmother's home, they found a dresser drawer with a false bottom, under which were documents and press clipping related to the Johnny Bob case and evidence that she was one of the petition's originators.[62]

Earlier, while he was in the Chicago area, Johnny Bob also took time to stop by the local office of the FBI to complain of the numerous threats he and his family were receiving downstate and to allege that his telephone line was tapped. Much to Johnny Bob's ire, the FBI never launched an investigation into any of his concerns.[63]

Despite the personal attacks and numerous setbacks, Johnny Bob Harrell continued on with his political campaign and his localized campaign against communism.

The news, rumors, and scandals that were being generated reached, not surprisingly, every corner of the town of Louisville. Codean Baker and her husband, Warren, were long-time Louisville residents and members of the Methodist Church. Like everyone else in town, they got caught in the crossfire. Mrs. Baker would later describe it quite succinctly: "The whole town went mad!"[64]

Despite a lot of negative press coverage and endless gossip, Johnny Bob still had his supporters and believers, especially in the Methodist church, where about half the congregation fully supported Harrell, his causes, and his radical views. However, those believers often got harassed themselves via crank phone calls and other bullying tactics.[65]

Meanwhile, those who criticized Harrell as, as one local once put it, "a crackpot on communism," started getting their own late-night crank phone calls.[66, 67] Whether the harassment was from actual church members or just some kids or others having fun, no one was ever sure.

Obviously, news of all this activity and controversy could not be contained within small town southern Illinois for long. In December 1959, Johnny Bob's pastor and close friend, Rev. Vance Comer, found himself summoned by letter to appear before the Methodist bishop in Chicago. The presiding body of the church had become concerned about the stories of faith healing and prophecy supposedly being generated out of Comer's Louisville parish.[68]

Though the reverend was very well-liked and respected within his church, his church's increasing focus on the communist threat was seen by many as being in conflict with church orthodoxy.

Though it was just Reverend Comer who was being summoned, Johnny Bob knew that the major issue was actually him. Hence, not long after, one Sunday, in church, with 250 parishioners in the pews that day and just prior to the Chicago meeting, Johnny Bob stood up in front of the Louisville congregation. Then and there, Harrell offered his resignation as

Sunday School Superintendent if that is what the congregation said they wanted. He then called for a standing vote.[69]

According to Harrell, only fifteen stood up to demand his resignation. Again according to Harrell, most of that number were individuals who themselves were guilty of many of the things that he and the preacher had recently been preaching against. Later, Harrell stated that of those who objected to him it was because "their plans were being upset and exposed."[70] With only fifteen people supposedly wanting Harrell's ouster, Harrell decided to remain with the church.[71]

Regardless of the (alleged) vote of confidence in Louisville, Rev. Comer and Harrell, as head of the church's pastoral relations, were still being called to Chicago.[72] For his and Comer's trip to Chicago, Harrell was joined on the trip by his wife and his son, Tod. Later, Harrell would categorize the meeting as little more than a witch hunt. With an extreme level of disdain, Harrell would lash out at the church elders that he and Rev. Comer met with, calling them a "Kangaroo church" and concluding that "the hierarchy of the Methodist Church was aligned with the local Louisville conspiracy."[73]

That meeting in the Windy City, at one time, became so heated that Johnny Bob would report later that things even came to fisticuffs. He reported, "the District Superintendent lost his temper, rose to his feet and seized both my arms [and] bent me backwards over the chair in which I was sitting."[74] Harrell would also later accuse the church powers of trying to have him committed to a mental hospital.[75]

Before Harrell and Comer left Chicago that day, the bishop made a decision and ordered Rev. Comer to cease all his sermons on the topic of communism.[76] The church hierarchy also—supposedly—tried to bribe Comer with a raise and a transfer to a different church if he would sever all his ties to Louisville. Comer flatly refused.[77]

According to Harrell, the Methodist organization gave Comer an ultimatum—agree to be reassigned to another church or forfeit his credentials.[78] Comer refused the church's offer. Allegedly, he said that the Lord had told him to stay in Louisville and continue this local mission. Shortly thereafter, Comer surrendered his church certificate before it could be revoked.[79] Later, Comer wrote a letter to the church's organization stating his reasons for abdicating. He wrote, "I would rather leave the Methodist Church and walk with the God than stay in it as a back-slider."[80] The following Sunday, when Comer attempted to enter the church in Louisville, he found himself physically barred.[81]

Though Comer seemed to be banned from the Louisville Church, Johnny Bob and his family were not. So, on December 20, 1959, Johnny Bob Harrell went to the church.[82] By that time, the church had not only lost its long-time and very popular reverend but it had been firmly split into two nearly-waring fractions: those who supported Johnny Bob and those who did not. It was a situation that had proved to be untenable to all.

That day, before the service began, Johnny Bob stood on the church steps and handed out copies of his letter from Dr. Busby "clearing" him.[83] Then, inside, Johnny Bob stood up and proceeded to make an announcement. He announced that we would be leaving the church for good to start his own church, a "church to warn about what was to come," he said.[84]

He then invited any and all members of the congregation who wanted to follow him. As one witness recalls, at that moment about half of those present—about 175 people—stood up and walked out, declaring themselves loyal to Johnny Bob.[85]

The newly hired pastor, Rev. Vaughn Brown (Comer's replacement), was schooled quickly in local church politics. Years later, he elaborated on the deep division within his congregation, "The people that stayed were more or less opposed to Johnny Bob and they probably were glad to get rid of the people who left with him."[86]

Harrell later declared, "You can't preach forcefully against Communism and stay in the church today."[87]

As Johnny Bob was splitting from his local church, he was also continuing his political campaign. During the months of January, February, and March 1960, Harrell traveled all over the state of Illinois, "flying, and driving thousands of miles, speaking to thousands upon thousands of people," according to him.[88]

Throughout all his whistle-stops, which extended all the way up to Illinois' Cook County, Harrell spoke—mainly in places of worship and always with his "terrible sincerity"—about the threat of communism and the urgent need to return God to government, explaining "the Lord God Jehovah was getting ready to move into the political arena and take wrong from the throne and remove truth from the scaffold!"[89]

Throughout his campaign, Harrell was constantly being asked about his mental health. He seemed to always be ready to show off Dr. Busby's letter and to let voters know that he was the only candidate in the race who had been certified in such a manner.[90]

Alas, on Election Day, April 12, 1960, Harrell lost the primary. In the final count, John R. Harrell secured only about 37,000 votes (in contrast, the winner, Samuel W. Witwer, got over 250,000 votes).[91] Harrell finished fifth in the six-man race.[92] The defeat was especially humiliating once the ballots were broken out by county. In his home county of Clay, Harrell's obtained only 315 votes, and if approximately 115 of those came from Harrell's own congregation, this meant he was only able to garner about 200 additional votes among every other registered voter in the region.[93]

At the time of his loss, Harrell blamed the rumors about his mental health for costing him the election.[94] Later, however, Harrell charged mass voter fraud and ballot tampering and stated that, in actuality, he had secured more votes than the other five candidates combined.[95] He also stated that the campaign had cost him personally over $20,000.[96]

Still, despite his defeat, as was becoming very clear to all by this point, Johnny Bob Harrell was not one to simply disappear quietly. Only days after his loss, Harrell announced that he was starting his own political party to continue his fight to reunite God and government and stop the spread of communism.[97] He stated that the Republican and Democratic parties were the same thing anyhow, essentially one party operating behind two fronts.[98] He said he was christening his new political party the Christian Conservative Party.[99] The party was united for "God and country against foreign obligations and against encroachment on individual liberties."[100] Under the banner of the new party, Harrell said he would run as a third party candidate in the senate election. His placement on the ballot however could only occur if he gathered enough signatures from registered voters to support him. The possibly of that happening was never doubted by Johnny Bob. He said, "The Lord will help me win the nomination!"[101]

Harrell further stated to the press at the time that the mystical vision he received to enter the race originally was still guiding him and leading him to victory. Harrell said, "I was told I was being sent to the Senate for work but I was not told I would win the primary." He added that his earlier defeat was only a "stepping stone" and that he had already had "numerous calls from influential persons all over the state supporting a [new] party."[102]

Years later, Harrell became philosophical about his election loss, seeing it as only part of the Lord's much larger plan. He said, "God told me to run but He never said I'd win… The Lord said I would win if certain things came to pass. They didn't."[103] Despite his loss, Harrell remained deeply concerned about the state of the state and of the country and about the still-thriving communist threat.

Along with his own political party, and now divorced from Louisville's Methodist church, Harrell also decided to found his own church which he named the Christian Conservative Church. Rev. Comer and those who had left the Methodist church would soon join him.[104]

Harrell later reported of his new endeavor, "The Lord then directed that a small country church approximately two miles east of Louisville, formerly known as the Coles Chapel Methodist Church, which I had purchased earlier, was to be repaired and opened."[105]

Harrell explained, "The Lord gave the name 'Christian Conservative Church' for a two-fold purpose—Christian for the meaning we all know,

'Christ-like'—Conservative to let it be known it was taking an active part in political affairs of the nation."[106] Later, Harrell announced that Coles was just the start—he planned to establish other CCC churches in the nearby towns of Kinmundy, Claremont and Shobonier, Illinois.[107]

The very first service for the newly-configured CCC was held on Sunday, July 10, 1960.[108] As would soon become the norm, Rev. Comer presided and preached that morning. After Comer's sermon, Johnny Bob would rise and also address the parishioners. As one worshiper would later recall, while Comer's Sunday sermons always addressed exclusively the teaching of God, Harrell's inevitably took on a far more political turn, usually focusing on the eminent dangers of communism and its presence within this very community.[109] Often Harrell's rhetoric was dire in its prediction—upheaval was coming and war will be waged. As he often warned, "the streets of Louisville will run red with blood!"[110]

Come on Up to the House

In my Father's house, there are many mansions.

John 14:2

Back in 1958, it was not just politics and communism that God was talking to Johnny Bob Harrell about. Among other things, the Lord also told Johnny Bob to start investing in gold and silver.[1] Then the Lord started to give Harrell fleeting and disturbing visions, visions of foreign armies marching through American landscapes—a result of communism's unchecked growth.[2]

Then, in one of his most ambitious and grand visions, Harrell said that God told him to build a new home—a massive mansion, modeled on George Washington's famous Mount Vernon estate only 20 percent bigger than Washington's original.[3]

As Harrell had already visited the real Mt. Vernon several times and was a great admirer of the nation's first president (Harrell claimed that he once received a vision of the nation's future just like Washington claimed to have had at Valley Forge in 1777), the Lord's instructions seemed to make a kind of logical sense to him.[4] This house was to be built on land alongside the north side of Louisville, the combination of two parcels that Harrell purchased from John Zink, Sr., a local businessman.[5] That property was already the site of the brown-brick building that served as Harrell's business office. The finished home on the expansive plot would become, Harrell originally said, the residence of him, his wife, and their children.[6]

As Harrell was already in the construction business, the building of such a massive abode was not as pie-in-the-sky as it might sound. First, Harrell reached out to an area architect that he knew, Leland O'Dell (no relation to the author). O'Dell researched the original Mt. Vernon structure and then drew up the first architectural plans for the home. Harrell would insist later though that much of the house's building was guided by God.[7]

Though one might assume that such a great manor would be purposely set off in a secluded area someplace, tucked away in the woods perhaps to add to its grandiosity, the (still standing) Harrell–Mt. Vernon manor actually is not. Though the home is not, technically, within the city limits of Louisville, the land is buttressed right up to the city line. In fact, the home is only about three blocks east from the city's central courthouse. On a clear day, one can stand at the end of Louisville's town square and see the rooftop of the Harrell house. The house's proximity to the town is probably something that, ultimately, added to some of the mutual fear that the home's occupants and the town's residents eventually developed for each other—they were both just so close.

In fact, every location that would become vital to the story of Johnny Bob Harrell in Louisville is startlingly close by. Not only was his estate a stone's throw from Louisville's main business district but the church he worshipped at was just down the road, a quick bike ride away, and the roller rink he owned no more than 1 mile from his Mt. Vernon property.

Harrell broke ground for the giant home in 1958.[8] Its placement was near the center of Harrell's large Louisville lot, more or less directly over where a thirteen-room ranch-style house had originally stood before burning to the ground a few years prior. The Harrells had been living in that home when it burned; no one was injured though the home was a total loss.[9]

To build the grand structure, Harrell employed his own construction company employees who worked on the home—with salary—during times they were not at work on other builds. According to Harrell, building the house became a religious experience for many of his carpenters who, shortly after they started on the job, began to relate stories of their own spiritual revelations.[10]

The real Mount Vernon, in Mount Vernon, Virginia, has twenty-one rooms; Harrell's larger version has twenty-four rooms spread out over three floors. Harrell would later boast that one room was more than 40 feet long. The house's main floor has seven rooms including a massive entryway that is anchored at one end by a large fireplace—ultimately, the home's only source of heat. The second floor—oddly, only accessible via an outside staircase—has ten rooms. The third floor is one large space. The observation cupola of the house (round, glassed in on all sides) is located at its tip-top and can be reached from the third floor only via a steep spiral staircase.[11]

The house also has a basement. As the home was built almost directly over the foundation of the previous ranch house that had stood there—and the basement to the earlier home was still intact—during the build, these two underground areas were connected by a tunnel. Then, like something out of a spy novel, the entrance to the old underground area was blocked by a bookshelf that could be swung open to reveal its entryway. It was never completely clear what this was meant to be—a fallout shelter, an overly indulgent pantry? According to Angie Comer Garcia, daughter of Vance Comer, who largely grew up on the property after moving to Louisville at age five, the underground vault, though hidden, was no secret; "Everyone knew it was there," she says.[12] This below-ground tunnel would later play a vital role in the Harrell saga.

In keeping with Harrell's original vision, the house was a direct (albeit larger) replica of Mount Vernon complete with bright red-colored roof, sixteen front-facing windows, double front doors and eight tall, square, and imposing-looking wooden posts that held up an over-hanging roof that sheltered the grand porch underneath.

As can be imagined, this mammoth house in the middle of a community that was mainly made up of small tract homes or farm houses eventually attracted considerable press attention. As the edifice of the home neared its completion in mid-1960, various area newspapers sent reporters and the story of Harrell and his new home, and the reasons he said he was building it, was widely disseminated. For example, Jim Doussard of the *Decatur Herald* reported:

> The political hopeful said he is building the house "because the Lord told me to."
>
> He said he does not know how much it will cost. "Say several thousand dollars," he said, "that ought to cover it."
>
> The home is on a 40-acre tract of land. To the north of the house is the Little Wabash River bottom and Harrell's private airstrip.[13]

Doussard reported that Harrell's finished home would contain over 10,000 square feet.[14]

Sometime later, Harrell would state that though the Lord had instructed him to build the house, he had not—yet anyway—revealed what its full, eventual purpose was to be.[15] Yet ultimately, for all its space and external grandeur, inside, the Mt. Vernon home of Johnny Bob Harrell was never fully finished. The home was never equipped with electrical wiring nor was it ever plumbed for running water. The home never acquired a proper kitchen. No doors were ever installed in the roughed-in doorways and though the upper floors were completed with wood flooring, the main level never acquired more than a subfloor.[16]

As work on the mammoth house continued, Sunday services of the newly-configured Christian Conservative Church proceeded as well. They were held at Coles Chapel. Though the country church was open to everyone, most Louisville citizens stayed away and Comer and Harrell proceeded only with their original core group, the ex-members of Louisville's Methodist.

With the erection of the house being done by Harrell's own company and the little country church a ways from town, few non-Harrell followers knew fully what was going on or why. Even Johnny Bob's near daily news coverage did not fill in all the gaps. Hence, what was happening at the church and in that fast-growing mansion often led to confusion.

The increasing isolation of Harrell's group and the rest of the people of the county soon got the CCC dubbed a "cult," a term Harrell strongly resisted. Meanwhile, the vacuum of information regarding the group and that house quickly got filled in—with rampant gossip and rumor.

One rumor stated that part of the house included a secret tunnel that was being dug from underneath the new house to the basement of the Louisville courthouse—with the purpose of the tunnel, never fully explained. Besides, Harrell would later call the local courthouse a "den of iniquity" anyway.[17] Another unsubstantiated tale involved the presence of various, huge snakes supposedly being kept at the big house, perhaps for use in religious ceremonies. Along with the alleged snakes, the grounds were also supposed be the home to a pack of vicious guard dogs, ready to pounce on any unwanted interloper. A big steel safe was supposedly located in the big house too in which Harrell had stacked all the worldly wealth of all his followers; only Harrell knew the combination. Harrell was also, allegedly, stockpiling dynamite and hand grenades. Another far more salacious rumor involved untoward sexual acts supposedly going on among and between church members; these particular rumors have always been vehemently denied by both Harrell and members of his church.

Others could not help but wonder how Johnny Bob, even with his personal wealth, was able to support his family, support the church, and build this giant new home.[18] No one could ever recall him ever doing any fundraising for his church.[19] Again, in the absence of any information, rumors flew and involved accusations that the church was running various mail order scams, placing ads in cheap magazines where people could mail in $5 to get a "Solar-Powered Clothes Dryer" only to receive a single clothes pin back in the mail, or they could send away for an authentic "Southern Fire-Starter," only to receive a single matchstick in return. Another alleged product was the "Guaranteed Insect Killer"—which turned out to be two small pieces of wood to smash a bug between.[20]

Yet despite the widespread and persistent nature of these particular rumors, no solid proof has ever been found to link the Harrell organization to any of these various scams. Still, even today, sixty years after the fact, these allegations cling tightly to the Harrell legend.

Some critics of the community assumed that Johnny Bob was simply bilking the savings of his followers, making them turn over all their assets in order to join the group.

At times, though, Harrell seemed to suggest via the press that he would welcome the influx of additional funds to fight the red menace. He said once, "Maybe some others of wealth will realize it's their country too and join in the campaign."[21]

In early 1961, God was, again, speaking to Johnny Bob. This time, He told him that he should use his church to spread even further warnings about communism. Hence, in the early months of 1961, Harrell announced that we would be personally sponsoring various guest speakers to come and speak at Coles Chapel to educate the populace about communism's great and dangerous reach. One of his first speakers, speaking on three consecutive nights, would be Kenneth Goff.[22] Goff was a minister and social advocate who Comer had met a few years prior at a church conference in Colorado.[23]

By 1961, Kenneth Goff was already quite famous, and notorious. A one-time member of the U.S.'s Communist Party (1936 to 1939), he later became a rabid anti-communism crusader. In 1939, he testified in front of the Dies Committee and later proudly boasted that his testimony saw to the dismissal of 169 federal employees for alleged communist ties. In 1951, he was arrested in Colorado (where he headed his own church, the Soldiers of the Cross Tabernacle) for seizing and slashing a Russian flag that was being displayed for United Nations Day.[24, 25] In 1954, he published a book titled *Hitler and the Twentieth Century Hoax*, which denied that the Holocaust ever occurred.[26] He also spoke out from time to time on the dangers of fluoride being put in the water supply, saying that that, too, was a communist plot as were attempts at racial desegregation.[27]

In early 1961, Harrell invited Goff to Louisville. It was an invitation Goff accepted. The first night of the speaking engagement was set for the evening of Monday, February 20, 1961.[28] The title of his lecture was to be "Moscow's Master Plan for Conquering America." The second night's topic was to be "Brain Washing in Schools and Colleges," and Wednesday's talk was titled "From Communism to Christ: My Life Story."[29] For those nights, nothing out of the ordinary was expected, but for those who were coming to see Goff that first evening, it would turn out to be a terrifying and unforgettable evening.

It was just after dusk and members of Harrell's flock had barely exited Louisville to get to the Goff lecture at Coles when they encountered a deeply disturbing site. As they neared the bridge, just before the church, they saw something hanging there off the bridge's scaffolding. It had the form of a person—a dummy, an effigy. The stuffed, life-sized figure was covered with crudely drawn swastikas and had an arrow piercing its chest.[30] Though no one knew who the effigy was supposed to represent, there was little doubt what it was meant to do—it was to warn and scare off anyone coming to see Goff.

Though quite young at the time, Angie Comer, daughter of Vance Comer, who delivered that evening's opening prayer, still vividly remembers the drive to the church that night and the fear and uncertainty that shrouded the church after everyone arrived.[31] Despite that foreboding sight, a crowd—a "capacity" crowd according to Harrell—went on to the church to hear Rev. Goff give his first night presentation.[32]

Immediately after Goff's speech, Johnny Bob got up and stood in front of the congregation. For their safety, Harrell invited everyone in attendance to come back to town and to spend the evening at his large estate. He assured them they would be safe there.[33]

That evening was the first time that people used Johnny Bob's property as a refuge, but Johnny Bob's Mt. Vernon home only offered a partial peace. As the night wore on, the home began to be barraged with crank phone calls and cars driving by on the road outside, their tires squealing, their passengers yelling from them. Sticking together, the churchgoers felt protected as they bedded down for the evening inside Johnny Bob's large (but unfinished) Mt. Vernon mansion. As the home was still not yet equipped with electricity, most of those who had come to the house slept on the first floor near the home's large fireplace to stay warm on that cool February night.[34]

As many of the church-goers bedded down at the estate, Harrell and Goff made their way to the local sheriff's office to file a complaint. At the courthouse, however, Rev. Goff was no more warmly received than he had been at the church. Local lawman Walter Welch said that there was little he or his office could do; no one could identify any of the marauders.[35]

Later, Goff would state that he was forced to undress and empty all his pockets and that he was physically threatened while inside the courthouse and even "roughed up."[36] Yet States Attorney H. Carroll Baylor countered, "There are 15 witnesses who say he wasn't!"[37] Goff said he was also ordered by the local police to issue a retraction about statements he had already made about the authorities in Louisville.[38]

While Goff was inside, word had spread quickly about him at the courthouse, and soon, the sidewalk in front of the building was crowded with a rowdy group of townspeople. By the time Goff was exiting the building, a mob of around 150 people had formed. Suddenly, Goff found himself in the middle of a booing, jeering mass. Along with their vocal jeers, the crowd, at one point, surrounded Goff, and a short panic developed when someone in the mob threw firecrackers into the throng.

The fireworks sparked and blasted when they hit the sidewalk, alarming everyone.[39]

Everyone it seems was on edge. Later, the Louisville sheriff said, "Guns were tucked in a lot of pockets that day. Folks'd had it with Johnny Bob and his kooky friends."[40]

That was Goff's first night in Louisville, and as Angie Comer relates, "that was the quiet night."[41] The next morning, this unprecedented disturbance was the talk of the region. Stories on the incident appeared in newspapers in Effingham, Flora, Alton, Mount Vernon, and Mattoon, Illinois. In the press, Harrell blamed area communists for the trouble the night before. Rev. Goff, meanwhile, demanded that both local and federal law enforcement immediately look into the incident and establish a grand jury if necessary.[42]

As the news swirled and more gossip was born, John Harrell announced that he and his church would not be deterred; Rev. Goff would be heard again that night on schedule.[43]

That evening, this time under local police protection, Rev. Goff returned to speak at Coles Church. Goff stated that it was the first time in his career as a touring speaker that he needed a police detail.[44]

Yet that night, churchgoers on their way to hear Goff were met with another disturbing sight. Again as they approached Coles Chapel, they found, dotted alongside the road, fully aflame, a series of three burning wooden crosses.[45]

Surprisingly, defiantly, a capacity crowd turned out to see Goff that night but, for every person who had come to hear him, just about as many people showed up to heckle him, disturb the service, and try to force the evening into cancellation.[46]

Even as the churchgoers attempted to drive up to the front of the chapel, they found themselves suddenly continually cut off by a circling caravan of other vehicles determined to block them. As wheels squealed and car horns blared out, the disruptors also yelled from their cars.[47]

Amid the ongoing noise and cars zooming by at high speeds, constantly driving by, the parishioners made their way into the church, but once inside, Rev. Comer had no sooner began the opening prayer than he was repeatedly drowned out with the sound of cars, yells, firecrackers, and flares coming from outside. Rocks also began to be thrown against the church's windows.[48]

The meeting was soon curtailed as the churchgoers fearfully left the church and attempted to gain safety in their own cars. Once again, Johnny Bob instructed all of his worshippers to repair to town and go directly to his estate.[49]

For security, all the worshippers tried to depart at the same time, falling into a single-file line, one after another, until their cars formed a long procession back into Louisville and to the presumed safety of the Harrell estate.[50]

Afterward, Goff again demanded legal action. He went to the Louisville courthouse to file charges against James Morgan, who Goff said was the leader of the unruly crowd.[51] According to Goff, once again Carroll Baylor said he could find no evidence to support issuing any sort of arrest warrant against Morgan or any other man.[52]

Harrell and Goff pressed on the next day and, again, announced that the church event would take place that evening as planned.[53]

At first, when the crowd arrived that third evening, all seemed to be calm; there were no crosses or crowds. Yet no sooner had Goff begun his talk than he was suddenly interrupted when someone set off the building's fire alarm.[54] Johnny Bob announced in the press the next day that the false alarm was the work of some of the city's cowardly communists; Clay County Sheriff Walter R. Welch, however, said it was probably just a teenage prank.[55] The fire alarm summoned the city's fire engine, which roared out to the church with its siren wailing.[56] Soon, the local police were also on the scene as well, their sirens all on full wail.[57] To this day, opinions differ on whether the fire and police were there to safeguard the church service or disrupt it.[58]

Reportedly, even when the fire engine left, it reactivated its siren, its high pitch adding even more to the deafening din.[59] Amid the noise, a horde of demonstrators returned and wreaked havoc just like the night before. They remained on the church property late into the night, not finally dispersing until about 2 a.m.[60]

Once again, those in attendance inside the church retreated, for their safety, to Johnny Bob's estate; by this time, he had also drafted two of his followers to act as guards, giving them rifles and telling them to protect everyone inside.[61]

The next morning—Thursday the 24th—Goff finally departed the region. Local police agreed to escort him out of Louisville and to Effingham in order to board a train toward Chicago. He would go from there to Delaware for another speaking engagement.[62]

Ultimately, those responsible for the burning crosses and for the effigy and for the other harassment were never apprehended.

Goff later recounted of his time in Louisville:

I never saw such a night! I thought I was behind the Iron Curtain instead of in the Corn Belt. The Sheriff, Police Magistrate, and the States Attorney all refused me protection against mob heckling and even refused to register my complaint! They kept me there [at the police station] an hour and a half, grilling me, badgering me, and refused me even a drink of water or anything to eat, though I told them I had not eaten since before the meeting and, being a diabetic, I had to have soup or something to sustain me....[63]

For Johnny Bob Harrell, his family, and his nascent church congregation, those three days in February 1961 changed them forever.

Only days after Goff's departure, Harrell was in the news again, this time announcing the immediate start of a retreat on his property to "teach Christians how to survive a Communist revolution."[64] The retreat was to consist of both prayer and periods of fasting.[65] As the number of people on the grounds increased, the Louisville police began to provide protection to fight off potential hecklers.[66]

Originally, newspapers reported that the retreat was to be a two-day event.[67] However, this seemed to change and expand very quickly. Subsequent reporting shows that the retreat had been almost immediately extended by Harrell to two weeks.[68] Finally, it was being reported that the session on the Harrell estate would be a permanent one.[69] Harrell proclaimed his property a "permanent haven for anti-Communist workers" and said he would soon begin the construction of "several dozen" cabins on the property to house the new permanent residents.[70]

Raised at a rate of about two per week, a total of twenty-four cabins would eventually be set up on the Harrell grounds.[71] The cabins, made from lumber cut from the property, would be built in two rows facing each other; the final lane of cabins would stretch a full quarter-mile.[72] Harrell added that more cabins would be built as the need arose.[73]

The majority of the cabins were one-room models measuring 10 × 24, the remaining were two room structures.[74] Cabins were equipped with electricity and had running water if not indoor bathroom facilities. If residents were not going to live in cabins or in "the big house," they lived in trailers pulled in and parked onto the property. Eventually, about fifteen trailers would join the landscape.[75] Harrell went on to say in a March 1961 newspaper article, "I have spent $250,000 so far in this fight and I'll spend more."[76]

Stating that their original place of worship, Coles Church, had been repeatedly vandalized with "hundreds" of bullet holes, shattered glass, and a damaged fuel oil tank, Harrell also disclosed that, from then on, all services for the Christian Conservative Church would be held on his property, under the protection of local police.[77] The change in venue took place around March 6, when Harrell brought his latest guest speaker to talk to his congregation.[78]

That speaker was Bill Beeny, a radio minister and founder of the anti-communist Missouri Youth Ranch. Beeny would later become a well-known segregationist and an advocate in favor of the Vietnam War. Today, he is best known for his various theories about Elvis Presley still being alive.[79]

Beeny later claimed that God Himself told him to come to Louisville for this speaking engagement, despite someone from the Clay County government supposedly calling him and warning him ahead of time not to come and being told by some of his radio bosses to not go to southern Illinois or even mention Harrell and his followers on his radio show.[80]

After first scheduling the Beeny lecture to take place at Coles, Johnny Bob later became concerned about more disturbances; on the day of the talk, he posted a sign on the front door of the chapel stating that the talk would now take place at his estate.[81] Yet Beeny was fearful that the people coming to see him would not follow through on the change of location and, instead, chose to remain and speak at Coles.[82]

Hence, that night, Beeny spoke at Coles in an unheated building and with its many shattered windows covered with newspaper. He spoke to a crowd rumored to be as many as 100. Along with his remarks, Beeny showed a short propaganda film titled *Communism on the Map*.[83] No major disturbances were reported. Johnny Bob did not attend and instead remained at his estate.[84]

For his visit, Beeny asked for and received from the city a police escort into and out of Louisville.[85]

By this time, the Harrell compound was now home to over a dozen people. The original group would soon be joined by others, turning it, in Harrell's words, into a "holy refuge."[86] For Harrell's followers who were not yet living on the grounds, they were told that the day would soon arrive when they, too, would have to come there to live.

In December 1960, again according to Harrell, the Lord had directed him to draw up a plan of action titled "Red Alert."[87] The "Red Alert" was a notice to all CCC members—about 300 at that time, most from the state of Illinois "as far north as Chicago and as far south as Carmi," according to Johnny Bob.[88] The "Red Alert" would be the signal from the Lord (communicated through Johnny Bob) that the fight against communism and for personal and spiritual safety was nigh. As soon as they got the call, church members were to drop whatever they were doing and rush to the Harrell estate—that would be the only place they would be safe, according to Harrell. When they came, they had to bring enough food for at least two weeks—for, among other things, the government would soon be shutting off food distribution to its citizens. The call could come anytime, day or night. Time would be of the essence, so they must always be ready.[89]

Awaiting that call, area families kept their cars fully loaded with any possessions they hoped to bring with them and with enough food stuffs to sustain them.[90]

Then, only days after the Goff incidents, Johnny Bob felt the power of the Lord and the need to enact the "Red Alert."[91] The call went out at 12:30 a.m. on the morning of Friday, February 24.[92] Almost immediately, headlights began to pierce the dark around the estate as cars began to pull onto Harrell's property. By dawn, the property was awash with vehicles and people.

As soon as the call had come, people did as they were told to. They rushed to their cars and trucks and left everything they owned forever behind, often disturbingly so. Some families, in their haste to make it to Harrell's, left behind pets and livestock, all of which eventually died of starvation and neglect.[93]

Some of the arrivals brought tents with them and set them up on the property as if it was one giant campsite. Others dragged trailers that they parked on the property. Some slept in their cars. Most though moved into the Mt. Vernon home, sleeping on floors or on a few scattered, second-hand beds.[94]

Harrell's reach was mighty. While a large group of estate dwellers came from Louisville, others came from outlying towns. Arthur Leib and his family came from Robinson, Illinois; the Kellums family came from Mt. Vernon (Harrell knew Mr. Kellums from their military service), and the Murie family had come all the way from California.[95] Robert Murie had earlier been introduced to the church via a sister of his who lived in southern Illinois.[96] Many had started following Harrell after learning of him during his political run or by attending one of his sermons/lectures on his spiritual healing. They then joined the CCC.[97]

Not only did Harrell's church cover a great geographical ground, it also seemed to bridge denominations. Coming to the house included not only those of the Methodist faith but also Protestants, Catholics, and other religions.[98]

After getting settled, all of the new arrivals mixed in with those already on the property and began observing a worship schedule drawn up by Johnny Bob. It included (originally) four church services a day, fasting every other day and praying "by twos" around the clock, twenty-four hours per day.[99]

Johnny Bob, his wife, and children resided in living quarters located above the property's large garage.[100] The majority of the others lived in the Mt. Vernon house (or, the "big house," as it was known). However, even for those in that structure, life on the estate was far from luxurious. As mentioned, the interior of the Mt. Vernon house was not yet finished. Some "rooms" were achieved only by suspending sheets to serve as walls. There were no doors either; individuals wanting privacy tacked towels over the doorways. Electricity in the building was obtained only by dragging a suspended cable over from the nearby garage, and even then, that only powered the first floor. For light, kerosene lamps were used and were carried from room to room. There was no running water or indoor plumbing.[101]

On the estate's big house, entire families often all lived in one room. This was true of Vance Comer's family of three who had previously been renting a home in Louisville. Yet for Comer's young daughter, Angie, despite this extreme change (previously she had a room all her own in a house that was just her family's), she does not recall feeling jarred or frightened by this great upheaval. She says, "I was with my mom, my dad, I felt very safe. I guess because I was with them, it didn't feel that unusual. It was an adventure to me." Later, the Comers were able to "upgrade" some and they moved into a trailer they purchased and then placed on the property.[102]

In the big house, there were no kitchen facilities either and, as mentioned, no running water. The occupants of the house made due with chamber pots. Family members who didn't wish to use the pots, could visit the communal outhouse outside, located a little way from the back of the home.[103]

Originally, all residents made use of a washing machine located in one of the other buildings on the property. In time, this machine was moved to one of the cabins. As was the norm for that era, clothes were generally dried on an outdoor clothes line.[104]

On Sundays, after church, a meal was usually cooked and eaten communally. At other times, people mostly ate their meals only with their family members. Yet cooking was not done every day; Harrell and his followers followed a schedule of religious fasting—one day with food, the next day without.[105] Children on the grounds, however, were always exempt from fasting.[106]

Yet before anyone believes that life at the estate was a complete throwback, it should be noted that even as late as 1961, many homes in the area did not yet have indoor plumbing and were not yet fully wired for electricity. For many, then, this was the norm. Furthermore, the entire estate was stunningly pretty, even idyllic. Every building was new, the lawns were meticulously kept, the scenery around it pristine and botanical.[107]

For the faithful of Johnny Bob's, life in the compound followed a straight-forward routine. Eventually, the flock shifted to a bi-weekly church service schedule (Wednesdays and twice on Sundays) but during times of stress, or what was perceived as rising turbulent times, additional services and prayer sessions would be added.[108]

The services, always presided over by Rev. Comer and Johnny Bob, were held on the large main floor of the Mt. Vernon house, where borrowed chairs from one of Johnny Bob's theaters served as pews and the walls, according to one newspaper article, were plastered with various newspaper clippings about Johnny Bob and his breakaway church.[109] They were posted there, said one parishioner, as a "reminder of our duty."[110]

Along with the large main house and the twenty-four cabins, the property also contained or would soon contain: a four-car garage with living quarters above it (where Harrell and his family lived), a large (50 × 100 feet) "pole-barn" for storage, and a shed to cover the various small aircraft that Harrell owned at the time as well as a private landing strip near the back of the property. Added quickly after all these structures was a tall water tower, about four stories high. The water tower became necessary after the town shut off Harrell's supply of water over a disagreement. In defiance, Harrell simply decided to dig his own well.[111] Harrell frequently exhausted the patience of local utilities and others. He was known to send invoices back scribbled with the message, "This morning the Lord told me not to pay this bill."[112] He also sometimes refused to sign his tax returns.[113]

Eventually built into the side of one of the hills on the grounds were various tunnel-like "bomb shelters," each stocked with canned food and containers of water. Every family had their own shelter so that they could endure and survive a nuclear attack. They were each responsible for keeping it well stocked with their needs.[114]

In front of the great house was an oversize—but working—"Liberty Bell." It not only symbolized freedom, it could be used as a warning system if the compound was ever under attack.[115] Next to the bell there was added a sign where, in script, it stated: "Upon this flag pole was raise[ed] the first flag of REGATHERED ISRAEL in ceremonies ... June 13, 1961."[116]

Finally, the entire perimeter of the property was surrounded by fencing made of barbed wire and wood. A metal gate blocked the front entrance to the grounds. It was, eventually, flanked on both sides by two small guard houses. Harrell and company even built three guard towers, set atop telephone poles, 40 feet high in order for lookouts to be posted in them and have a better view. The high towers gave the entire estate a fortress-like feel. The property's second entrance was somewhat more concealed and sat directly behind the Chestnut Street house that Harrell's company once built. After Harrell repeatedly ran afoul of local government, that building's original renter—a federal agriculture agency—left and Harrell took the building over as the headquarters for his construction business. In front of this building, over its driveway, Harrell would also erect a tall metal archway with the words "Christian Conservative Center" spelled out on the arch.[117]

The construction of these buildings and the maintenance of the expansive grounds occupied the majority of the daylight hours for all the men who now lived on the estate. For their labors, the men living in the compound received a small weekly stipend paid to them by Johnny Bob.[118] In 1962, Harrell noted that each of the members of the group living on the grounds earned around $112 a month, out of which they were asked to pay $1 for water as well as "their share" of the electric bill.[119] For Harrell, himself, maintaining the CCC and the grounds was probably costing him about $10,000 a month.[120]

Another not infrequent activity on the grounds, according to one source, were the practicing of military maneuvers where the men living on the estate trained themselves to do battle in case of enemy attack or invasion. Who they were prepping against is open to speculation—townspeople? foreign invaders?[121] One can imagine how, for those outside of the compound and looking in, these mock battles appeared.

At one point, in an attempt to make the compound further self-sufficient, Johnny Bob even set up a small general store on the property that was available to anyone living on the grounds.[122] The presence of that store has been often assailed by Harrell's critics. Here was proof, they maintain, of Johnny Bob's omnipotence over his disciples, of him taking advantage of them, of making everyone dependent upon him. Yet Harrell and his son Tod maintain that the store—given the quaint name "The Trading Post"— was only set up for the convenience of those living on the property, saving them from having to journey into town for sundries and protecting them from the growing harassment that many members received whenever they ventured back into the confines of Louisville.[123] The store eventually proved to be too difficult to keep well-stocked; Johnny Bob pulled the plug on it after only a few months.[124]

Despite the group's reach for self-reliance, they were not beyond bringing in help when necessary. A local doctor, Dr. Curtis, would come periodically to attend to the medical needs of anyone and everyone.[125]

Except for a few inconveniences, many found the estate quite livable. The children of most of the new residents adapted quickly. Though some people had sadly left their animals behind, others brought their pets with them. Angie Comer specifically remembers a collie that arrived at the estate with one name but was quickly renamed "Lassie" by all the kids living on the grounds. Another family retained their pet parakeet and it was soon adopted as a group mascot.[126]

Additionally, on the property there was a sparkling man-made pond with its own diving board as well as a sand box and a set of swings. To kids, the estate was like the world's biggest backyard. The basement of the big house was even big enough to roller-skate in.[127]

Since all the resident of Harrell's estate lived together, ate together, and worshiped together, the residents of Harrell's estate, not surprisingly, seemed to start to experience a kind of "group-think."

Originally, the group's church services, conducted in the chapel area, were relatively staid affairs, similar to other Methodist churches, but as other joined the estate/church from different areas and backgrounds, they brought with them their own worship practices. When a group of Southern Baptists—practitioners of speaking in tongues and sometimes violently throwing themselves to the ground, prostrating themselves to the Lord—joined the Harrell congregation, they brought those behaviors with them. Soon other members of Harrell's congregation were, also, speaking in tongues and rolling on the floors of the church. To Priscilla Laughton, whose Louisville family eventually moved onto the grounds, these new behaviors were, at first, deeply jarring.[128]

Additionally, as Johnny Bob often spoke about his visions from God and his messages from God, many others in the camp, then too, began to "receive" visions and edicts from the Lord.[129] The round, glassed-in upper cupola, the highest point of the Mt. Vernon house, became a popular place to pray, commune with God, and obtain visions and directions from the Lord, with the women of the order receiving the greater number of holy visions.[130] At other times, the cupola would also serve as a watchtower, staffed by followers with binoculars and guns at the ready.[131]

Though for many now on the grounds, the estate was their new and "forever" home, the populace of those living on the grounds did ebb and flow, ranging from about sixty to (at other times) near 100.[132] Harrell would often round up considerably when stating the number of people living on the estate; he sometimes stated that its total was as high as 150.[133]

According to Johnny Bob's eldest son, Tod, while some individuals and families were "long-term," others stayed for only a week or two. For some, the retreat lasted only as long their vacation time from their jobs lasted. Once those vacation days—maybe two weeks' worth—were exhausted, they returned to their homes, jobs, and lives.[134] For some others, sometimes their family members became apprehensive and would come to the compound and coax them out, never to return.[135]

Johnny Bob later stated that of the 300 people originally notified by the "Red Alert," between 100 and 150 eventually came to the estate; those who did not come or stay were, according to Harrell, simply not strong enough in their faith to hold on. Again, the Lord told Johnny Bob, "the weak would drop out on the way" and "Some phonies will appear but we will quickly find them out and deal with them. They won't stay."[136, 137]

Harrell would later contend that a few who came to the grounds came under fake names, only to satisfy their curiosity and then leave disappointed when they discovered the group was only interested in prayer and the earnest fighting of communists.[138] Sometimes even some of the truly devout did not last long; they found this highly spiritual existence just too much for their personal liking.[139]

Although some members did leave, many held the faith. Johnny Bob reported that the Lord was slowly revealing why they were all called there and that "people should not leave but hold."[140] As noted, many did. If the followers had not already, after the "Red Alert," many now on the estate resigned from their jobs (some supposedly leaving careers earning as much as $20–30,000 a year) and ordered their old homes sold.[141] Those who were in for the long haul moved into the recently completed cabins on the property or, like the Comer family, they eventually purchased trailers to live in.[142]

Despite the safety in numbers and communal understanding that all the estate residents had with each other, there was one worrisome part of life on the compound: there was a constant, underlying sense of ill-ease, especially at night, as those from town often continued with their harassment.[143] As soon as people began to move to the estate, a deep divide—literal and figurative—emerged that solidly separated them from those living in town. While the townspeople called the Harrell group all sorts of names, the Harrell group largely referred to those in town as "the Outsiders."[144]

The division between those on the outside and those on the inside manifested itself in a wide variety of ways. Since the turmoil of the Goff events, the area newspapers had been casting a harsh light on and applying a critical voice to Johnny Bob. The *Clay County Republican* published an editorial titled "Things We Believe and Do Not Believe," which, though it did not name Harrell specifically, certainly seemed to suggest him. Among other things, the editorial decried any and all communist conspiracy theorists whose warnings were "baseless, erroneous and out of order."[145]

However, if Harrell was not directly named, he certainly took it as an affront and quickly responded to the newspaper accusing it of a wide variety of lies. He wrote:

> I have followed with considerable interest some of the recent writings in your weekly newspaper and must confess that seldom have I seen such a conglomeration of misstatements and half-truths.[146]

Harrell concluded with a challenge to the newspaper:

> It would be fine if you would print the entire content of this letter without deletion in your newspaper, however I do not believe you have either the moral courage or the intestinal fortitude to do so.[147]

Outside of the war of words being raged in the press, CCC members began to feel the effects of the town's division in other ways. For example, as CCC members attempted to acquire lumber for their various on-site projects, they would often find local businesses refusing to sell to them.[148] Even various grocers were turning hostile and were turning away Harrell church members (resulting in short-lived general store on the property).[149] That was just the beginning.

Though the Harrell group took to the grounds originally for safety and abandoned Coles Church due to the ongoing vandalism of the chapel, the Harrell estate itself was still frequently the target of violence—BB guns being shot onto and into the property, fire crackers and garbage tossed onto the grounds, and boys in cars driving by and yelling at the children on the property, either threatening them or their pets. Some people even drove by in broad daylight, proudly brandishing their shotguns.[150]

Harrell said that he and his group were being watched and harassed constantly; city officials said that the majority of people going by the property were just curious onlookers doing no harm.[151]

The ongoing troubles and harassment from "the Outsiders" eventually necessitated not only the building of the 5-foot tall, barbed-wire fence and the guard towers but also the establishment of twenty-four-hour guards, men from the colony who were each given guns and trained in target practice. They then, each and every night, continually walked the perimeter of the property to ward off intruders.[152]

If by this time, in the ongoing saga of Johnny Bob Harrell and the Christian Conservative Church, Harrell was doing and saying many things that were making people uncomfortable and drawing a degree of unwanted attention to the area, he had not, yet, done anything deemed illegal. However, that was about to change. It changed when Johnny Bob began flouncing local truancy polices when he pulled his children out of the local schools in order to teach them at home.[153]

Harrell's comments, as covered in the press, about why he had pulled his kids from the local schools changed over the course of time. The "Red Alert" had occurred on Friday, February 24, a day that the Clay County public schools happened to be closed for a teacher's conference. On Monday morning, after Harrell discovered that many of the people now living on his property had formerly taught in Illinois schools, he decided it was not necessary—or, one assumes, safe—to send the children from the compound to the public schools. Instead, they should be educated right there on the estate—at least until the end of the retreat.[154] At least, that was the story Harrell relayed in the beginning.

Yet this justification was soon replaced and, instead, the purpose of Harrell's on-site school changed. Soon, Harrell was saying that the reasons for his actions were because local schools were overrun with communists all pushing their communist agenda.[155] Therefore, his children and the children of his followers would no longer be attending area public schools. Considering Johnny Bob's singular concern about communism, such a justification, from him, seems quite plausible. He also—happily—added that the teachers and administrators of his school were of far higher "spiritual and moral standards" than any other area school.[156] He then proceeded to call out the local school's high drop-out rate and to lambast schools that taught evolution over creationism.[157]

Various other localized articles published around that time state that Harrell's original reason for withdrawing his children from public school was the fact that they were being bullied and harassed by other students— another reason that is quite believable. Harrell is to have once said, "It's simply too dangerous for them [my children] to attend [regular] school."[158]

Finally, another possible reason emerged years later. Around the time that Harrell founded his own school, June Morgan, wife of prominent Louisville businessman and former Harrell friend, Jim Morgan, was teaching home economics in the area school system. She had also just been accused of inappropriate behavior with some of her female students. Though charges were, seemingly, never filed against her, it did lead to Mrs. Morgan's resignation from teaching.[159]

As a member of the school board, Johnny Bob would probably have known all about these accusations. If he was already suspicious of some members of the local school faculty, this, obviously, only added fuel to his fire. If he, as a board member, pushed for Mrs. Morgan's dismissal, it also explains the deepening dislike that was taking place between Harrell and those affiliated with him and the Morgans. Later, Mrs. Morgan would claim that her dismissal from teaching was simply Harrell's retaliation for the mental-health petition she had helped circulate during Harrell's run for political office.[160]

What is important to note though is that Johnny Bob was not wrong, or off base, at least not in this particular case. Knowledge of Mrs. Morgan's conduct seemed to be then (and now) an open secret within Louisville.[161] Over the years, various local women have come forth stating they had either knowledge of some of Mrs. Morgan's inappropriateness or had been the victim of it.[162]

In any event, for whatever reason, Harrell's "school" opened on his estate on March 6, 1961. Vance Comer was to serve as the school's principal.[163]

By this time, it was estimated that close to seventy people were living on the estate, including about twenty-five school-age children. These children would be the school's first pupils taught by four teachers specially retrained by Harrell.[164] Harrell stated to the press that his school would "teach the basic subjects. We will not teach anything that tends to destroy a child's faith or which leads to materialistic goals."[165] He described the school's curriculum as the "Three R's plus music, art, physical education and the Bible."[166] *McGuffey's Reader* was the school's primary reading textbook, but most other public school texts, according to Harrell, were rejected for their alleged communist leanings.[167] Later Harrell was quoted as saying the intent of the school was to fight the encroaching "communist menace."[168] The school would begin teaching only the primary grades but high school-level classes would be added in time.[169]

The launching of his private school—which eventually shifted locations from the Mt. Vernon house to the large building Johnny Bob had long used as his construction business offices located on Chestnut Avenue—immediately drew the ire of Clay County School Superintendent Robert Brissenden.[170]

Within days of the new school's opening, Brissenden issued a series of complaints against Harrell demanding that Harrell's two school-age children (Tod, thirteen, and Xon, ten) return immediately to Louisville's public schools. Harrell flatly refused and cited several reasons why he was not breaking any law. First, he maintained, it was not unusual for Clay County parents to pull their children out of school for extended periods—such as vacation—and those parents were never penalized.[171] Harrell said, therefore, he was, yet again, simply being harassed by the local government. Along with stating his school was part of his constitutional Freedom of Religion rights, Harrell noted that there was no law at that time mandating that children attend a public school, only a school of similar curriculum.[172] Harrell was quoted in the press as saying, "I do not propose to be taken into custody for breaking a law that is not on the books."[173]

Brissenden argued that if there was not a law about attendance, there were laws about a school's qualifications and specifications, which did exist, and that these requirements were not being met by Harrell.[174]

For the next few weeks Harrell and Brissenden argued back and forth mainly via the local media. The conflict became so contested however that it was eventually featured on Dave Garroway's *Today* show. NBC-TV sent a crew to Louisville to report on the educational stand-off. Some of their footage was shot in one of the "classrooms" at the Harrell school.[175]

Days later, Brissenden expanded his complaints to include the parents of the other children attending the CCC school. On March 8, 1961, formal criminal charges were filed against Harrell, Vance Comer, Carl Stanley, Flora Rowan, John Laughton, and Ralph Boose. All had children who had either previously attended school in Louisville or such nearby towns as Sailor Springs or Flora; all were now residing on the Harrell estate.[176]

A court date for all the parents to appear before Louisville judge Prentiss Cosby was set for March 20 at 10 a.m.[177] Harrell responded to the charges in the press via his attorney John Unger. It was conveyed that Harrell and all the others would be pleading innocent to any and all accusations.[178]

Jury selection for the Louisville-based trial commenced on schedule. On the morning of the 20th, a jury of seven men and five women was empaneled.[179] Yet of the six defendants ordered to appear, only three actually showed up for court that morning. Notably absent was Harrell himself. In a statement from Johnny Bob released to the press that morning, Harrell said: "We are moving on divine direction.... Local officials [are] using the courts for harassment and intimidation. No law says that you have to send children to a public school..."[180] Later in the statement, Harrell reiterated his claims that his children were the victims of harassment from various communist agitators. Harrell also stated that he believed that the children were receiving improper instruction in area public schools.[181] Harrell would later claim that the defense was forbidden from introducing many of his arguments at the trial.[182]

Besides Johnny Bob, also not in attendance at the trial that day were Vance Comer and Ralph Boose. Presiding Judge Cosby immediately stated that all three men would be tried with or without their attendance and that the absentee three would still be bound by the jury's decision.[183]

Press reports on the truancy case—some reprinted as far away as Lincoln, Nebraska—labeled Harrell as a "Red Fighter" either "hiding" from the law or defying it from inside his Louisville "fort."[184] Newspaper accounts went on to state that armed guards with "high-powered rifles" were now guarding the Harrell estate around the clock and that Harrell had said clearly, yes, "there are guards ... and they have their instructions."[185]

As the trial got underway, more was at stake than just the fate of Johnny Bob's handful of students. Should the trial be decided in favor of Harrell, it would thereby validate and legalize all non-state run schools throughout the state of Illinois.[186] Hence, with so much on the line, States Attorney Baylor mounted a full prosecution, calling to the stand nine different grade school teachers from the area in order to establish the legality of Clay County Schools and the validity of the state's charges against Harrell.[187]

It was not until the trial's third day that Harrell's attorney, John Unger, called his first witness. Dr. Clayton Curtis, a physician and surgeon from Grayville, Illinois, then took the stand and testified that he was the head of Harrell's private school.[188] Though Curtis was deemed the defense's star witness, he did concede under oath that though he was teaching on the grounds, he himself did not possess a teaching certificate, nor, in fact, did any of the other "teachers" active at that time in Harrell's school.[189] In fact, of all the Harrell teachers, only Curtis had any sort of advanced degree.[190] Furthermore, on the stand, Curtis could not name any of the textbooks any of the instructors were teaching from.[191]

Prosecutor Baylor further charged that one of the teachers on the property was a seventeen-year-old high school girl from Clay City. "She's an intelligent girl," he said, "But she hasn't even completed high school herself."[192] The girl in question was Priscilla Laughton, a seventeen-year-old girl living on the estate who was pulled in to teach music in Harrell's *ad hoc* school.[193]

Shortly after Curtis's testimony, the case was turned over to the jury. The verdict was delivered swiftly. The jury (who had reportedly been sequestered for the duration of the trial) deliberated only about two hours before they returned to the court room on March 22 and delivered their verdict in front of a courtroom, which was said to have been jammed with over 500 spectators, some of whom had brought their lunches with them.[194]

All the defendants were found guilty of truancy, and each was fined $20 a day for each day of school their children missed; Harrell, himself, was fined $360—$180 each for his two sons.[195] The defendants were also ordered to pay for court costs; the three-day trial had cost the county about $1,000.[196] The jury's ruling effectively made Harrell's school illegal. All of the children were ordered to report back to public school the following Monday morning or their parents would face additional fines and new truancy charges from the county.[197]

Regarding the decision, Harrell was quoted at the time as saying, "The verdict shocked us."[198] Harrell also divulged that he had no intention of discontinuing his school—even if it was now deemed "illegal"—and he would continue to fight.

In the wake of the trial, States Attorney Baylor announced that he was prepared to seek "state assistance" if Harrell and the others did not obey by the recent verdict.[199] Though Baylor did not elaborate on what type of assistance he would ask for, he did say that the county was prepared to seize property of Harrell's and sell it at public auction if Harrell refused to pay his fines—or his mounting back taxes which at that time totaled just over $1,000.[200]

In the wake of the trial, Johnny Bob announced that, to the surprise of no one, after serving for three years, he would not be seeking re-election to the local school board.[201] It was noted at the time that Harrell had only attended two board meetings in the past two years anyway.[202]

Almost before the ink had dried on the truancy judgement, Harrell found himself in the news again. On March 26, John Laughton of Sailor Springs, who had been a resident of the Harrell compound and one of the original defendants in the truancy case, left the camp.[203] It was reported that along with leaving the estate, he would also be re-enrolling his children in a "legal" public school. Laughton announced that his ten-year-old son Tommy would be attending a Clay County school starting the next Monday and that his seventeen-year-old daughter, Priscilla—who was the young music teacher discussed at the trial—would be moving to the Chicago area to live with relatives and she would be enrolling in a high school there.[204]

One day later, Ralph Boose, also one of the original defendants, disclosed to the local press that he, too, was leaving the Harrell estate and would be paying the truancy fines he accrued ($40) and pulling his children from the Harrell-estate school.[205] After leaving the grounds, Boose and his family relocated to Elgin, Illinois.[206]

However, if the splintering off of some of his group made people think Johnny Bob would start to weaken in his stance, they were greatly mistaken. Instead, Harrell seemed to double-down on many of his views. The same article that sited Boose's and Laughton's exit from the estate quoted Harrell as saying he was ready to take his school fight to the Illinois Supreme Court if necessary: "The only way they will get me to return my children to public school is to shoot me down in cold blood."[207]

Harrell would also go on to minimize the recent exodus from his group stating, "John Laughton got scared. He got jumpy. He figured if you can't beat 'em, join 'em." Yet Harrell added about his retreat, "People come and go here. The Laughtons are welcome anytime."[208]

Meanwhile, one day later, again in the press, States Attorney Baylor announced that, if necessary, he would file suit against Harrell and his followers again and that fines would again start to be levied against Harrell and other parents who continued to withhold their children from local schools.[209]

Always happy to speak to the press, and anticipating an upcoming legal battle, Johnny Bob quickly announced that he would immediately be implementing some changes to his on-site school, among them: the hiring of qualified teachers ("We have interviewed some," he said, "But the people in town frightened them away").[210] He maintained, however, that the school would continue to teach a basic curriculum concentrating on the three most important patriots in American history: George Washington, Abraham Lincoln, and the late Senator Joseph McCarthy of Wisconsin (who Harrell said he believed had been killed by communists, though medical records point to cirrhosis of the liver).[211] Harrell further stated that the school's main goal was to preach against communism and socialism.[212]

That same day, through his attorney, Johnny Bob filed for an appeal to his truancy conviction on the grounds that the proceedings were unfair.[213] On April 8, that appeal was denied by Judge Prentiss Cosby; he ruled that Harrell and his co-defendants had received a completely fair trial.[214]

The following month, clearly inspired by the Harrell controversy, Dwight Friedrich, a Republican Illinois state senator from the Centralia area, introduced two bills in the Illinois state senate that would increase truancy fines and make the act of willfully keeping children out of school a jailable offense for their parents.[215] Testifying in support of the bills were Robert L. Brissenden and H. Carroll Baylor. Despite this though, true to form, Johnny Bob vowed to continue his fight.[216] "[This is] only a skirmish," he said in his larger battle against communism.[217]

Similarly, though, Johnny Bob's legal foe, Carroll Baylor, said he would continue the fight as well: "I want two things—the children on Harrell's estate back in public schools where there are qualified teachers and facilities—and for Harrell to quit hollering that there are Communists around here."[218]

Throughout the rest of the spring of 1961 and well into the summer months, Johnny Bob remained firmly in the local news. First, in early April, he complained to the press that a house he owned on the outskirts of Louisville had been vandalized to the tune of $1,000.[219] The home, unoccupied at the time, saw its windows broken, walls battered, and front porch supports knocked loose. According to Harrell, the home was not insured at the time as various insurance policies of his had recently, unexpectedly, been cancelled.[220] Meanwhile, another home he owned in the area was the victim of arson. Harrell stated in both cases that the crime was the work of an old foe. He said, "Communist pressure continues to mount. A five-room house I own west of Louisville was damaged by Communist vandals over the weekend."[221] However, Clay County law enforcement scoffed at Harrell's claim. Baylor said, "If it's one of those old vacant houses, the whole thing isn't worth $200." Baylor also wondered why the damage was not reported to them before Harrell reported it to the newspaper.[222]

Then, in June, *The Decatur Daily Review* reported that various tax records of Johnny Bob's were currently being reviewed by the Internal Revenue Service.[223]

Speaking once more to the press, Harrell insisted that he was completely paid up with his federal income taxes though he did concede that he had refused to pay some of his local taxes due to the "Communist conspiracy" afoot in Clay County government. "Why should I finance this rat race?" Harrell once asked.[224] Harrell stated that he believed the IRS investigation into him was born from his open criticism of then President John F. Kennedy.[225] About JFK, Harrell once said, "We don't have a President, we have a Russian ambassador in the White House."[226]

Harrell also used that interview to complain that he and his followers were under almost daily attack from hecklers and people throwing rocks and firing guns into his property.[227]

In July 1961, it was reported that besides running afoul of local politicians and the IRS, Harrell was also embroiled in a conflict with the local Clay County State Bank.[228] The bank, acting on a defaulted loan, had seized the local, fifteen-room motel that was owned jointly by Johnny Bob and his mother. At the time of its default sale, the motel was not operating—it had been closed down due to a "message from God" that Harrell said he had received. On July 31, the bank sold the motel at an auction held in front of the Louisville courthouse.[229] It was sold for a final bid of only $6,300.[230]

The purchasers (among a total of five bidders) were two businessmen out of Fairfield, Illinois.[231] Under Illinois law, however, the Harrells had the right to reclaim the deed to the property if they repaid the loan within the next twelve months.[232] Johnny Bob said that that was his intention and that he had only gone into arrearage due to a "strained relationship" with the local bank. He elaborated by saying, "[This] forced sale of our motel is all part of the conspiracy against us."[233]

Later the same month, a photo of a well-suited Johnny Bob was reproduced in the Decatur newspaper to announce the debut of his church's new flag. In the photo, Harrell was pictured alongside the wife of Vance Comer. Together they held up the newly christened, newly fashioned flag that would now be flown over the Harrell property.[234] Modeled in part on the U.S. flag, the flag consisted of three white stripes alternating with four bold navy-blue stripes. In the flag's upper corner, against a background of blue was one large white Star of David surrounded by eleven smaller white Stars of Davids arranged in a circle. On the other side of the flag, according to the caption accompanying the photo, in its upper corner was a white twelve-pointed crown seen sitting atop a white cross. According to the photo's caption, "Mrs. Vance Comer … sewed [the flag] on Harrell's direction … Harrell said he commissioned the flag at the direction of God."[235]

Immediately, the newly configured flag was being hoisted every day on the estate to fly alongside the property's regular red, white, and blue stars and stripes. As can be surmised, all of this Harrell-based controversy soon brought with it an unprecedented degree of attention onto Louisville, previously a very quiet town of about 900 people. Soon, various newspapers throughout the region were writing about the unprecedented events taking place and about the town's most infamous resident, Johnny Bob Harrell and his group of devoted followers.

An Associated Press article from March 24, 1961, was widely reprinted throughout Illinois and the Midwest. In the Decatur newspaper, the article was given the title "This Man, Johnny Bob," and it attempted to profile this small-town troublemaker who had so willingly segregated himself off from the rest of the town. Harrell is quoted in the piece as saying, "I haven't set foot on the town square since 1960. The last time I was there, a man threatened me with a club." Harrell would also claim that he was once shot at—in fact, three times in one day.[236] The article went on to make mention of Harrell's fortune—"[I have] hundreds of thousands of dollars"—and the divine direction he (and his wife) often received. Harrell said, he "hears the Lord speak in an audible voice" along with regularly receiving "spiritual manifestations and visions."[237] The article recounted Harrell's large estate, his ongoing religious retreat, his recent battle over schooling, and his determination to fight communism in all its many forms.[238]

Other observations were made by Associated Press reporter David C. Breeder:

> Families live among carpenters' tools…. Housewives shuttle up and down makeshift stairs with buckets and chamber pots…. Two teen-age boys, armed with military rifles, were standing guard Thursday in the cupola….[239]

Breeder also made mention of the silvery, long-ish, almost shoulder-length hair that both Johnny Bob and his eldest son, Tod, were now sporting. Harrell once defended his long locks by saying, "Bach, Beethoven, Washington and Jefferson—they all wore their hair this way."[240]

Reporter Breeder then journeyed into Louisville, proper, for feedback from the local citizens regarding Harrell and his crusade. One Louisville citizen stated about Johnny Bob and his personal movement, "We don't deserve this kind of attention." Others stated that Harrell's antics were driving people out or away from Louisville and affecting the town's economic equilibrium. One person said, "Folks from out about half way to, say, Farina (18 miles west), now go there to shop. Some are afraid to come here."[241] Other locals were quoted as saying, "It used to be funny. It's isn't funny anymore" and "We wish Johnny Bob no harm. We just wish he'd be like he used to be."[242] One person interviewed just seemed to shake their head at the whole thing: "This is something you read about or see on television, but never dream it is really happening."[243]

Once again, local business owner James Morgan and his wife, June, were open in their criticism and were even pictured in some copies of the article. For the piece, Mr. Morgan went with Breeder to the front of the Harrell compound where Morgan was angrily confronted by Johnny Bob's mother, Natalia. Mrs. Harrell was quoted as saying, "Take a picture of him [Morgan]! He's the main trouble around here."[244]

Mrs. Morgan added, "He accused Jim of being the Communist Party's head and said I was second in command."[245]

Others from the area seemed to concur about the recent troubles in Louisville and largely blamed Johnny Bob. Vaughn Brown, manager of the Wabash Telephone Company, said, "I've got a stake in this town. So have the Morgans here. He's not going to run me out."[246]

The local Louisville newspaper also seemed to have had enough. They eventually published an editorial stating that they would no longer cater to or cover Johnny Bob: "We do not intend to publish any of his messages, letters or news releases that we feel is detrimental to our town, our state or our nation."[247]

Outside of Louisville, the press was often no kinder. One editorial out of Maroa, Illinois, went so far as to compare Harrell to Hitler.[248] Other newspapers might not have been as direct as the Maroa newspaper but sprinkled their Harrell coverage with not-so-subtle criticisms. They called Harrell's retreat "supposedly" religious and called Johnny Bob the "loose-talking, sooth saying Mr. Harrell."[249]

Area reporter John Temple also visited the compound around this time and filed a story. After first being told by the locals that he better call first—"the Harrell estate is guarded"—Temple noted that he first gingerly made his way to the construction offices on the grounds before, there, being told by Harrell's mother to make his way to the big house. She said, "Yes, you can go right up to the house. But when you get there stay in the car. Don't get out. It's not safe. There's a dog and he hasn't had his dinner."[250]

Following orders, Temple drove up to the Mt. Vernon house and met the "husky, handsome" Johnny Bob, further describing him as "a quiet, intense, friendly man and a persuasive talker."[251] Harrell told Temple, "I know that God is guiding my life for a purpose and I am in His Hands. I can't tell you all I know that is to come to pass."

In his story, Temple noted that Harrell saw his Louisville outpost as only the first in what was to become a series of seven or eight sanctuaries spread throughout the nation. Temple also noted that, despite forewarnings, he saw no armed individuals on the property.

All this swirling controversy eventually—as it inevitably would—attracted the national media, or at least a certain segment of it.

Though not quite yet the colorful supermarket staple it is now, the *National Enquirer* was already a popular, widely read tabloid by the early 1960s that gave readers a hearty mix of celebrity gossip, true crime, gore, and other salacious topics. The cover of their June 4, 1961, issue featured a provocative portrait of actress Terry Moore where she claimed, via a blazing headline, "I'm Haunted By My Past." Inside that issue, there was a well-illustrated article on Johnny Bob Harrell under its own blazing headline: "House of Fear."[252]

Under that headline, printed in all caps, there was more over-sized print. It read: "Rich Johnny Bob Built It to Escape The End of the World ... And He Invites You to Join Him."[253]

The accompanying text to the article related much of Johnny Bob's story—his miraculous cure from cancer, his failed political bid and his ongoing crusade against locally-based communism.[254] The story read in part:

> He has barricaded himself behind a wall of armed guards who stop everyone except the press (Johnny wants his story told) from setting foot on his land.
>
> "I talk to the Lord each day," he says, "Just like I'm talking to you."
>
> "When the Lord told me that he had picked me to fight communism, he told me that I would be the most hated man on earth."
>
> "But I can take it. I've got a thick skin."
>
> This year John Harrell has become convinced the end of the world is due. He has invited all who would listen to protect themselves from the holocaust by camping outside the huge replica of George Washington's Mount Vernon estate he built.[255]

Years later, Harrell stated that much in the *Enquirer* article was highly inaccurate.[256] For example, it repeats the rumor of the large pack of guard dogs on the property. Nevertheless, it was Harrell's greatest marketing tool up until that time, spreading news of his new home and religious movement from coast to coast and to an untold number of readers.

One of those readers was a young, then AWOL marine named Dion Davis.[257]

4

The Traitor

All men should strive to learn before they die what they are running
from and to, and why.

James Thurber

Today, Dion Davis lives in a very small town in Texas. Except for driving
a school bus during the school year, he is largely retired. Though he has
had a long and colorful employment history, the majority of his working
years have been spent as a driver for various companies who maintained
the vast oil fields of the Lone Star State. Today, he is a long-married man
(twenty-five years and counting), a step-father, and a step-grandfather.[1]
Neither his children nor his grandchildren were ever told of his one-time
notoriety, and surprisingly, no member of the press had ever hunted him
down before.[2]

Dion Gaylord Davis was born on January 3, 1943 in Greenville,
Pennsylvania. He was the youngest of three children, and the family's
second boy. He was raised in the Lutheran church. According to Davis,
his father was a life-long alcoholic who could turn violent when he drank
too much. Growing up in such a volatile situation, Davis said he often
dreamed of getting away.[3]

At that time in American history, young people desperate to get out
of bad home situations had very few options. For girls, they could get
married, often, with an eye more for escape than for love. For boys who
wanted out, they could join the military, which is what Dion did. "I lied
about my age and enlisted when I was sixteen," Davis says. "Then they
found out and wouldn't take me. So I sat around the house for a year
and waited to turn 17 so they'd take me."[4] According to military records,
Davis was enlisted in Pittsburgh, Pennsylvania, on June 14, 1960.[5]

However, if home with his "crazy" Dad was hard, the military was little better. After his intake into the corps, Davis and other new recruits were sent to Marine Corps Recruit Depot at Parris Island, South Carolina, where, only four years earlier, six young marines died during a training exercise in the infamous Ribbon Creek incident of 1965.[6]

Davis maintains that little had changed since then. He says that at least two other recruits died in the boot camp during his time there. Those fatalities were part of the reasons for his later running away from his camp.[7]

After his basic training, Davis was transferred to Camp Lejeune in Jacksonville, North Carolina. He arrived in Jacksonville on October 7, 1960.[8] There, Davis continued his service with the 2nd Marine Division, which included guard duty and training as a military sniper, a skill he excelled at.[9] Davis's military records also indicate his participation as a bandsman in the music corps; he had played clarinet in his high school band and still remembered how.[10, 11]

Despite the firm structure of the military, Davis's youthfulness still seemed to get the best of him at times. One night, around April 4, 1961, Davis and a pal of his, "on a whim," wandered off the grounds of the base into town and engaged in a drinking spree or as Davis has called it "an extended drunk." They never returned to base. Davis says, "By the way, that was my third AWOL. I wasn't what you would call the most dedicated soldier…."[12]

Previously, Davis's two prior AWOLs were shorter, more localized, and—allegedly—ended the same way. A newspaper account from the time states that Davis told a reporter, "Both times my parents turned me in."[13]

After his second AWOL, Davis reported he "got off pretty easy" with only a punishment of sixty days of hard labor and "I had to sign a paper saying I would be classified as a deserter if I went AWOL again."[14]

Now on his third flight from camp, with no firm plans about where they were going to go but no plans either to return to their base, the two men just began to wander. Eventually they made their way from North Carolina to Virginia, where they settled in Richmond. In Richmond (ironically only about one hour from the real George Washington Mt. Vernon homestead), Davis and his buddy took up residence in a run-down, skid row boarding house. An older widow had opened her home to tenants—most of them much older men, most with serious hardly-hidden drinking problems. She gave them a roof over their heads and one warm meal a day in exchange for a monetary remuneration.[15]

In Richmond, Davis took on odd, short-term jobs and his buddy got a job driving a Mr. Softee ice cream truck. Davis recalls, "I'd ride along with him in the truck sometimes. We'd eat some of the ice cream for dinner."[16]

Then, one day, somewhere, Davis or his buddy picked up a copy of the *National Enquirer* and came across the article about Johnny Bob Harrell and his Mt. Vernon-like home located in Louisville, Illinois.[17] The two men were inspired.[18]

Today, Davis says that he and his fellow AWOL marine phoned Johnny Bob after reading the article and finding a phone number for him. Davis says, "We called him. And in one phone conversation he talked us into [it] ... convinced that we should come live there. That he'd give us a place to stay and protect us."[19]

Later literature generated by Harrell (and some contemporaneous reporting) says he did not actually receive a call from Davis but, instead, received a letter from Davis, one possibly addressed as simply as: "John Harrell / Louisville, Illinois" and postmarked from Richmond.[20] In 1962, Harrell said, "While many letters were received ... [most] are not answered because the direction of the Lord is contrary, nonetheless instructions were given to write this boy and invite to come, which he did."[21]

Harrell was also quoted as saying, "The Lord told me he would send people here and He told me I should protect them with my life." Regardless if Davis wrote or called, in any event, he and his buddy (curiously, Harrell's literature says nothing of the second man) hit the road for Illinois.[22]

In the early 1960s, two young men, needing to make their way halfway across the United States without any money, had only one option open to them, and they took it. The duo hitchhiked from Virginia to Illinois.[23]

Today, Davis does not recall how long it took the two of them to make it to Illinois, though he does recall getting many a ride from lonesome truck drivers, many of whom took them great distances. The nights they were not in a truck cab or car, the men slept outside alongside the highway, always keeping an eye out for wolves or other animals.[24]

Once the two men finally arrived in Louisville, it was not hard for them to find Johnny Bob's large estate. Once at the compound, Davis and his buddy were apparently warmly welcomed and given both food and clothing. They were also, supposedly, even given a little spending money by Johnny Bob himself.[25] They soon then took up residence in one of the newly built red-colored cabins that had been equipped with twin cots and a hot plate, the only "luxury" that the small shack had. The men later made a mistake when they tried to take in a wild raccoon as a pet. "Yeah, he eventually chewed up everything," Davis recalls.[26]

It has now been over sixty years since Dion Davis took up refuge (or whatever you want to call it) at the Harrell estate in Louisville. Davis admits today that his memories of that time are fuzzy and have only grown cloudier due to some of the subsequent experiences he later endured. He cannot recall the name of his fellow traveler nor, seemingly, can anyone else. Most from that time believe that the other man's first name was "Jim" (or "James") and his last name might have been "Young." What is known is that he hailed from Memphis, Tennessee, and that he phoned his parents not long after his arrival in Louisville. His parents immediately drove up—in a fancy 1960 Ford Fairlane, which everyone does recall—and reclaimed him. Neither Davis or Harrell or anyone else connected to the Louisville cult, ever heard from that man again.

Davis also is not completely sure how long he was actually on the Louisville property, but various records and timelines suggest that Davis's time in Louisville was extraordinarily brief—perhaps little more than two weeks.[27]

Regardless, Davis, while there, immersed himself in church activities and worked on the property. He says, "I remember driving around in a jeep and making deliveries."[28] Davis also remembers sitting on the front porch of the big house talking with many of the compound's other residents and he recalls the large, fully populated church services that they all attended, he says, three times per week.[29]

Eventually, Davis even took his turn on guard duty, walking the perimeter of the property at night. He says, "Everyone slept with a gun near their beds, ready for anything. We were armed to the teeth."[30]

According to Johnny Bob, the CCC also put Davis's artistic talents to use. They had him paint a large wooden sign to post on the front of the Mt. Vernon house.[31] It read:

Construction of this house began in the fall of 1958 upon the direction of the LORD GOD of HOSTS and is an enlarged replica of George Washington's Mt. Vernon. It had a direction relationship with the establishment of GOD'S KINGDOM upon Earth and the ultimate defeat of Satanically inspired Communism. This is in accordance with Washington's vision of Valley Forge in 1777 as he was shown the destiny of the United States of America.[32]

In some Harrell-sanctioned literature from the era, Johnny Bob goes on to describe Dion Davis:

He was a fine young lad, who did have great artistic talents...

After he had been here a short time, he revealed to me that he had been in the Marine Corp and because of what he knew he left.[33]

Today, there is speculation (and fading memories) about if Johnny Bob knew Davis was AWOL before he arrived at the estate or, as Harrell published above, learned this information only after Davis's arrival.[34]

Regardless, later, Harrell said, ultimately, it would not have mattered to him anyway as the estate was open to anyone seeking sanctuary—and this was especially true once Harrell learned of Davis's boot camp allegations and discovered this was not a "normal" type of desertion.[35]

Allegedly, Davis related to Harrell the horrors of the marines and his base camp. When Harrell heard these stories, he offered Davis full refuge.[36] Harrell later said:

> The Lord then instructed the group that Mr. Davis came for a purpose in order to bring before the minds of the American people the sordid conditions within our Armed Forces…
>
> The conditions of our training camps are no better than what we are being sent to fight.
>
> We want the world to see what is happening in our training camps.[37]

As with his fellow AWOL buddy, once Davis got settled in Louisville, he, too, reached out to his parents, who, he says, he had not spoken to for several months, to let them know that he was not "missing" and was, basically, okay and now residing at a religious retreat in an obscure part of southern Illinois. The last weekend of July 1961, Dion's father (reportedly the manager for an A&P grocery store in Pennsylvania) came from his home to Louisville to try to get his son to surrender or, at least, return home with them.[38] According to one source, the meeting of father and son was less than cordial.[39] The elder Davis is said to have mocked his son's religious beliefs and to have said he would prefer to see his boy in an asylum rather than continuing to reside in the Louisville estate.[40] Still, Davis's dad, Ted, supposedly "pleaded" with his son to leave the compound, but to no avail.[41] Afterward, Ted Davis wondered to the press, "how [can] such a place exist where the government can't go inside and get my son?"[42]

Davis was also the recipient of a phone call from his mother. She, too, failed to talk her son into turning himself in.[43] Later, Dion's mother was quoted in an article as stating that her son, "must have had a mental breakdown and can't be responsible for what he has done."[44]

Eventually, the U.S. military learned of Davis's whereabouts. How the U.S. military learned this is not fully known. Davis himself has stated, "I wouldn't be surprised if it was Harrell himself who contacted them!"[45] Also, in at least one published account from many years later, it does state exactly that.[46] However, it has also been reported that it was actually Dion's father, who, after he came back from Illinois, alerted the authorities about his AWOL son's current location.[47]

Another plausible theory is that when Davis's AWOL buddy left Illinois for Tennessee with his parents, he would, probably, have had to answer to someone eventually, with one of their first questions no doubt being about Davis's then whereabouts.

In any event, police and military authorities were informed of Davis's location on August 1, 1961.[48]

As this was a federal matter, the task of retrieving Davis fell not to local police, but to an FBI agent from the Centralia, Illinois, office named Manley Hawks (FBI No. 1,452).[49] Hawks later said that he knew little of the situation before he first arrived at the Harrell estate on that Tuesday afternoon around 4 p.m.[50]

Again, finding the Harrell estate was no trouble at all. Met at the gate by estate residents, news of Hawks's arrival was then conveyed to Johnny Bob's mother in the brown brick office building on the grounds in the foreground of the massive Mt. Vernon house. Then Johnny Bob's mother called up to either the main house or the living quarters of the garage to summon her son.[51]

Shortly thereafter, Johnny Bob came down to the front gate. It was at that front entrance, its driveway blocked by a wide metal-and-wood lift gate, that Hawks first met Johnny Bob Harrell.[52]

No one quite knows what Hawks was expecting when he arrived—would this be an easy hand off? If that was what he was expecting, though, that certainly was not what he got. As reported in the press the next day, Harrell showed up to meet with Hawks flanked by two "guards," two of his church members, each holding rifles. Further off in the distance behind them were other Harrell followers, reportedly as many as twelve, allegedly armed and looking on from behind the trees.[53]

The first local news of the runaway marine taking refuge in Louisville hit the newspapers on the morning after that meeting, on Wednesday, August 2, 1961.[54] It was reported that, at the meeting, Harrell confirmed that Davis was indeed inside but that he would not turn Davis over despite the fact that the FBI agent informed Harrell that in not doing so he was aiding and abetting a wanted criminal.[55]

Harrell was quoted in the press as stating that the young man had arrived at the estate approximately two weeks earlier, telling tales of "debauchery, atheism and brain washing" as well as other "ugly vileness" at the boot camp in Virginia.[56] According to Harrell, Davis had taken refuge from the "immoral activities" of the marines that "trained men so they can turn on their own people like in Communist countries...."[57]

Harrell would go on to say that he was not holding Davis (or anyone else) at the estate against their will and that the young man was free to go anytime he wished, but so far, Davis did not wish to leave, supposedly stating, "I'll be here for quite a while."[58]

Later, Davis was quoted in the press as saying that the marines "flaunted sin right in your face" and that the camp's nearby town was a busy den of prostitution and that the camp regularly provided meeting spaces to area atheists.[59] Davis is said to have said that it was not right in normal circumstances to go AWOL from military services but "in this case it is right."

Harrell later elaborated and said that Pvt. Davis had fled to escape atheism, debauchery, and immorality.[60] Harrell went on to state that the young marine would be allowed to stay at the estate for as long as he wished and then repeated what would become a familiar line, "They'll have to kill me to take this boy out of here."[61] Harrell would go on to add:

> We have people here who will fight at the drop of a hat. Anyone coming in peace will find kindness but any looking for trouble will find a reception as cold and hard as steel.
>
> Davis is just another victim of communist infiltration.... We can't spend one cent to fire a bullet at Khrushchev or Castro but we'll spend billions to break the hearts of these young boys.[62]
>
> ... This is the Lord's fight. We are few against many because the Lord wants credit for the victory.... The next move is up to them [the FBI], I guess they'll send a contingent here to try to take Davis, I won't permit them to use force to take him.[63]

Further labeling any attempt to take Davis as an "invasion," Harrell went on to say:

> I'm not angry at anyone, I'm just angry at the system. There are literally tens of thousands of boys in the service who are being brainwashed, hurt, bruised—physically, mentally and spiritually....
>
> The Communists say, "Better be Red than dead." Well, I'm not going to live that way. I'll take "dead."[64]

Then, just in case, Harrell had not been clear about his position, it was reported he also invoked the will of the Lord: "I had a direct message from God ordering me not to surrender Davis!"[65]

It is believed that this initial meeting between Harrell and Hawks was quite brief and quite cordial. And that Hawks did not even lay eyes on Davis at that meeting, speaking only to Harrell. Harrell though promised to show Davis to Hawks—but not give Davis up—if Hawks returned the next day.[66]

That next day, at approximately 11 a.m., G-man Hawks returned, bringing with him Louisville's local sheriff Walter Welch.[67] Once again,

Hawks met with Harrell at the front gate entrance to the estate. Once again, Harrell—who would later question the true identify of Mr. Hawks and if he was really with the FBI at all—was adamant in his convictions and in his refusal for them to meet with Dion Davis or even to see Davis.[68] Harrell also denied them entrance to his property unless both men agreed to lay down their firearms.[69] Both men refused, and soon after, they departed from the grounds.[70]

That evening, Harrell later reported, he received a phone call from Manley Hawks asking if Harrell would be willing to speak with FBI senior agent Robert Gibbons the next morning. Harrell said he would, provided that the man arrived carrying proper identification.[71]

The next day was Thursday, August 3. In the morning, Hawks (or the "so-called Hawks," as Johnny Bob would later call him) phoned Harrell again and told him he would be coming to the estate later that day with Agent Gibbons (or the "so-called Agent Gibbons" as Johnny Bob also call him).[72]

That day, the meeting at the gate commenced at about 4 p.m. Hawks and Welch were joined by Agent Gibbons.[73] All three men were also joined by members of the local press, including a camera crew from a TV station out of Champaign, Illinois. It was suspected that Harrell himself had called the media.[74] Harrell supposedly wanted them to witness his refusal to hand over Davis. Welch would later publicly denounce Harrell's publicity-seeking and grand-standing techniques.[75]

As at the prior meetings, Harrell was flanked by shot-gun holding guards from his church/estate.[76] That day the men were also joined, finally, by Dion Davis.[77] In their reports, the press described Davis as "slender, side-burned" and "pencil-mustached."[78] Although Davis says today that he does not remember uttering one word at the meeting—letting Johnny Bob do all the talking—he was quoted in the press as stating he had fled the marines because they were "trying to teach me to be a killer and I wanted to be a missionary."[79] His parents ridiculed and laughed at this desire, according to a published source.[80] Davis also added, "If the Lord wants me to cause trouble, I'll cause trouble. If He wants me to leave, I'll leave."[81]

"Do you refuse to come with us voluntarily?" Gibbons ultimately asked of the young man.

"I refuse," Davis allegedly replied. "I don't trust the Marine Corps one inch."[82]

Gibbons and Hawks continued to try to reason with Davis, supposedly pointing out that Davis's refusal "could lead to something that might mean your life or my life or the lives of those across the street."[83] The two officials added that he was "hurting the military with the publicity" that he had created with his actions.

Later, the law agents attempted another tract with Davis. Gibbons appealed to Davis's sense of loyalty, saying, "After all, we're [the FBI] fighting communism too."

To this, Davis is said to have replied, "Then join us!"[84]

The methods of the FBI did little to impress Johnny Bob, who later said to the press, "[They] are trying the soft-sell approach to get the boy from me…. If they can't fill men with the love of God, they have no business calling them into service."[85]

Harrell further stated to the press that "I won't permit them to use force to take Davis" and "It's possible they might bring up an armed contingent. But we're ready for them. We have supplies to hold out for weeks."[86, 87]

Davis has said in recent years, "Harrell tried to tell them that his house was a sovereign state and that they had no jurisdiction over him."[88]

It was also reported that, at one point, Davis did say he would return to his base in Virginia if he was promised no punishment and an honorable, or even dishonorable, discharge. Otherwise, said Davis, "The Marines will literally work me to death if they got hold of me."[89] However, the FBI men did not take Davis up on his request. The meeting between law enforcement, Harrell and Davis is said to have lasted about forty minutes.

While Manley Hawks and the other men were blocked once again from entering the estate, Harrell did not bar the news media, including an Associated Press photographer, who was invited into the grounds and took several snaps of the various people gathered at the gate that day for the face-to-face meeting. Later, the photographer was invited up to the house to take shots of Harrell and Dion Davis, both posing in front of the massive Mt. Vernon house and staring out defiantly. These photos would soon be seen from coast to coast.

To those same media outlets, Robert Gibbons stated that in his twenty-seven years in the FBI, he had never been forced to use violence in making an arrest but that it was quite possible that a fight would soon be necessary in order to retrieve this AWOL serviceman.[90]

Another attempt by Hawks to obtain Davis from Harrell took place later that evening. This negotiation took place over the telephone and it saw Hawks, once again, rebuffed by Johnny Bob.[91] That was the evening of Thursday, August 3.

Johnny Bob Harrell would later report that that evening, after the FBI men had left, the Lord impressed upon him a great sense of "something wrong" and of approaching "danger." That night, Harrell instructed that three automobiles belonging to residents in the compound be parked in front of the front entrance to the estate to form an imposing blockade, just in case.[92]

The next morning, the early morning raid began, not surprisingly, with military precision. After the over 100 men—twenty-five FBI agents and

103 state troopers, some only deputized the night before—were known to be in place, FBI special agent Robert Gibbons gave the "go" at 4 a.m.[93]

The attack was multi-pronged; the attack was simultaneous with teams of men, guns drawn, storming the Harrell grounds from, at least, four different entry points—the main gate; the grounds' secondary gate, just down the road; from across the Wabash River; and even from the air.[94]

For those living on the grounds, all they recall—at first—was the cacophony of noise that devastated the calm, quiet night—the crashing of metal, the shrieking screams of their friends, the yells from inside the cabins and rooms, and the shouts of deep, foreign voices coming suddenly from all sides from out of the darkness.[95]

The metal arms of the front gate and the parked cars were no match for the tank-like army half-track that barreled through the compound's main gate—the noise of metal on metal, being crushed, ricocheted throughout the property.[96]

From the back of the half-track where he was, Illinois State Police Officer Joe Middleton used a megaphone and ordered all those on the grounds to immediately surrender. Also at the front guard gate, State Trooper Wilfred Rauch called from his position on the half-track and demanded that the two boys, standing guard and holding rifles, drop their arms. The boys did as they were told though not before one ran and set off the alarm on the grounds that alerted everyone to the attack.[97]

As the half-track moved into the property, a phalanx of ten police cars followed it in, and dozens of men spilled from each of the vehicles. Toting guns and other weapons, groups of men rapidly fanned out to all parts of the compound, rushing in all directions, running to every corner. Some stormed down the long row of cabins, kicking in their doors and smashing the glass of the windows with the ends of their rifles, one after another.[98]

Overhead, a low-flying airplane swooped down. The plane came so close, it felt like it was grazing the ground. Equipped with loud speakers on its wings, a resounding voice yelled from above "COME OUT—YOU'RE SURROUNDED!" and the plane's giant searchlights flooded the scene with fractured beams of blinding light.[99]

The group of soldiers that rushed the Mt. Vernon house entered its front door while another set scaled its back, external staircase to get to the second floor. Inside, they ran down its halls, room after room, their footsteps pounding and echoing through the wood floors as the home's residents scattered, fell to their floor in prayer, or gripped their bed frames in terror. Some of the men who lived inside reached for the guns or knives that they had been told to keep handy. Some lunged for the invading soldiers. Some rushed from the house ready to do battle on the lawn. They swarmed out "like flies," as one solider later related.[100] Johnny Bob had warned them about this, but what was going on? Who were these people? Townspeople? The long-feared communists? Vance Comer would later relay that he thought the invaders were members of "the gang we had been guarding against."[101]

Confusion reigned as the blaring of sirens and the estate's own "warning bell" added to the deafening noise. Shouts were heard: "Drop those guns!" and "You're not going to take Dion!" Children screamed or ran or clung to their mothers. As Harrell's followers—all still in their night clothes— emerged from their cabins, most were quickly tackled and taken to the ground. Tod Harrell was hit on the head, allegedly when he tried to come to the defense of his pregnant mother. Harold Leib's skull was cut open. Soon man-to-man, hand-to-hand struggles were seen all over the grounds. Agent Gibbons climbed up the property's water tower to gain a better vantage point.[102] From there, he saw the rays of the many army flashlights mainly focused on one cabin along the estate's southern edge—Dion Davis's cabin, the man they had come for.[103]

As residents began to pour from their campers and cabins, other teams of army men marched onto the grounds from a secondary entrance, using wire cutters to tear away parts of the estate's fence, while still another battalion marched up the hill from the river.[104] Harrell's mother later described the incoming horde, "They were as the sands of the seas."[105]

All over the property, guns were drawn and fists were raised. Men stood, frozen, at gunpoint—soldiers had their weapons fixed on them. Besides the rifles they carried, the soldiers had brought with them canisters of tear gas, axes, and baseball bats. Through the noise and confusion, the women and children of the estate, most in nightgowns or pajamas, were forced out of their cabins and then moved, as a group, to various trailers, one after the next, before being ordered to stand under a large oak tree on the property. They did this, gathering tightly together in the hot early morning air.[106]

Then, being seen being pulled from the Mt. Vernon house, was Johnny Bob himself. He had been found in the basement of the main house, inside the underground "tunnel" where he was said to have surrendered without incident.[107] As he was being lead from the home, both of his arms restrained by soldiers, he cried out to all his followers, "Do not fire your weapons!"[108]

Later, Harrell would state that he had been alerted by one of the guards on the grounds earlier that night about some headlights seen just outside the property. Harrell reported that this had been reported to him at about 3 a.m. Concerned and propelled by the Lord, he said, Harrell had quickly dressed and had made his way from the separate garage building to the basement of the Mt. Vernon home.[109]

The first thing Dion Davis remembers of that morning was being yanked awake "surrounded on all sides, four people standing above me with rifles pointed down at me.[110] They hog-tied me and dragged me out of bed. I didn't have a shirt on, and they tore the pants I had on."[111] Later, it was reported that, at his capture, Davis "struggled violently" and had "refused to walk" when apprehended.[112] Eventually, Davis was locked into leg irons.[113]

The attack was headed up by FBI special agent Robert Gibbons. Along with Rauch and Middleton, also part of the raid team that morning were Illinois State Policeman William Morris; Frederick Draper, an FBI agent out of Carbondale, and State Trooper Kenneth Groff.

As dawn finally broke, much of the commotion—if not the fear and shock—of the raid began to die out. Estate members could finally see the amount of damage that had been done to the property by the vehicles, the half-track and all the marauding soldiers. They could also see, parked at the edge of the property, two bulldozers, each at the ready to demolish any or all of the compound's cabins and other out buildings if necessary.[114]

If the raid was an utter surprise to the members of the Harrell community, others in area were well aware of the government's plans.[115] Not only did the local and state police and Louisville's mayor know of the upcoming mission, so did some area businesses. Rather disturbingly, the local funeral home, Neal Funeral Home, was notified and prepped to act as a hospital triage in case there were any injuries among the soldiers or the residents. They were also told to be prepared for the possibly of causalities.[116]

Additionally, the military had expected so many people to be arrested as a result of the raid that they assumed that the local jail wouldn't hold them all. So, Louisville's roller rink (ironically a business John Harrell once owned) was commandeered to use as a temporary holding center for the police.[117]

After his arrest, the injured Harold Leib was taken with the other handcuffed men to the roller rink, where they were ordered to sit on the rink's skating floor. By that time, though, Leib had been injured and his head wound was bleeding badly. After he leaned his head back against the wall of the rink, he left behind a large blood stain that would remain faintly visible on the roller rink's wall for several years to come. Leib says that he was hit on the head and knocked to the floor when he momentarily panicked and attempted to grab the barrel of one of the soldier's guns.[118]

As Tod Harrell was one of the very few others injured during the raid, the 6-foot, 200-lb teenager was first transported to the local funeral home and then to the hospital in nearby Flora, Illinois, where he received four stiches to seal up the wound on his head. Finally, he was returned, after "a couple of hours," to the then filled-to-capacity Clay County Jail in Louisville where he rejoined the other arrested followers who had already been moved there. Today, Tod takes the blames for his injury.[119] He says, "I lunged for one of the guns and I got mouthy."[120]

Originally, it is believed, the authorities planned to arrest everyone residing on the estate—men, women, and children—but once there, they realized that that was completely impractical as there were too many people living on the grounds. The plan was then immediately altered, and it was decided to only apprehend all the males on the land, leaving behind all women and children. Eventually, they were told to arrest only those men who offered resistance and/or brandished a gun or other weapon.[121] Ultimately, along with Johnny Bob and Tod and Dion Davis, sixteen other men were arrested.[122] Published reports differ in regard to if any of the compound's women were armed or not; regardless, no women were taken into custody that morning.

As the raid played out, Dion Davis remembers being only "in shock" before finding himself thrown into—he believes—the local Clay County Jail where he obtained a shirt to wear from a fellow prisoner.[123] Later, photographs of Davis, seen both in custody and exiting the jailhouse— the latter in his borrowed shirt—and flanked by MPs would appear in newspapers nationwide. A later newspaper reporter stated Davis looked disheveled from "wear and tear" and as being attired in "dark trousers," with some articles making note of the sizable rip in his pant leg.[124]

In retrospect, it is nothing short of miraculous that not only was no one seriously injured in the raid, but not one single shot was ever fired by either side. Not that the events of that morning did not come to close to ending in massive bloodshed. Everyone who lived through the raid still vividly recalls the tension in the air during those early morning moments. Though it was rumored that there were over 100 people living on the grounds, there were actually only about sixty. Regardless, though, when those sixty people were rushed by 100 armed men flooding the grounds in the dark of night, bedlam and havoc was inevitable. Tod Harrell says, "A firecracker could have set it off."[125] Even an accidently fired weapon, by either side, could have resulted in the tragic loss of life. One estate resident has since said, "It could easily have become another Waco."[126]

Asked later why they did not utilize any of the guns they had at their disposal, a Harrell follower stated, "The Lord did not tell us to fire the first shot."[127]

For Angelyn Comer Garcia, the then eight-year-old daughter of Vance Comer, who by that time was living on grounds with her mom and dad in a trailer they had purchased, it would take her almost twenty years before she was ready to speak about the morning of the raid. Garcia, whose father was one of the guards on patrol that night, still has a clear memory of being suddenly awoken by her mother, and being told to quickly get dressed and of then peeking out the slanted window of their trailer to see an array of army men and police marching, moving in mass, towards their home. Angie's dad would be one of the men arrested that morning.[128]

Today, Garcia firmly believes that much of the before-dawn invasion was total overkill. She says, "The doors of those cabins didn't even have locks on them, there was no reason to kick them in or go around knocking out windows with the ends of their rifles...."[129]

Lester Kellums, who was also living on the grounds with his family, echoes her thoughts. He remembers Davis on the grounds and often of making trips into Louisville. Kellums wonders today, "If they [the military] wanted him so bad, why didn't they just grab him sometime when he walking down the street?"[130]

In retrospect, the collective military might that the authorities utilized that morning does seem extreme, but the intel the authorities had on the group was either scant or disproportionately based on rumor. For example, many of the soldiers that morning had been equipped with heavy bats because rumors of vicious guard dogs living on the grounds had been widespread. The Harrell estate was also rumored to be an arsenal of guns and many townspeople had told stories of seeing daily target practice occurring on the grounds. Furthermore, Harrell himself had, allegedly, threatened force against any forceful attempt to disrupt the camp or apprehend Davis.[131] The army and police did not want to go in without being prepared for the worst which all the more adds to the extraordinary fact that there were no major injuries or fatalities occurred during the mission.

After they were arrested, all of the men were transported out of town and to East St. Louis for arraignment. Ironically, the author's uncle, Kent O'Dell, co-owned one of the service stations in the nearby town of Kinmundy at that time. He happened to be working at the station the morning of the raid when the long, unprecedented line of police cars came through Kinmundy as they drove on to East St. Louis. O'Dell distinctly recalls the site of Harrell in the back seat of one of the black and whites, arms pinned behind his back, his long Jesus hair falling and resting on his shoulders.[132]

Along with Johnny Bob, Tod, Davis, and Vance Comer, the other men arrested that morning were Thomas H. Ladley, James F. Gillard, Carl E. Stanley, Charles C. Childers, Lloyd W. Stanley, Harold B. Leib, Robert Murie, Jim C. Kellums, Robert D. Grosnick, Roger Moore, Arthur Leib, William Kuhlig, Lester Kellums, and Gene Densmore. Excluding Tod, who was still in his teens, the men ranged in age from twenty-three to fifty-eight, including Johnny Bob. They were all facing charges of harboring a deserter, a crime that, if they were convicted of, could send them each to jail for three years. Young Tod was charged with one count of assaulting a federal agent. Six of the men were charged with resisting federal officers. Bond for each of the men was also established and ranged from $2,500 to $7,000. A preliminary hearing was set for August 14.[133]

Along with various members of the sect, the feds also confiscated a cachet of rifles, side arms, and "thousands of rounds" of ammunition.[134] An Associated Press photograph taken that day shows an assortment of rifles being loaded into a police car, but quite clearly, many of the guns are still in their boxes, hardly battle-ready.[135] This fact gives credence to a later claim from Harrell that many of the guns seized in the raid were not the property of compound members but inventory for his mail-order sporting goods company.[136] It was reported in the news that also taken in the raid were "several" unspecified "pieces of equipment."[137]

News of the large raid was a national and international story; nearly every newspaper in the U.S. made mention of the government storming into this small-town compound, most of the papers reported it on their front pages, and many referred to it as a "smooth" military operation.[138]

For their coverage, some newspapers dug out photos of Harrell from back during his senate race or the popular shot of Harrell standing in front of his Mount Vernon home still under construction. For a photo of Dion Davis, some papers went so far as to obtain a copy of Davis's high school senior photo to run on their pages.

Later, the press got their hands on a handful of photos of Davis, Harrell, and sometimes Davis and Harrell pictured together taken on the grounds. In one, a defiant-looking Davis stands clutching what appears to be a Bible and is seen in front of a large plaque then hanging on the Mount Vernon house. The hanging spoke of the home's deliverance "upon the direction of the Lord God and of Moses and is an enlarged replica of George Washington's Mount Vernon."

In the days immediately following the raid, more information about it came to light. The raid had been authorized by none other than founding FBI director and then head, J. Edgar Hoover, who was quoted as saying that the actions of Harrell and his followers were "in a state of armed insurrection against the United States." When the press later inquired of Johnny Bob if Hoover's was an adequate assessment, Harrell responded, "Not even remotely."[139]

The night before the raid, the majority of the soldiers had been readied in Effingham before being brought to Louisville.[140] Immediately before the raid began, they gathered at the local roller rink just down the road from the Harrell estate.[141] From there, the troops were mobilized to their entry points and told to hide in any undergrowth available until the airplane was almost overhead and the half-track was at the ready at the main entrance. When that time arrived, the men would be simultaneously deployed.[142]

Of the followers, those who remained on the property began to tell their stories to the press as well. Johnny Bob's wife, Betty, who was at that time expecting the couple's fifth child, was quoted as saying that there were others injured in the action including Mrs. Ruth Leib, who was struck down for no reason. Mrs. Harrell said, the woman was "just praising the Lord with a Bible in her hand" when the blow came.[143] Along with Mrs. Leib, the Harrell Family's longtime housekeeper, Flora Rowan, reported various smaller injuries or near injuries when shards of glass went flying after being shattered by the incoming troops.[144]

Fifteen-year-old Ruth Ann Stanley, who lived on the property, told the press that her mother saw some of the soldiers about fifteen minutes before the attack. "The Lord had placed white shirts on those men for my mother to see them in the dark," she said.[145]

Others still on the estate put forth the party line by saying, "If they would use all that energy against communism there would be none left in the state."[146] Others swore to their perseverance in light of the recent events, "The Lord told us they would come and do just what they have done. We are not discouraged...."[147]

Thirteen-year-old Linda Rowan said, "God has a purpose for it. We're the chosen."[148]

Mrs. Lester Kellums said, "They'll be back. And we'll carry on. After all, Mr. Harrell is with us. He knows."[149]

Once in East St. Louis, all members of the arrested Harrell group were photographed walking in an orderly formation into the courthouse. The Louisville group was so large they filled an entire cell block. Johnny Bob insisted that his son, Tod, be kept with him.[150]

All of the men were then processed, photographed, and fingerprinted. They were arraigned in the office of U.S. commissioner Elvira Fellner, at the East St. Louis federal building.[151]

Reporters were on the scene in St. Louis as well, but according to Johnny Bob, he and all the other arrested men were barred from talking to them, though that did not prevent one newspaper as describing Harrell's appearance as "gaudily dressed in cowboy boots, khaki trousers, and a lavender work shirt."[152] Harrell was photographed holding a Bible in his hand.

Someone was able, however, to gain access to Dion Davis, who was described as talking "freely" to reporters before being arranged.[153] Allegedly, Davis told reporters, "I can't fight God and country with the marines. I have to stay here with Mr. Harrell where there's no excuse for being shot."[154]

The afternoon after the raid, a reporter for the UPI news services located Davis's parents in Greenville, Pennsylvania, to inform them that their son had been captured and was now in police custody. Dion's father, Ted, was quoted as saying, "That's good. I'm glad to hear it. Naturally, we're going to work with the FBI and the Marine Corps and find out what happened and bring [Dion] back to the way he was when he left us—a good, clean moral fellow."[155]

Dion's mother was also spoken to, telling the reporter, "I can't decide at the moment if I'll go visit him, although I certainly would like to see him."[156]

Davis was not among those arraigned that day. Instead, he was dispatched from East St. Louis to St. Louis and, from there, turned over to the military corps; they would handle him themselves.[157] After being separated that day in East St. Louis, neither Dion Davis nor Johnny Bob Harrell would ever see or speak to each other again.

Hunted

[In a crisis] a man always falls back upon what he knows best.

James Thurber

As Harrell, his son, and the sixteen other men went through the system in East St. Louis, back in Louisville, Natalia Harrell, Johnny Bob's mother, mobilized quickly to be able to bond them out. She would do it by putting up as collateral various parts of Johnny Bob's businesses, property, and land holdings.[1] As she set about gathering up all the necessary deeds, titles, and tax records, it was a task, she said, that was now far more difficult as the men who had stormed the grounds the day before had recklessly seized and scattered files and papers throughout the house while also upturning furniture and dumping out dresser drawers. Mrs. Harrell was quoted as saying, "They searched everywhere. They even searched the refrigerator."[2]

The time it took her to procure all the necessary paperwork meant that her son and grandson would have to spend at least one night in the East St. Louis jail.

As the older Mrs. Harrell took to that job, the other women in the camp announced that they would immediately begin a fasting and prayer vigil.[3] Patricia Gilliard, whose husband was one of those arrested that morning, stated, "We will fast and pray until the Lord tells us to stop." It was noted, however, that Johnny Bob's wife, Betty, many months pregnant, did not take part in the fast due to her condition. But Johnny Bob's mother refused any food and sustained herself only by drinking milk.[4] That night, for the sake of safety and community, all the women left their cabins and trailers and took up residence in the big Mount Vernon house.[5]

Eventually, via a Western Union money transfer, Mrs. Harrell was able to post the $9,500, which allowed for the release of Johnny Bob and Tod.[6]

The other men, however, would have to wait until the other additional bail money could be generated. Eventually, the Mt. Vernon house was put up as collateral.[7]

After posting bail, the Harrells, father and son, immediately returned to the Louisville compound where their arrival back on the property was greeted with cheers from all the followers.[8]

Harrell's night in jail had, seemingly, done little to dampen his zeal. After first complaining that his jailers refused to supply him with a Bible after he specifically requested one, Harrell was then quoted as saying that he was now in fear of a mob of citizens from Louisville attacking his homestead. Yet if that happened, he said, he and his group would again be ready. "We won't fight the FBI, but a local mob is something else."[9]

Harrell also stated that, at that time, he did not know if the women on the grounds would conclude their fast or not.[10] "There will be instructions. They'll know themselves. They're close enough to the Lord to know," he said.[11]

That same day, Harrell went on the offensive again. Harrell took to the phones and called every media outlet in the vicinity to condemn the raid and the government that authorized it.[12] After he pledged that he would pay for all legal fees that might be incurred by Dion Davis, Harrell accused the U.S. government of mail tampering. He said that his letters "had been steamed open and you could still smell the tea kettle when I got them."[13] In that same interview, Harrell also stated that various communists were still active in the local government and that they had successfully blocked $200,000 due to him in royalties from his mausoleum patents. "The Communist conspiracy has done everything it could do to break up this retreat, but we are stronger than ever," he asserted.[14]

In order to prove his case, Harrell offered himself and his followers as subjects of a lie detector test—as long as he could be assured that the administrator of the test was fair and impartial.[15]

Harrell then went on to state that he had yet to see any warrant for his arrest or any warrant to come onto his property in regard to the raid. Did one even exist? Later, he would also state that not once during any of his meetings at the compound's gate was he ever explicitly asked by police or the FBI to turn over Dion Davis.[16] He said of the raiders, "[They] came onto these grounds slashing, knocking down women and children ... like Hitler moving into the Rhineland.... Any Christian work that amounts to anything must be preceded by persecution."[17]

Also the day after the raid, it was reported in the press that U.S. postal authorities (who were supposedly alarmed by the extraordinary amounts of mail found on the Harrell grounds) and the IRS had both begun investigations into the Harrell-CCC operation.[18] Describing the business records seized as a "mess," federal tax auditors had also begun investigating some of Johnny Bob's businesses as the government—like various Louisville citizens—had begun to wonder just how Harrell had been able to bankroll all his extensive estate and church activities.[19]

Harrell responded to all these reports in an expected fashion. He said, "They want to find enough to put me in the penitentiary," adding, "if they couldn't find anything wrong, [they'll] make something wrong."[20] Later, Harrell would accuse the FBI of looting his estate of not only his (legally owned) guns but also of paper currency and silver dollars. Harrell then threatened legal action against the government if his property was not returned in due course. His attorney also attempted to have suppressed from the trial any and all seized items.[21]

On August 7, Harrell announced that bond was being posted for the remaining men still in jail in East St. Louis. Harrell said he would be putting up his entire estate—valued at $105,000—in order to secure the group's release.[22] Additionally, while in the St. Louis jail, Harrell had met an eighteen-year-old who was being held for stealing his sister's car. Harrell later announced to the press that he would pay for this youth's bail as well if the young man would be willing to return to Louisville with him.[23] Nothing seems to have resulted from the offer.

The next day—August 8—Johnny Bob and several members of his group traveled to East St. Louis and delivered the necessary deeds to Commissioner Fellner, who then released the other men. Those who had come from Louisville that morning also delivered to the men clean clothes and some spending money.[24] Upon their departure, the men were quoted in the press as saying that during their three-day incarceration, they had been treated well but they did complain that no Bibles had been issued to them and that their pillows and mattresses were dirty.[25] After the bond was posted, all of the men returned to Louisville.

The day prior, Harrell did something quite unexpected—he announced that, beginning the following Sunday, he would be opening his Louisville estate to any and all members of the public for guided tours.[26] Along with being able to see the grounds, visitors would also be able to attend daily lectures by Johnny Bob.[27] The mission, according to Harrell, was to correct any incorrect impressions the public may have about him or his retreat from all the "slanted" press coverage and for people to see the extensive damage inflicted on the grounds, its buildings, and one of his airplanes by the government raid.[28] The military would never admit to causing more than "minor damage" to the property.[29]

Inexplicably in the press, the Harrell estate was now being increasingly referred to as "Mount Zion," though this was never a name used by Johnny Bob or the CCC.[30] The estate was, however, now being characterized by Harrell as a "citadel of anti-communism."[31]

The size of the crowds that showed up for the twice-a-day, free tour of the "citadel" that weekend were double what was expected and may have totaled as many as 2,000.[32] Johnny Bob said, "They came from as far away as Connecticut and California."[33] Especially popular was the cabin where Dion Davis had resided, which was now, according to the press, being treated as a "shrine."[34] Johnny Bob took the occasion of the tours to announce that he was establishing a "Dion Davis Freedom Fund," to pay for the young marine's legal defense. Early donors to that cause were Mr. and Mrs. Clifford Sharp of Waterman, Illinois, and Mr. and Mrs. Frank Thompson of Shabbona, Illinois.[35] They visited the estate after reading about the raid in a northern Illinois newspaper.[36] Today, Davis says he never received any funds.[37]

Amid all the news being generated by and around Johnny Bob, major news for him personally was reported on August 14, 1961, when he announced that he and his wife, Betty, had, the day before, welcomed their fifth child, a girl that they named Deborah.[38]

That same month, with everyone reacting to Harrell's new notoriety, Johnny Bob was asked to speak to a meeting of the Danville (Illinois) Jaycees.[39] He accepted. The meeting was crowded and Harrell's spoke for nearly two straight hours on such familiar topics as God, war, communism, patriotism, Christianity, taxes, and education.[40] The next day, the event was written up in the Danville newspaper, where a reporter in attendance said:

> Though praised on some opinions, his logic on others escapes some listeners.... He jumped from one subject to another using ... stock phrases, frequent quotes from historical figures in US history and the bible.[41]

Among other various predictions that Harrell offered up that day was the "fact" that the U.S. would be at war by the end of the year.[42] It was noted in the article that while the Jaycees sponsored the event, many members of the group refused to be photographed alongside their guest speaker after the talk.[43]

Other Harrell news arrived on August 18, 1961 when it was reported that Harrell and his group of followers had waived a hearing of their charges that was to take place on August 21 in Benton, IL. As explained by U.S. Commissioner Everett Lewis, the case would therefore immediately proceed to a federal grand jury in East St. Louis.[44]

After waiving the Benton hearing, Harrell said he would though be requesting a change of venue from East St. Louis to Danville, IL. He stated, "It would be more convenient for us. My attorney, John Unger, lives in

Danville."[45] Additionally, Harrell said he would not be able to obtain a fair trial in St. Louis due to all the pre-trial publicity surrounding the case. Harrell also said that he and Unger would be filing a motion to suppress any evidence seized during the raid by the FBI or the police, namely any mention of the rifles and other fire arms as they were illegally seized since no warrant was ever issued for those items. Harrell also continued to maintain that the guns taken were for the sporting goods business he and his mother had run since 1946. He said, "[My mother] is a business woman. We didn't have an arsenal here."[46] Credence to this argument was obtained when the Jefferson Arms Corporation filed suit against the FBI and the Illinois State Police for return of many of the guns that had been seized. The company maintained that they had been shipped to the Harrells for sale but since they had not been sold, they were still part of their company's inventory and they were entitled to them back.[47]

Also filed that day was a motion by Harrell's lawyer to obtain the names and address of the 100 or so men who participated in the early morning raid and another motion which asked for the dismissal of all charges.[48] Harrell added at the time, "I wish you could sue the President. He sent the raiders here. We are almost ready to fight. The move is almost ready to proceed against communism."[49]

Though the magnitude of the pre-dawn raid and subsequent news coverage greatly upset many of Louisville's citizens some of them—at least those willing to speak to the press at the time—seemed relieved by the arrest of Johnny Bob and the others. One said, "It should teach 'em a lesson!"[50] Another—local salesman George H. McGee—said, "I hope it's over. I had enough a long time ago."[51] Even Johnny Bob's own aunt, Mrs. Ira Eaton, said, "I think the raid should have happened sooner. It was past the time to stop."[52]

Another echoed an earlier sentiment by stating, "We haven't deserved this."[53] Also, according to that same article, many in town just could not figure out what had gotten into Johnny Bob. Though some said they once admired him, "now he has changed so much."[54]

As always in regard to the saga of Johnny Bob and his so-called cult, rumors flew out fast and wide about goings-on at the compound. As the Harrell group awaited trial, it was rumored that Harrell and every one of his followers were planning to flee the state, or the country, in one of Harrell's airplanes.[55] However, Harrell was the group's only pilot and none of his planes could seat more than six, which would have required innumerable (and very costly) repeated trips.

One of the most tantalizing—and enduring—of the various rumors that has sprung up over the years was a theory that Dion Davis was not a wayward serviceman at all but was, instead, a government plant, that the U.S. government had been monitoring Harrell and his cult and were looking for a good reason to go in and break it all up. Therefore, they sent Davis in as an undercover agent—a way of justifying their eventual actions.[56]

That particular theory became so strong it was even adopted, at times, by Johnny Bob himself, who would go on to espouse it in various interviews he would give in later years. He stated on more than one occasion that he believed the raid was a set-up, orchestrated in retaliation for statements he made about John F. Kennedy, Robert Kennedy, and Illinois State Senator Paul Douglas.[57]

Harrell had long made accusations against JFK. At one time, he said that Kennedy sent a Secret Service agent to warn him against speaking out against the government infiltration by communists. Of course, if that was true, it was certainly not advice heeded by Harrell.[58]

As thought-provoking as the "double agent" theory is, Davis's own story belies it and his personnel files from the military support only his account, not any alleged conspiracy.

As for Davis, he remembers his first days after the raid as a giant blur. Released into government custody, he was quickly hauled out of Illinois.[59] He was soon sentenced by a military court to six months in jail. In a subsequent news story, it was reported that his attorney, Glen Hooper, was planning an appeal.[60] Regardless, though Davis next found himself in a military prison that, only later, did he discover was in Ohio.[61] As for his time in jail, Davis conveys:

> I was really brutalized there ... by the guards. They knew my story and they liked to throw me up against the cement wall or hit me on the back of the head and say things like "You seein' God? ... You seein' God now, boy?"[62]

Davis adds, "I was there [in prison] for a while...."[63]

According to Dion Davis's military records obtained via the Freedom of Information Act and Mr. Davis's permission, his time in prison seemed to last from the time of his capture in Illinois until October 1961, at which time the records show his transfer to what Davis now calls "the Funny Farm," a military-run mental hospital located in Philadelphia.[64] Davis continues:

> I was diagnosed by them as being schizophrenic or paranoid schizophrenic or something, and they started to dope me up with Thorazin. It made everything foggy. But I knew I wasn't crazy, it was those pills that they gave me.[65]

Eventually, Davis began to hide his daily medication pills rather than swallow them. His mind immediately cleared, he says, and without too much effort, he was able to walk away from the mental hospital one night. A sympathetic psychologist lived near the hospital grounds and Davis went to his house and convinced the man to take him off the pills and reevaluate him.[66] Davis's calm argument was successful. Not long after, he was released from the institution.

Though now out of the "Funny Farm," Davis was not yet out of the military. He was eventually put in front of a military tribunal to discuss his situation. Davis says today, "I was given a choice to stay in the service or be a civilian again. I was young and I wanted out. I should have stayed. I could have put in my 20 to 25 years and had a nice pension."[67]

The military panel further determined that whatever Davis allegedly suffered from, he had been afflicted with before his entry into the service. Hence, the U.S. government was not to blame—and neither was Davis. Therefore, on July 5, 1962, Dion Davis was honorably discharged from the U.S. Marine Corps. He says, "Yeah, I was released, given one set of clothes, $150 in cash and a bus ride."[68]

Though now free, Davis could not yet get on with his life. There was still a lingering proceeding against him in Illinois. In mid-August 1962, Davis and his parents returned to East St. Louis to appear in a courtroom where he was facing a prison term of ten years and a fine of $10,000 for resisting a federal officer on the morning of the Harrell raid.[69] According to Davis, it was only his mother's impassioned plea to the presiding judge that prevented him from spending the next decade of his life behind bars.[70]

After his very brief return to Illinois, Davis returned to his Pennsylvania hometown and moved in again with his parents. However, the same troubles that Davis had with his father as a youth were even worse now that he was a grown man. He says, "My dad was not a good guy. My mom, though, was a saint."[71]

"I had a real attitude," he says. "I got into a lot of fights in Pennsylvania. I spent six months in jail again up there for [getting into a] fight." Later, after another infraction, a judge ordered him again into a mental institution for two months. There, Davis would undergo at least one round of electro-shock therapy.[72]

After his release from that facility, there would be another prison stint of about three months before a kindly judge, Davis says:

Saw something in me. And trusted me and even allowed me to be released on my own recognizance. And, believe it or not, that's what it finally took. I didn't want to let him down. Even now, I get choked up thinking about it. I sent him a Christmas card every year after that....[73]

Eventually, Davis would work in an auto body shop and even, briefly, pursue a career in fine art. Art had always been a passion of his but, he says, "I almost starved." For a time, he traveled as part of a carnival hauling two ponies around in a truck with him. He finally settled in Texas and spent about thirty-five years driving trucks around the oil fields of the state or, also for the oil companies, driving elsewhere within the continental U.S. and Canada.[74]

In the passing years, Davis never spoke to or saw Johnny Bob or any of Harrell's other followers again. Davis says he is now an atheist and has been one for many years. He says, from the vantage point of today:

> It's probably good what happened happened. I wonder if it could have been much worse if it might have gone the way of David Koresh or something. Why did I go? Probably for the same reasons anyone else went. We were not in a good place in life, and looking for refuge and answers that Johnny Bob seemed to have.[75]

Despite his brief time in Louisville, Davis remains still troubled by the things he witnessed there. He says:

> I really think Harrell was brainwashing people. He saw himself as some sort of messiah. And he convinced everyone—and these weren't dummies living there. They were professionals who left their jobs, one family had come from California to live there…. If I was messed up before, I really messed my mind up there.[76]

In Southern Illinois, in late 1961, Johnny Bob Harrell and his group continued to generate news stories about their "cult" and the raid. By this time, the press seemed to enjoy slowly chipping away at Harrell's story and credibility. Gradually, in reports about the morning of the raid, Johnny Bob went from (according to his followers) being found "meditating" in the tunnel under the house to (according to early press reports) being found "hiding" in the tunnel to (eventually, in later news reports) being found "cowering" in the long, dark concrete tunnel.[77, 78] Even the tunnel got relabeled as a "dark room."[79] Later it was reported that a loaded Mauser rifle was next to Harrell when he was discovered in the tunnel and that seven clips of ammo rested on the floor next to him with Harrell, momentarily, thinking of grabbing and firing the gun.[80]

Harrell also saw himself described in the press as everything from Dion Davis's "protector" to a "militant religious sect leader."[81, 82] Almost no press, however, failed to point out Harrell's personal wealth (still estimated by some to be around $200,000) or his unique ability to generate publicity for himself and his group.[83]

Yet if the military attack on the Harrell compound was meant to end or disband the group, it did not. Though the population on the estate dropped slightly, the great majority of Johnny Bob's followers returned to the estate. As one-time follower Johnny Leib has said, "We had no place else to go."[84]

The raid also, no doubt, helped unite the group together as never before. They now had first-hand evidence of the evil potential of communism.

Despite the commotion and the ongoing legal battles, Johnny Bob kept preaching and rallying against evil in all its forms. As many of the followers on the compound attended to the now-needed repairs—replacing the destroyed front gate, for example—Harrell announced plans to reopen his on-site school in late August.[85] Along with boasting in the press about his school's eight-room learning space, its air conditioning, and his recently purchased collection of 1,000 library books from a nearby Decatur school system, Harrell said he also dreamed of establishing a "vast educational institution." In terms of the latter, Harrell appealed to the public to side with him against the local Clay County officials who still deemed his school "illegal."[86]

While he was at it, Harrell also appealed to the local community, Illinois Senator Everett M. Dirksen, and other officials for assistance and help regarding his charges against the FBI for the damage done to his estate during the raid and to cease the "harassment and intimidation" he said he was still receiving from the local government.[87]

Harrell's private school opened for a new school year on September 1, 1961, and consisted of four teachers and twenty-five pupils (the small class size the better for "individual attention," Harrell contended). For whatever reason, Harrell and company were not fined this time for the school's operation.[88]

Then, on September 26, after various inexplicable delays and postponements, John Harrell, Tod, and the other men arrested were indicted with harboring a deserter from the U.S. military.[89] The Harrell group appeared in court in East St. Louis *en masse* on October 5, 1961.[90] Before going into the courthouse, however, the men were photographed posing on the building's front steps. In their suits and ties and with their neatly combed hair, the group looked more like a church choir than a band of radical government resisters.[91] Inside, each of the men and boys entered a plea of "not guilty."[92]

Outside, after the hearing—which was once again in front of Judge William Juergens—Harrell (true to form) handed out a printed statement criticizing the federal government for its weakness in combating communism.[93] Harrell went on to say that his estate back in Louisville had just completed building a set of nuclear fallout shelters as Harrell was sure that a nuclear attack against the U.S. would begin any day now; "the Lord told me," he said. "In fact," he added, "we will be fighting the Russian troops on American soil by Christmas. They will be coming via Cuba and Mexico."[94]

Later, from his estate, where six American flags were now flying above the Mount Vernon house, Johnny Bob told one reporter, "The Lord has told us that the United States will be subjected to a 7,000-megaton nuclear attack."[95] He later added that the Lord had just sent him a message that "Russian paratroopers will be dropped and will conquer the United States from the Atlantic to the Appalachians and from the Pacific to the Rockies."[96]

Then, to truly prove that he was truly unbowed in front of all the attacks against him, in November 1961, Johnny Bob announced he was considering another run for the Senate, unless, he said, another "outspoken Communist-fighting patriot volunteers to run."[97]

Though, by the start of 1962, he was already under a litany of lawsuits, ongoing court proceedings, and blazing headlines, Johnny Bob Harrell still found it possible to draw even more controversy unto himself.

On January 9, with the new year barely begun, Harrell announced in the press that he would be providing a $1,000 bond for some friends of his.[98] Mr. and Mrs. Edgar Johnson of nearby Flora, Illinois, were being charged with contempt of court for refusing to turn over some of their financial records that were being demanded for an investigation into their taxes.[99] Harrell knew compatriots when he saw them, and he delivered the bond for them himself at the East St. Louis courthouse where the Johnsons had a brief hearing in front of Judge William G. Juergens.[100] After the hearing, Harrell handed out a printed statement to reporters. That document stated that a "Communist Manifesto" was the source of the country's tax laws and that "the government is placing chains of slavery around its citizens."[101]

Later that same year, Harrell made another gesture of this sort. In October, he offered up his estate as bond for controversial general Edwin A. Walker who was then being held in a Springfield, Missouri, prison.[102] Walker had been arrested in September 1962 for his role in a fifteen-hour riot over the desegregation of the University of Mississippi. Walker did not riot himself but was charged with inciting insurrection and seditious conspiracy, which propelled approximately 1,000 students to turn violent. After being arrested, Walker was first sent to a psychiatric hospital for evaluation and then held on a bond of $100,000. Harrell's estate was, at the time, valued at $210,000. Harrell made his offer to Walker via Robert Welch, head of the John Birch Society, who had already offered to assist Walker.[103] Harrell was not affiliated with the Birch Society at this time or, directly, at any time, but did once remark about the group, "the more I hear of it the better I like it."[104]

As can be surmised, by this time, anything and everything done by Johnny Bob was not only major local news but also, in some cases, national news as well.

In February 1962, newspapers as far away as Oregon carried articles about Harrell. They reported that his compound was currently being prepared for an eminent Russian attack.[105]

To see to their safety after the start of the nuclear war, the CCC were hard at work digging out "15 to 20" bomb shelters carved out of the sides of the hills running along the edge of the property and along the Little Wabash River.[106] "The Lord is telling us to put in these shelters," Harrell is quoted as saying. "There are three gallons of water for each person, food for three days, beds, a lantern, one gallon of kerosene and three changes of clothing.[107] The Lord is having us watch this fallout caused by the Russian tests and there is a possibility we may use the shelter before the actual attack."[108]

Also quoted in that same UPI article was H. Carroll Baylor, who, once again, found himself answering allegations from Johnny Bob. "There's not a communist in the county," he said, "The FBI and state authorities have checked."[109] Later Baylor said of Harrell, "[He] wants to run the whole show. He's a publicity seeker."[110]

Harrell though responded to Baylor's declaration with full-on contempt. Harrell told the press, "Such a statement would be made only by a fool or to cover the communist conspiracy itself."[111]

As Harrell and CCC members dug further into their caves, on the other outside of the compound's walls, Harrell continued his various legal fights. On February 24, 1962, the Illinois Appellate Court at Mount Vernon upheld the convictions of Harrell and the others for their earlier truancy case. Upon hearing that news, Harrell announced that he would not be filing an appeal, saying this was due to the futility of it; he "no longer expects a favorable decision," he said, and added, in typical Johnny Bob fashion, "We are being denied our constitutional rights to even pursue the issue further."[112] Two months later, it was reported in the newspapers that not only did not Johnny Bob re-file, he even paid his old truancy fines, though H. Carroll Baylor noted at the time that he had yet to receive payment from any of the other defendants.[113]

Shortly after all this transpired, Johnny Bob was able to celebrate some good news about another one of his battles. For several months, both Harrell and his mother had been under investigation by the FTC, who had accused mother and son of engaging in unfair and deceptive acts in connection with interstate sales of their mausoleum plans and franchises.

In accordance with the investigation, the FTC had demanded that mother and son turn over all accounts and records pertaining to the business. It was a request that Harrell, who considered the investigation yet another witch-hunt against him, denied.[114]

In mid-May 1962, Judge William Juergens of Federal District Court agreed with him. He denied a petition by the FTC that would have compelled the Harrells to turn over the documents. Upon learning of this court victory, Johnny Bob said, "[it] was the first victory we have had in court for going on three years."[115]

Throughout the summer of 1962, Johnny Bob and the CCC continued to make headlines. In May, it was reported that Harrell still believed that a Russian atomic attack was "very close," and as such, his many followers (which supposedly at that time numbered around seventy-five living on the grounds) were now being taught survival training.[116]

Days later, various southern Illinois newspapers reported that Harrell's already vast land holdings were expanding even more. His mother was donating to the CCC parcels of land she owned in Clay, Richland, and Jackson counties; one of the parcels was about 500 acres near Claremont, IL. As the head of the church, Harrell was free to do what he wanted with the gift. He told the press at the time that the land would probably be sold. He said, "We have legal costs to handle."[117]

Johnny Bob's continued high profile though did not go without pushback from others. Only days after news of the land deal, Harrell complained of a fresh bout of vandalism and ongoing taunts from what he labeled a local "Communist-inspired goon squad."[118] Harrell said that pranksters had done damage to his estate's exterior fence and that someone had also been setting fires and the throwing rocks onto the property. He also noted that rifle and shotgun blasts were being fired into the grounds.[119] Later, Harrell claimed that five of the six dogs who lived on his property had been fatally shot.[120]

To combat the ongoing terrorism, Harrell bought space in an Effingham newspaper and called upon all "responsible and patriotic citizens" to help discourage and contain the vandalism.[121] He complained that the ongoing troubles were making his retreat "no longer a good risk to insurance companies."[122] Among others things, Harrell sited in the ad that someone had, again, knocked down his estate's front entrance gate.[123]

When reached for comment, however, Louisville authorities stated that some of the complaints made by members of the group had been "exaggerated."[124]

Harrell's name returned to the papers again on August 5, 1962, when it was announced that he and his wife had just had their latest child. A Decatur newspaper noted:

The boy, their sixth child, was born at 8:22 a.m. central standard time.

The eight-pound boy has been named for Jeb Stuart, the famous Confederate Army Calvary general, whom Harrell says he has always admired despite fighting for the Confederacy.

The new child is the fourth boy for the Harrells.

Their fifth child, a girl who also weighed 8 pounds, was born on Aug. 13, 1961.

It had been just one year ago today that more than 100 policemen and FBI agents smashed their way into his estate."[125]

Then, the following December, a birth of another sort got Johnny Bob mentioned in the papers once more. On Christmas Eve, when the regular physician who attended all in the compound was suddenly hospitalized himself, Johnny Bob had to assist in the delivery of a baby by one of his followers.[126]

Mrs. James Gillard went into labor at approximately 10:15 p.m. Her delivery was attended to by Harrell and two other colony women. According to one news account: "Harrell and the women took the doctor's place. They cut the umbilical cord with a pair of kitchen scissors, tied it with a borrowed shoe string, and sent the mother and her 8-lb boy off to a Flora hospital."[127]

Yet for Johnny Bob, all was not good news at the end of 1962. In early December, Harrell failed to appear at a court proceeding in Olney, Illinois, which pertained to his ongoing IRS investigation. The IRS wanted to question Harrell about his tax returns for 1958, 1959, and 1960, but Harrell refused to produce the records and declared that he would not do so unless taken to federal court.[128]

Harrell said to IRS Special Agent G. L. Quayle, that, during the raid in 1961, the FBI had "confiscated money, records and equipment." Then Harrell added, "And you continue to ask us to produce items that I think you well know are not in our possession."[129]

Despite that argument, the IRS continued their thorough vetting of Harrell and his finances. In early 1963, IRS division chief Robert J. Paulsen said that the Harrell tax returns from 1954 through 1959 failed to show a "substantial amount" of Harrell's income and that his 1960 return was not properly filed and lacked some required supporting information.[130]

Along with his battle with the IRS, Johnny Bob was also at issue with the courts over the charges pertaining to the 1961 raid. On December 7, 1962, Johnny Bob and the other men arrested at the 1961 raid appeared in court in East St. Louis—once again in front of Judge William Juergens—and asked for all charges against them to be dismissed.[131] Their argument for the dismissal was centered on the 1961 ruling of a military court regarding the status of Dion Davis at the time of the raid.[132]

Though often used interchangeably, being AWOL from the military and being a deserter are, legally, two different things. To be "AWOL" (absent without leave) suggests that one has left their post without permission but will probably, at some point, be returning, probably voluntarily. In contrast, being a "deserter" is interpreted as leaving one's post or one's unit without any intention of returning.

The military never charged Dion Davis with desertion, only with being AWOL. Their decision may have been influenced by Davis's two previous AWOLs (April 5–16, 1961, and another on May 8, 1961), from which Davis had both times returned to base voluntarily.[133] Additionally, after the Louisville raid and Davis being reclaimed by the military, he was given a psychiatric evaluation. Davis's "mental responsibility" at the time was called into question, and Davis was found of being incapable of desertion.[134]

Yet, Johnny Bob and his followers were charged in court with harboring a deserter, an offense that brought with it the possibility of three years in jail and a $3,000 fine.[135] Harrell and his lawyers—rightfully—asked, "If the boy was not convicted of desertion, how then can we be charged with harboring a deserter?" Harrell then, of course, added at the time, "It's another attempt by the government to disband and disperse our Communist-fighting group."[136] It was reported that the motion to dismiss the standing charges, based on that argument, were being "taken under advisement" by the court.[137] However, nothing seemed to ever happen to the case in regard to this discrepancy.

Throughout all his travails, Johnny Bob always knew the power of the press and the written word. He also took some matters into his own hands in 1962. That was when Harrell publish his own monograph explaining his side of the Louisville raid story. Titled *Persecution USA: People & Place*, the forty-five-page, photo-illustrated publication was written by David K. Stacey. It contains a preface by Kenneth Goff and has a dedication to Harrell.[138]

The "book" recounts various events leading up to the raid, including the miraculous healing of Harrell at the Mayo Clinic. It includes numerous photos of Harrell, Dion Davis, and the Harrell grounds. Many of the photos of Harrell depict him alongside his wife and children—the good family man.[139]

Persecution is not easy reading. Written as a series of questions and answers between Johnny Bob and Stacey, the text is quite strident and didactic, with an abundant use of exclamation points. Rev. Goff's preface sets much of the tone. Goff compares his experiences when he was in Louisville to entering the "dark ages."[140] Then, he rails against the "bigoted" law enforcement officials who harassed both him and Harrell.[141]

He compares Johnny Bob then to Joseph Smith and wonders where a man as persecuted as Harrell could turn—"To the United Nations, or to Russia?"[142]

In the book, Harrell himself compares the invading soldiers of that August morning to "Hitler's Gestapo" and accuses the majority of the soldiers on the grounds that morning as being visibly drunk from "hard liquor" supposedly consumed the night before. He also accuses the men of freely using profane and vulgar language in front of all of the grounds' women and children and running amuck with "smirks and sneers." When not yelling profanities, some of the soldiers were supposedly yelling "this is what we have wanted to do for a long time!" Harrell goes on to say, "[PEOPLE] WERE NEEDLESSLY INJURED. WOMEN WERE KNOCKED DOWN AND PROPERTY WAS DAMAGED!"[143]

In regard to the latter point, *Persecution* includes various photos—some featuring Bobby Ladley, the young son of one of the followers—of some of the broken windows, cut window screens, and busted wood supposedly done by the early morning raiders.[144]

Along with the damage to the property, Harrell/Stacey also lay out accusations that the military looted the property of business records, equipment, bows and arrows, rifles and other fire arms, tools, and even roofing supplies as well as a box of silver dollars and cash.[145] Of the large quantities of cash supposedly stolen, only $40 was ever returned to the church, according to Harrell.[146] Harrell charged that all these seizures were done without the presence of any legal warrant. Harrell labeled the entire action "legalized robbery" and claimed that there were underlying motives behind the raid other than simply retrieving Private Davis.[147]

Stacey also lists the various constitutional amendments that all these actions were in violation of: Article One (freedom of worship), Article Two (right to bear arms), and Article Four (the right to privacy).[148]

Interestingly, the narrative of *Persecution* shows that, at least for a time after the raid, Harrell and his associates attempted to follow the case of Dion Davis as it made its way through the military courts. The text makes note of Davis's sentencing to and then his release from a naval prison. It also describes Davis's later assignment to a "hospital," which Harrell takes as a sign that "[the military] do not desire the boy to be free."[149]

The author of *Persecution USA* was David K. Stacey, who was born and raised in Farmington, New Mexico. According to him, he had never heard of Johnny Bob or the CCC until news of the Dion Davis raid hit the newspapers. An ordained minister (at least according the book's "About the Author" section), Stacey became outraged at what he viewed as the "slanted" news coverage of the Harrell event. He then made his way to Illinois to "interview" Johnny Bob for this publication. He, too, would take up residence for a time at the compound, though his duration there seemed to have been brief.[150]

Before and after his time in Illinois, Stacey himself remained an impassioned anti-communist advocate. Later, he began to devote more and more of his "ministry" to preaching for the segregation of the races and against blacks and Jews. He was still active among the "Identity Church" movement as late as 2013.[151]

The *Persecution* book concludes with Harrell promising to be unyielding in his battle despite what he calls "GOVERNMENT HARRASSMENT." He states, "for we have determined and purposed within our own mind that we shall stay and hold even if we have to live on bread and water and turn the Fallout shelters into regular living quarters!"[152] Once the text was finished, thousands of copies were printed and mailed out to church groups and various media outlets.[153]

As 1963 began, the CCC seemed to be undergoing some significant changes. In early 1963, Harrell announced that he had decided to close his on-site private school.[154] Harrell said that the closing of the school had already caused some of the families living on his property to leave for "other states where Christian Conservative bases are being established."[155] His decision to close was, he said, due to ongoing pressure from Clay County officials. The closure had originally been disclosed as part of a recent, local court proceeding.[156]

That court cast was a child custody case filed in the first part of 1963 by Vernon Woomer of Xenia, Illinois.[157] Sometime earlier, Mr. Woomer's ex-wife, Velma, had come to live on the Harrell estate and brought her thirteen-year-old twin daughters, Bonnie and Connie, with her.[158] Along with living at the compound in a trailer with their mother, the girls attended the CCC church and, assumedly, also attended the compound's school.[159] Yet Mr. Woomer wanted to obtain full custody of his daughters and filed a motion with the court to do so. In the motion, Woomer referred to the Harrell estate as an "armed camp."[160]

On March 2, 1963, inside another packed Louisville courtroom, Circuit Judge Raymond Horn heard the custody case which exposed yet another sad and rather tawdry event involving Harrell and his Louisville estate.[161]

First, an eyewitness testified about a trip Mr. Woomer had made on February 8 to the Harrell house to see his girls. According to the witnesses, when Mr. Woomer arrived at the gate of the compound, he was confronted by a band of Harrell followers all armed with guns and clubs. Mr. Woomer would eventually be beaten by at least one of the men at the guard station before he was driven off.[162]

Later, under cross-examination, Velma Woomer said that she had come to live at the Harrell estate because she feared her daughters were being led into the use of narcotics and becoming prostitutes, but she caused the greatest controversy in her testimony when she was asked about enrolling her daughters into Harrell's school. She replied, "There is no school there."[163]

When the trial ended, the court awarded permanent custody of the children to Mr. Woomer.[164] The next day, accompanied by the local sheriff, Mr. Woomer went to the Harrell estate and reclaimed his two daughters. Woomer and his daughters soon returned to Xenia.[165]

The news of the school's closure, now made public, seemed to hasten the decline that the Harrell estate was experiencing. By this time, according to reports, those residing on the property had greatly dwindled—once as many as seventy, Harrell now stated there were only "about a dozen" living on the grounds.[166]

Additionally, with the IRS decidedly not backing down, Harrell had grown fearful that he might lose his compound entirely. He said at the time that he "firmly believes" that the government would eventually seize his estate to satisfy its income tax claims.[167]

Hence on March 3, 1963, the same day as the custody decision was handed down, and claiming that he, his family, and his followers were still the recipients of harassment as well as "death threats," Johnny Bob Harrell announced that (not unlike the one-time Mormon migration westward) his church would be leaving Louisville to establish a new religious colony in New Mexico.[168] He added, "We are waiting now for the Lord to tell us when to go."[169]

According to Harrell, a church had already been purchased on a mile-long tract of land in the desert near the tiny town of San Fidel, New Mexico, about 60 miles west of Albuquerque; "as God directed," he said.[170] Harrell said, "Buildings have been leased and rented and we soon will be ready to start constructing others," though he added, "Our people would rather live in a foxhole of the desert with the heavens as a roof and be free, than to live in the finest mansion and be slaves."[171]

Harrell stated that the migration of his group had already started and that twelve to fifteen church members were already on their way west.[172] He stated that only about a dozen of his followers would remain behind in Louisville, one of them being his new-born son, Jeb.[173] Harrell explained, "They had told us we are going to have to fight or move and if we fight and hurt someone, even in self-defense, we would land in prison."[174]

One of the first families to be dispatched westward were the Comers, who were part of a convoy of eight vehicles that left Illinois for New Mexico in April 1963.[175] Leading the parade of cars was David K. Stacey, author of *Persecution USA*, who was returning to his home state of New Mexico but who would now be taking up residence in San Fidel.[176]

At the news of Harrell's leaving got reported, newspaperman Mike Carr filed a vividly descriptive story about the compound in the *Decatur Daily Review*:

> This reporter rode to the estate in the company of one of the few persons left who share Harrell's friendship without sharing his beliefs. Bud Zink, son of lumberman John Zink.
>
> Around the grounds, the only sign of life was a line full of drying clothes. Only two of the long line of rough cabins looked as if they might be occupied and about a half-dozen house trailers, mostly empty, remain.
>
> The door of the converted garage was opened by an elderly woman, who immediately gave way to Harrell's mother.
>
> ...the smell of kerosene fumes was overpowering.
>
> The entire scene was a far cry from a visit of a Decatur reporter and editor 23 months ago. Then, accompanied by Jim Morgan—one of Harrell's archenemies—the news team was barred at gunpoint.[177]

Carr went on to quote one Louisville resident, still smarting from all the activity and notoriety, who said, "I wish you newspaper people wouldn't call it an estate. I'd call it a mess."[178]

The compound was due to become even more barren shortly as Harrell announced his family was among the next set of people to leave the area and relocate to the American southwest.[179] To the press, Harrell stated that they would be departing shortly after an upcoming meeting with IRS representative Robert Paulsen that was to take place in Springfield, Illinois.[180]

Originally that meeting was scheduled for March 11, but Harrell, by letter, had earlier had it successfully rescheduled for April 9, 1963.[181] However, on April 9, Harrell did not show up for the meeting.[182]

In fact, though he and his family (his wife, his mother, and five of his six children) had left Louisville on the afternoon of Sunday, April 8—after taking part in a prayer circle at the house—and headed up towards Springfield, no one had seen nor heard from them since their leaving and driving north. The family never arrived in Springfield and had not returned to Louisville.[183]

The family, it seems, had vanished.

Walls of Time

Surviving is perhaps the strangest fantasy of them all.

The Optimist's Daughter by Eudora Welty

Originally, the abandoned vehicle—a 1954 dark green sedan bearing Oklahoma plates, its key still in the ignition—did not attract too much notice.[1]

It was first noted by police on April 12, 1963, on Illinois Route 66 near Glenarm, Illinois, about 10 miles outside of Springfield.[2] At first, local law enforcement just assumed it was a breakdown and would soon be reclaimed by its owner, but after four days, when no one ever returned to the vehicle, it was towed away to a garage in Springfield.[3] In impound, the vehicle was searched, and although no blood was found, those who searched it quickly became concerned for the car's owner and one-time passengers.[4] Various things had been left behind. Inside, they found papers, clothing, shoes, and a Bible embossed with a name on it: John R. Harrell.[5]

Though one investigator labeled the whole situation "a screwy deal," Johnny Bob Harrell, his wife, their children (Tod, fifteen; Xon, twelve; Cathy, ten; John five; and Deborah, one), and his mother were soon classified as "missing persons."[6] As can be imagined, the news of Johnny Bob's sudden vanishing was a major story all over the country, especially, of course, in Illinois.

Quickly, the police began releasing whatever information they had. First, it was soon learned that only five of the Harrell's six children had been with them; their son, seven-month-old Jeb, was still safe at home in Louisville.[7] Second, police did not believe that Harrell had purposely disappeared despite the fact that the car showed no visible sign of violence and it was said Harrell was traveling with around $14,000 in cash, monies from some recently sold properties that Harrell said would be needed in the new colony in New Mexico.[8]

Surprisingly, even a letter that Harrell had written on March 30 and mailed from Salem, Illinois, and which was described in the press as a "statement of departure" did not make investigators believe Harrell had simply run away.[9]

In the letter, on Harrell's personal, eagle-embossed stationary, Harrell stated that he and his family would be leaving Illinois in the very near future—"to avoid bloodshed," he said.[10] Very soon, the letter said, they would be living at 429 Nimitz Drive in Grants, New Mexico, and that, there, they would devote themselves to building various church buildings including an orphanage for Navajo Indian children.[11]

IRS man Paulsen said that the meeting he and Harrell were to have on the 9th was simply routine: "There was nothing about the conference set up for last Monday that would cause Harrell alarm."[12] Paulsen also stated that the meeting had been scheduled at the request of Harrell, not at the request of the agency. Paulsen also believed that Harrell, prior to the meeting, had alerted some members of the news media about the appointment.[13]

Still, not only were none of the Harrells seen in Springfield, none of them had ever arrived in New Mexico either. The presence of Jeb still in Louisville supported the notion that the Harrells might have been the victims of foul play. Furthermore, when police canvased all the area hotels and motels, they found no trace of the family.[14] They also checked the logs of all local trains and airports—still nothing.[15]

When news of the family's disappearance reached the compound in Louisville, the remaining residents there immediately began another prayer vigil—praying for the safe return of Harrell and the others.[16] Vance Comer, for one, feared the worst: "I don't know who got him but the Communists are back of it."[17]

The Harrells's long-time housekeeper, Dorothy Payne, was quoted in the press:

> We began to worry late Wednesday when part of our advance group in New Mexico telephoned asking if we knew where Mr. Harrell was. He had not arrived there.
>
> Our worry mounted when the Harrells failed to arrive by Thursday morning. Then we notified state police. We had not heard a thing until this morning when news reporters telephoned us. We are really worried about the Harrells.[18]

Payne added that the car the Harrells had been driving was recently purchased by Mr. Harrell after his previous vehicle broke down on a trip

Right: The estate of John R. Harrell in Louisville, IL, *c.* 1960.

Below: John R. Harrell with his wife, Betty, and son, Tod, *c.* 1959.

Vote For

JOHN R. HARRELL

REPUBLICAN CANDIDATE FOR

U. S. SENATE
FROM ILLINOIS

✝

I H S
(IN HIS SERVICE)

— PLACE GOD BACK IN GOVERNMENT —
(over)

Business card/campaign item from Johnny Bob's run for office.

Johnny Bob outside his Mt. Vernon replica, then under construction.

The Harrell estate, c. 1960. Note the estate's tall water tower at center of the photo.

The courthouse in Louisville, IL, as it appeared *c.* 1961.

Johnny Bob preaches at the church on his estate.

Johnny Bob at one of his estate's newly constructed bomb shelters.

Above left: Dion Davis just before he enlisted.

Above right: Johnny Bob and Dion Davis in front of the Mt. Vernon house.

Above left: Dion Davis in custody.

Above right: Some of the rifles and other guns seized the morning of the raid.

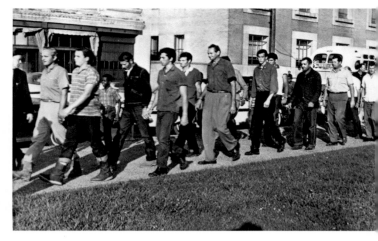

Above left: Johnny Bob and his son, Tod, the morning of their arrest.

Above right: Johnny Bob and Tod Harrell and others from the CCC arrested the morning of the raid.

Above left: Dion Davis in custody in East St. Louis.

Above right: Johnny Bob in handcuffs.

The house and estate after the raid.

Above left: Dion Davis exits the courthouse.

Above right: A gawker looks into the Mt. Vernon house shortly after Johnny Bob and his family disappeared.

Above left: Mrs. Lester Kellums is photographed in rural Missouri.

Above right: Harrell's attorney Robert Rice.

Johnny Bob's "WANTED" poster.

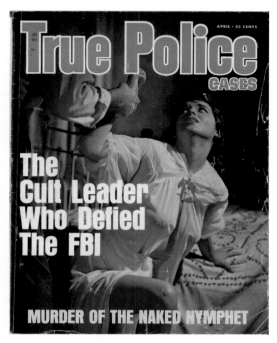

Above left: Johnny Bob as he looked at the time of his arrest in Arkansas.

Above right: The cover of *True Police Cases* magazine from April 1965.

Right: Johnny Bob speaks at one of his annual Freedom Festivals.

Above left: The home on East Chestnut Street in Louisville, where Johnny Bob lived the last years of his life.

Above right: One of the guard stations at the main entrances to the estate; it is no longer standing.

The Mt. Vernon house as it looked in later years.

The estate of John R. Harrell, *c.* 2015.

Front entrance to main house on the estate, *c.* 2015.

Side view of the Mt. Vernon house.

Back of the Mt. Vernon house.

One of the many discarded vehicles that once littered the property.

One of Harrell's airplanes still parked on the grounds.

One of the remaining cabins.

Also on the estate, the one-time offices for Harrell's construction business; it later served as the HQ of the CCC church.

Front door of construction offices.

The garage building above which the Harrell family lived for many years.

Johnny Bob Harrell, *c.* 2016, in front of the former Coles Church. The church has since been razed.

Another view of the Mt. Vernon house, *c.* 2021.

back from New Mexico.[19] She also stated that Jeb stayed behind from the trip to Springfield as he was considered too young to travel that far.[20] Finally, she said that, just days before the Harrells left for Springfield, Mr. Harrell was the recipient of two "threatening" phone calls from an unidentified person or people.[21]

Yet while Harrell devotees worried and prayed, others voiced skepticism, believing that Harrell had simply stage-managed his exit and shuffled off with not only his family but with plenty of other people's money as well.[22] Credence to that latter theory arrived when, the day after the disappearance, police captain William Hall, who was heading up the investigation alongside police sergeant Elmer Emerson, went looking for one of the two small personal aircrafts that Johnny Bob owned.[23] One of them was now missing, too. That single-engine, silver green Cessna was not at the Louisville compound, but police did not necessarily believe it was part of the Harrells's disappearance.[24] It was noted that the plane could only seat a pilot and three passengers—it would not be able to accommodate the entire missing family.[25] The Cessna later turned up, with no explanation, at a rural airport near Houston, Missouri. It had supposedly been parked there since March 1963.[26]

As Illinois police and the FBI kept an eye on the Harrell estate in Louisville, Sgt. Bud South of Grants, New Mexico, was reported in the press as keeping a "wary" eye on the comings and goings of families near the new CCC settlement.[27]

As days turned into weeks since the family's disappearance, neither law enforcement nor those with an opinion on Harrell (devotees or critics) quite knew what was going on.

At the start of the missing persons case, Decatur newspaper reporter Charles E. Albright visited the Louisville compound.[28] There, he found a strangely desolate scene among the now debris-strewn grounds. Those still in residence at the estate (only about five adults at this point) were attempting to be brave, he said, when asked about the Harrell Family. He wrote, "my questions brings lumps to their throats and handkerchiefs emerge to brush wet eyes.... You learn they fear for the safety of their leader."[29] One disciple then went on to say, "We're willing to fight, bleed and die for our country in this fight against communism."[30]

Along with those on the estate, others, too, were rallying to find Johnny Bob and his family. The Minutemen, an anti-communist movement headquartered in Missouri, offered up a $5,000 reward for any and all information about Johnny Bob's whereabouts.[31] The Minutemen, then helmed by its founder, Robert B. DePugh, even went so far as to send out letters to around 200 Louisville residents soliciting information from any citizen who might have any useful intel.[32] Their letter read in part:

"Our organization has reason to believe that the Harrell family has been brutally murdered. We have further reason to believe that persons residing in Louisville have knowledge of this crime."[33] The five-paragraph letter was accompanied by a return envelope.[34]

Not everyone in the area was so convinced. Many in Louisville were arch skeptics. A newspaper quoted various residents as saying, "He's just seeking more publicity" and "He's skipped the county in fear of his income tax problems" or "We're just glad he's gone."[35]

One major critic of Harrell went even a step further. In an area newspaper, local attorney James F. McCollum placed a large ad and offered a $5,000 reward to the various, local community groups (including the Lions Club and the Chamber of Commerce) if Harrell and his family "stayed away" for the next seven years.[36] McCollum went on to label Harrell's disappearance a publicity stunt.[37]

Gradually, other tidbits of news leaked out. In April 1963, assistant FBI agent Elmer Linberg and other agents and officers conducted a "systematic" search of the Mt. Vernon house, the compound, and other known Harrell-owned properties in search of any sign of Johnny Bob—they found nothing.[38]

On April 18, 1963, it was disclosed that Johnny Bob had recently made several large purchases of gold and silver ("up to six figures," according to one report) just prior to his vanishing.[39]

On April 23, 1963, Thomas Ladley—who was still living on the Louisville compound—reported being the recipient of a threatening phone call stating that Ladly and his family were "next"; local police regarded the alleged call though a prank.[40]

In early May 1963, it was reported that John Harrell's last will and testament, dated March 31, 1963, had been located—by Lester Kellums—at the Mt. Vernon residence.[41] Harrell's attorney, Robert Rice, did not disclose any of the will's contents but did say that it was created by Harrell due to the increasing number of threats on his life he was now receiving. Rice did release the following except, words written by the now-missing Johnny Bob: "For three years I have pleaded for the protection of my family, both by mail and in person, all the way to the authorities in Washington, D.C., and have been refused."[42]

For members of the CCC still living on the compound in Louisville, the disappearance of Johnny Bob did more than just make them worry about the safety of their founder and his family; it largely also ended their way of life.

With Harrell M.I.A., the monthly stipends issued to all the members of the church halted. With time, both their cash and food reserves were depleted. All members now had to find new ways to support themselves and their families.[43] As Harold Leib bluntly put it, "We had to go out and get jobs!"[44] Leib went to work in a local sawmill and held other jobs though he later admitted that he sometimes found himself suddenly unemployed when bosses discovered his association with Harrell and the CCC.[45]

While continuing to live on the grounds, most of the other followers took jobs inside of Louisville or in other nearby towns—if, that is, they could get them. The controversy that had surrounded them, their sect and Johnny Bob did not dissipate quickly. The members were, at times, the victims of shunning. Many businesses in the area still held a grudge, and as Leib experienced, employment by CCC members was often hard to come by.[46]

Meanwhile, out in New Mexico, the residents of the CCC's new planned retreat continued their work of building buildings and fashioning wells. In New Mexico at that time were Vance Comer, David Pinkstaff (originally from Idaho), Gene Densmore (originally of Olney, Illinois), and Charles Rowan (originally of Louisville) along with their families. According to a newspaper article from April 26, 1963, this group was soon to be joined by David Stacey (who had assumed much of the group's leadership role in Harrell's absence) and Mrs. Florence Rowan, who was to bring little Jeb Harrell with her.[47] Only two people (two men) were to stay behind in Louisville to act as groundskeepers for the Mt. Vernon homestead.[48]

Establishing a brand-new colony in a new state was not proving easy. The location was remote and the terrain was difficult. Not helping, of course, was the fact that the group's benevolent leader was nowhere to be found. As with those in Illinois, without their weekly stipend from Johnny Bob, the new residents of New Mexico were forced to take outside jobs in order to afford food and shelter. During their time in New Mexico, the Comers lived in the back of a local convenience store located on Rt. 66. When not working at their "day jobs," they and other members of the church went about making clay bricks and drying them in the sun. The bricks would be used to construct the sect's new church.[49]

In the same newspaper article that noted the migration of members to New Mexico, it quoted another long-time Harrell associate, Lester Kellums, as saying that he and his family would not be going to the southwest but, instead, to the town of Rolla, Missouri. They were set to move there in the very near future.[50] The town of Rolla, Missouri, is about 100 miles southwest of St. Louis and in 1963 had a population of approximately 11,000. Rolla would be the location of the next interesting development in the Harrell saga.

By mid-June, along with Lester Kellums and his family, several other one-time Harrell estate dwellers, including Dorothy Payne, were now living in Rolla.[51] Kellums had leased a local business, The Trading Post (ironically the same name as the Harrell's one-time on-compound store), a post office/general store hybrid, in Rolla and said he did so simply because it was a good business opportunity.[52] He had also taken possession—and title to—one of Harrell's old Cessna airplanes; it had been sitting parked on a private airfield outside of Rolla, allegedly undergoing repairs, since the previous March.[53]

Soon, though, it came to light that a few years before, in 1957, a J. R. Harrell had purchased an 80-acre farm near Missouri's Big Piney River.[54] Then, about four months after Johnny Bob and his family disappeared, a man who identified himself as "Robert Edwards," but who many thought looked a lot like Johnny Bob, was seen in and around town.[55] The mysterious "Edwards," who sported long blond hair, long sideburns, and reading glasses and who drove a white Cadillac, had just purchased additional acreage in the area and paid cash for it.[56] Edwards augmented his purchases with a large cache of lumber.[57] Edwards was also the one who had originally leased the Trading Post property according to its owners, Mr. and Mrs. N. E. Hancock; Mr. Hancock, ironically, was a former St. Louis police officer.[58] Later, when she was shown a photo of John Harrell, Mrs. Hancock said that the man in the picture resembled Edwards.[59]

Additionally, a Volkswagen that was used by "Edwards" to secure the lease was discovered to be registered in the name of Natalia Harrell.[60]

Later, still, it was reported that a boy resembling Tod Harrell had been seen as had a woman who resembled Dorothy Payne.[61] Also, the woman had sometimes been seen carrying an infant.[62]

All this speculation was enough to attract a few intrepid reporters to the area who hoped to catch a glimpse of the "missing" Harrell. In Rolla, those press members doggedly pursued Mr. and Mrs. Kellums in hopes that they would lead them to the missing family.[63]

It was further reported that Kellums was sometimes seen allegedly taking many of the items from the Trading Post and driving off with them, late at night, into a remote part of the Ozark Mountains. It was also reported, by a specially sent *St. Louis Post-Dispatch* reporter, that large groups of people were often seen, late at night, inside the store. Large quantities of guns had also been reported as being seen in the presence of these various visitors and that a van with the initials "CCC" painted on its side had also been sighted in the area.[64]

Around the perimeter of the farmland, purchased by Harrell but now occupied by Kellums, various small, unpainted, clapboard homes began to sprout up. Families—new families, unknown to others in the area—were said to be living in them.[65] Later, when pressed on the issue, Mrs. Kellums did admit that many of the former Harrell-Louisville followers had relocated to this area of Missouri but she declined to say exactly how many.[66]

As stories of these activities spread, other members of the press, along with members of the IRS and a gaggle of curious tourists, also descended on the area, all in hopes of finding Harrell.[67]

Despite these intriguing developments, though, nothing much else was heard about the still-missing Harrells for the next two months. That was until early August 1963 when suddenly the Louisville grounds were once again bustling with activity.[68] Sharp-eyed citizens suddenly took notice of various autos entering and exiting the grounds, as well as how much of the on-site clutter was being purged and the overgrowths of weeds were being cut back. Even the huge log that had been placed to block the front entrance had been excised.[69]

People were also moving back into the big house. Among the first to arrive were Mr. and Mrs. Carl Stanley and Mr. and Mrs. Gales Newberry.[70] Even Lester Kellums had returned. Kellums informed the press that the group had returned because they were expecting the eminent return of their leader Johnny Bob, though they were vague on what they were basing this prediction on—a prophecy or word from Johnny Bob?[71] It was also noted that the promised return of their leader would coincide with Jeb Harrell's first birthday.[72]

Unfortunately, the much-heralded return of Johnny Bob did not come to pass. On the appointed day, only Harrell's most devoted were seen on the Louisville grounds. Still, Johnny Bob's failure to materialize did not dissuade any of his flock. Lester Kellums was quoted as saying, "Johnny Bob has promised resurrection. Even if Johnny Bob has met with foul play, he will be rise up again."[73]

By this time, it had been almost six months since the Harrell family disappeared. As CCC members awaited his return and police and FBI continued to work the case, it was decided that the legal charges against him and his followers would proceed—with or without his involvement. More than two years since its occurrence, a court date for the sect group for charges related to the harboring of Dion Davis was finally set for November 4, 1963. Authorities made it clear that if Harrell did not show up for court that day, his $52,000 bond would be forfeited.[74]

Then, in a bit of interesting timing, the next big development in the Harrell missing person case occurred. In mid-October, Johnny Bob's attorney, Robert Rice, came fourth with startling news—he had received a letter from Johnny Bob.[75] According to Rice, Harrell and his family were all hostages and were being held in either Chicago or St. Louis.[76]

Over the next few days, various letters were received by various Harrell associates. All three missives were described as being handwritten in pencil on "cheap, yellow paper." The first of the letters was received by Rice, who told the press that according to what Harrell wrote, he "has not seen his family but has been in communication with them." Harrell added that he had access to newspapers from both Chicago and St. Louis and that was what he was basing his possible location on.[77]

The second letter—about 1,000 words long—was received by Vance Comer.[78] In it, Johnny Bob wrote:

> After six months of being held I have found the way to get from one to three letters out.[79]
>
> ... I am under house arrest and so is my family, being grilled day and night concerning the divine revelations received during the past five years with regards to Communist aims, goals and troop movements undermining our economy, etc.[80]

Harrell also stated that he did not know if those holding him were part of the government or some nefarious group. He said he had not seen his family but had been able to communicate with them via an intercom. Harrell ended the correspondence by saying, "Our only hope Vance is that there will be an awakening and an aroused move in the ranks of the people."[81]

The third and final letter was sent to the United Press bureau in Marion, Illinois.[82] The UPI letter from Harrell's "prison-like" location had a post mark of Cairo, Illinois (stamped at 2:30 p.m.) and bore a three-cent stamp on it; it was delivered to the UPI office with seven cents postage due. The UPI's letter was the longest of the trio—twenty-three handwritten pages long.[83] The letter began:

> Greetings in the name of the Lord God of Israel, ... I am writing with the hope this letter can reach its destination safely. After being held captive for almost six months, I have detected a manner in which delivery may be possible.[84]

Later Harrell related that his captors wore masks and that some of them could not speak English. He also said he and his family had been abducted back in March while driving north of Taylorville, Illinois. They had stopped along the road, he said, when they heard a siren. A man in a state police uniform accused Harrell of speeding. Harrell was then, he said, the recipient of "hard blows upon my head" after which he "lost consciousness." When he awoke, he was bound, gagged, and blindfolded. He was then driven to his current location.[85] Harrell went on to say:

My cell room—windowless and soundproof—is comfortable with bath, bed, desk, Bible, books, pencil, paper and even envelopes to submit written statements to some of their questions upon request.

I have received my requested two meals a day except on the regular two fasting days per week. Treatment seems to be contingent upon giving them requested information, especially in the field of divine revelations....[86]

In the lengthy letter, Harrell would go on mention how the names of some of his old adversaries in Louisville had come up during his "house arrest":

Much questioning done concerning our knowledge of their local organizations in Louisville. The only names they mentioned were Ray Summers, James Morgan, State Atty. Carroll Baylor, Vaughn Brown, James [Bud] McCollum and some of the Kincaids. One of the men who was questioning me said there are others in Louisville who had failed in every task they have been given. How true.[87]

Near the end of the letter, Harrell wrote:

Many questions concern patriots and any connection to Bob DePugh, Carl McIntire, Ken Goff, Gerald Smith, Robert Welch and others. They are not sure our underground is not being financed with the aid of some of these. Many questions about my conversations with Paul Bosco, who was Gen. MacArthur's secretary, and with who my wife and I talked at the Waldorf-Astoria in New York in August 1959.[88]

Along with suggesting that he might have "figured a way" to escape, Harrell concluded the letter:

These prison walls shall remain only until they have served their purpose. Not one minute longer. Our stand has not been in vain. God shall raise up friends to fight our battles for us.... Encourage all whom you see to take up their cross and follow. Already I can see a silver lining around the dark cloud that covers America. God cares for his own. Yours for those of Israel and the Kingdom.[89]

In response to the letter, Illinois state police stated they had no evidence of anyone being stopped for speeding outside of Taylorville on that particular night.[90] The FBI, meanwhile, stated that they were not investigating any of these suggested occurrences near Taylorville.[91]

As the recipient of one of these mysterious letters, Rev. Vance Comer suddenly found himself under greater scrutiny especially from those who believed he knew where Harrell currently was. Yet Comer remained steadfast in both his faith in Johnny Bob and in his declaration that he did not know where Johnny Bob was. Comer was quoted in October 1963 as saying, "It's all conjecture. We don't know where he is. But Johnny Bob will show up for the trial and when he does, they'll [the authorities] make it look like he wasn't held captive all this time."[92]

Comer, in Louisville at the time, added, "They won't have any trouble getting those people [pointing toward town] to testifying against us."[93]

Similarly, Lester Kellums was being questioned often by the FBI and the IRS over the entire situation. Kellums, along with denying that Harrell was ever in the Ozarks, said, "I don't know where Johnny Bob is now, but my faith tells me that he and his family are all right."[94]

That same October, it was announced that the on-site school at the compound had been reopened and currently had twelve pupils attending.[95] About twenty-five people were said to be living on the estate again at this time. Among the teachers at the school at that time were Vance Comer and Mr. Comer's wife, Avelyn.[96] The school was necessitated as most of the followers had returned or were returning to Louisville from New Mexico in anticipation of their court trial scheduled to get underway at the start of November.[97]

Meanwhile, the entire estate was in jeopardy at about this same time. With Harrell's whereabouts unknown, his taxes obviously were not being paid. The county then stepped in and sold the entire Mt. Vernon property out from under him. It was purchased by a Mrs. Ruth T. Walsh of Decatur.[98] She obtained the land by paying off the estate's back taxes owed by Johnny Bob and Johnny Bob's mother, Natalia. Her total cost was only $2,053.[99] However, Walsh was not a real estate bargain hunter. Instead, she was a friend of Harrell's who purchased the property in order to keep it in the hands of the CCC.

Then, as if all that were not enough, at the end of October, members of the Harrell cult made nationwide news again. Long-time Harrell church member Dorothy Payne, then residing in a farm house in the town of Houston, Missouri, about an hour from Rolla, returned from the laundromat on the night of Tuesday, October 29, to find her living room furniture and floor rugs in disarray, suggestive of a struggle. Soon, she reported, she realized that her son, five-year-old Larry, her sister Linda Rowan, and her son's babysitter, fifteen-year-old Nancy Kellums, had all vanished.[100]

Local sheriffs Robert Van Dyke and Lem Wilson responded to Mrs. Payne's panicked phone call that night. Their early investigation turned up the discovery of three bullet holes (from a .22 rifle) in the front door of their farm house.[101] Officers reported not knowing if the two girls had run off and taken the baby with them or if they were the victims of foul play. The police also refused to state if they believed the disappearance of these three one-time Harrell followers was related to the Harrell family's missing persons case or not.[102]

After being alerted by Mrs. Payne, it was reported that Lester Kellums, his wife, and their two sons immediately drove over to Houston from their home in Louisville.[103]

In early November 1963, it was back to court for all the members of the Harrell group who were arrested the morning of the Louisville raid. Neatly suited and all carrying Bibles, the twelve men showed up at the East St. Louis courthouse on the morning of November 13. The trial was expected to last five weeks. All of the men conveyed that they were anxious to "learn the will of the Lord" via the trial's outcome.[104]

Johnny Bob Harrell, of course, was still missing yet despite his obvious absence from the courtroom, the bailiff still went through the ceremony of calling out his name to come forth. "John Robert Harrell!" he called. When Johnny Bob did not appear, as had been threatened, it led States Attorney Carl W. Feickert (who would soon be giving his thirty-minute opening statement) to ask that his bond be forfeited as well as a bench warrant be issued for his arrest. Judge William Juergens agreed to both motions and then proceeded to sever Harrell from the case before allowing the trial to continue with just the defendants who were present.[105]

In the courtroom, all of the defendants were once again appearing in front of Judge Juergens. All of the defendants entered a plea of "not guilty," except for Robert Lee Murie who had been residing in his home state of California since two months after the raid. Back in the area and at the courthouse, Murie pled guilty and then made an oral request for probation. It was a request that was honored by the court.[106] Obviously, however, Murie's plea deal did not sit well with his fellow defendants who quickly called Murie "Judas" and claimed "He's not a patriot!"[107, 108] After his plea, Murie left the courthouse and, soon after that, the state. It is believed he and his family moved back to California.

For the remaining group, the progress of the jury trial was slow as almost everyone from the jury pool had heard about the case and more often than not had already formed an opinion of it, too. On the first day, the pool of forty-one possible jury members was fully exhausted, necessitating the summoning of twenty-three other prospective jurors.[109] Among those from the original pool who were jettisoned were individuals from Effingham, Flora, Iuka, and other towns close to Louisville who said they had already read most of the Harrell news coverage.[110]

The final jury was chosen the next day and consisted of seven women and five men.[111] Before the trial got underway, the judge cautioned all of them not to be embarrassed or reluctant to find the defendants guilty, even if the defendants insisted they were acting on direction of the Lord.[112]

Finally, arguments could begin. All of the eight men on trial were seated at one table. Among them, were three father and son pairings.[113] In his ten-minute opening statement for the defense, Robert Rice, defended the values and principals of the men he was representing:

> These men are very truthful. They will not lie. Defendants do not have to take the stand in criminal cases because in doing so they bare their entire lives to examination. But you will hear from all of these defendants before this trial ends.[114]

Also, as part of his opening statement, Rice called into question the sobriety that morning of some of the soldiers and police officers who participated in the raid.[115]

Despite facing large fines and as much as two decades behind bars if convicted, all of the Harrell men proved unwavering in their commitment to God and Harrell. Nineteen-year-old Jim Kellums, the youngest defendant, said on the stand, "Of course, I don't want to go to prison but Paul and Silas underwent such ordeals, too."[116]

When he was questioned, Jim's father, Lester Kellums, echoed his son's convictions, "This is the Battle of Armageddon!"[117] Later, Kellums, who was described as "talking like a zealot," revealed that he believed Johnny Bob had been planning to release Davis to the military but the raid took place before the exchange could occur.[118]

Sitting in the court room, the defendants were described as looking a mix of "city people" and "rural oriented."[119] Young Harold Leib, twenty-one, was described as having a "nervous smile" and it was noted that his father looked far older than his sixty-one years because "he has no teeth."[120]

When Vance Comer was on the stand, he was interrogated about the number of followers in the church. Comer responds, "Our membership is informal, we don't keep rolls."[121] Later, though, he described the active congregation as numbering between forty and fifty. Jim Kellums added later, "But thousands [of members] in a sense."[122]

During breaks, it was mentioned that the defendants milled about in the hallway and talked among themselves. Most of the conversations were about the one man who was not there—Johnny Bob. According to one article, a man who happened to be in the hall asked one of the defendants, "Do you think he'll show up now that the FBI will be after him?"[123]

To this, one of the defendants responded, "It's about time they started looking."[124]

The trial's second day saw FBI Agent Manley Hawks take the stand. Hawks related that Harrell had told him that the Lord said for him to not surrender Dion Davis. Later, Hawks said that Harrell threatened that any "force" would be "met with force" with Harrell supposedly adding, "We have arms that we could use to carry out the instructions of the Lord."[125]

Also testifying was Walter Welch and another agent, Cecil Miller. Miller said he got into a scuffle with Lloyd Wade Stanley over a weapon the latter was carrying. "I grabbed the gun, and we had a general tug-of-war for about 30 seconds before he released his grip on it," Miller said.[126] The rifle's chamber was later found to be empty, a fact that Rice purposefully highlighted in his questioning.[127]

Stanley later testified that he had picked up his gun the minute he heard the call to "come out" and added, "I took a rifle to use if the Lord said so through Harrell or another intermediary."[128]

Harold Leib, who had obtained bodily injury in the raid, stated that he, too, acted immediately upon hearing the warning bell. He grabbed his gun and ran towards the "big house." He said, "I didn't know that there were any law enforcement on the place. I was worried about our lives. Our lives had been in danger many times, and I thought this was one of those times." Leib continued that he had started running towards a spot where he had heard a woman screaming.[129]

Later Leib recalled being hit on the head and being knocked unconscious by one of the raiders when he supposedly lunged for one of their weapons. Leib said he remembered nothing after being hit though he later heard, from witnesses, that he had been held down by two men while a third bashed him in the skull.[130]

FBI Agent Raymond Berneking and State Trooper W. E. Bailey both testified that they had each been struck by Jim Kellums and that Kellums yelled "Shoot 'em! Shoot 'em!" at his fellow followers as he was being subdued by one of the agents.[131] Bailey stated that Kellums had "advanced on me with a rifle which he pointed right at me. He also had a pistol on him. I grabbed the rifle."[132]

Agent Robert Collinberg said that he wrestled with Childers when Childers refused to drop his gun, "We wrestled for it and rolled down the incline."[133]

Later, under cross examination, Collinberg was asked if he kicked Mr. Childers while he was down. "Yes, sir, I did," Collinberg replied.[134]

Agent Charles Leatherwood said he could "see down the barrel" of the rifle James Gillard pointed at him.[135] During the course of all the questioning, much was made of whether or not the weapons the Harrell followers wielded were actually loaded or not.[136]

By the end of the trial, over thirty witnesses had been called to testify. Among those taking the stand was the Harrell's long-time housekeeper, Flo Rowan.[137]

In his closing argument, Rice laid out the various ways the prosecution had failed to make their case, saying that they had fallen short of proving that any of the defendants had attempted to conceal Dion Davis or protect him. Rice even stated that they had not proven beyond a reasonable doubt that Davis was a "deserter" at all.[138] Further, he asked the jury to keep in mind that, at the start of the raid, no one in the compound knew who the invaders were or what they had come for.[139]

In regard to the argument of Davis as either "AWOL" or a "deserter," the prosecution contended that Davis's status as a deserter or not had no bearing on this non-military court proceeding.[140]

The case was sent to the jury on November 20, 1963. Six hours later, the jury returned a verdict of guilty.[141]

Some months later, in March 1964, the judge meted out the punishment to the Harrell defendants. It could have resulted in each defendant getting twenty-one years in prison and being assessed a fine of $25,000 each. Instead, each received suspended sentences and three years of probation. They were also all given fifteen days in which to appeal the ruling if they so wished.[142]

In his ruling and sentencing, the judge seemed to place as much blame for the events of August 1961 on the people of Louisville as he did on the men who appeared before him. The judge stated:

> I strongly feel that much of what has happened must be borne by the people of the Louisville area ... I feel that some people in the area acted about as nonsensical as you did and their attitude does not seem to have changed much.
>
> It is none of their business if you want to belong to the Christian Conservative Church or don't.
>
> It behooves every one of us to respect the rights of the individual. We cannot stomp on the individual's rights to obtain our own.[143]

As can be imagined, the residents of Louisville did not take kindly to the judge's remarks. In response, "about 10" locals wrote to the judge protesting his criticism, while others wrote to their congressional representatives. One of those locals was long-time Harrell critic June Morgan, who wrote to her senator, Everett McKinley Dirksen, chastising Judge Juergens.[144] As one Louisville citizen put it, "Sure we're bitter. Why shouldn't we be? Louisville isn't the one on trial." Many locals also chafed at the suspended sentences handed down to the convicted men.[145]

Louisville's frustration with the judge's words is understandable—not only were they not the ones on trial, it was not them, but the U.S. government, that engendered the raid.

After the verdict but before the sentencing of those eleven one-time Louisville residents—and as if the town had not already experienced enough—the town suffered yet another extraordinary blow.

It was the morning of Friday, December 3, 1963, at 3:35 a.m.— the "coward's hour," as June Morgan would later call it.[146] Suddenly, an explosion of staggering size and volume tore through downtown Louisville.[147]

Felt as far as 10 miles away and heard even further, the early morning blast was the result of several (perhaps as many as forty) sticks of dynamite bound together and attached to a fuse or clock mechanism.[148] The bomb was placed on the west side of the town square in front of the hardware and sporting goods store owned by the Morgans.[149] The Morgans were described in the press as "arch foes" of Johnny Bob.[150]

The blast was so great that one man, asleep in his home near the bomb's epicenter, was literally blown out of his bed but was, thankfully, otherwise unhurt.[151] The downtown blast literally tore up the sidewalk, and after the explosion, pieces of wood, glass and other debris were, in some areas, piled up three to four inches deep.[152] Fifteen different buildings and businesses around the town square sustained damages; Louisville's central courthouse suffered ninety-two broken windows. In many buildings, foundations were cracked and even some iron work was destroyed.[153] Photos taken at the scene shortly after the explosion make downtown Louisville look like a warzone.[154]

The final tally for damages, according to insurance claims, was in excess of $100,000.[155] Among the businesses that suffered damages were: Kincaid Department Store, Wellmore Laundry, a pool hall, the V&M Café, Tigo Locker, Bunnell Drug Store, Burke Food Market, and the Louisville Dime Store.[156] Even businesses located on the other side of the town square were damaged.[157]

Miraculously, no one was injured in the blast. The town's cop, George Tolliver, who was usually on the downtown beat, had coincidentally just gone off duty when the explosion occurred.[158] Also, the occupant, Michael McFarland, of an apartment above the hardware store that was completely destroyed had, luckily, been out of town that particular night.[159]

Immediately after the explosion, area newspapers made note of the bomb's strategic placement directly in front of the Morgans's store and linked the attack to Johnny Bob Harrell.[160] James Morgan was quoted as saying he had long been expecting some sort of retaliation. He said, "I've been told plenty of times that I was going to get it." Morgan added that for years now, he had never been far away from his own loaded gun.[161]

However, there was one problem in blaming Johnny Bob—he was still missing. No one had seen him or his family for months. When Vance

Comer, who was residing on the Harrell compound, was sought out for comment, Comer said only that, like everyone else in town, he and the other people residing on the property were shocked by the bombing and had, that morning, been awoken by the extraordinary noise.[162]

Even though he was missing, the *Clay Country Republican* newspaper, in a blistering editorial, accused Johnny Bob of being at the root cause of the bomb blast:

> Because of his slanderous remarks, his apparent hatred for the citizens of this community who opposed his will, and for this [*sic.*] boastful remarks that he would make Louisville a ghost town, Harrell has become a prime suspect in the bombing at the Morgan Hardware Store ...[163]

State police immediately launched an investigation with the FBI announcing they had been brought in as it appeared that the explosives were transported across state lines. Whatever fragments of the explosive could be found were shipped to the Illinois State Crime Lab.[164]

Sheriff Van Dyke labeled the bomb a "home-made affair" and disclosed that an unfamiliar car was spotted leaving Louisville, headed north on Highway 45, immediately after the explosion.[165]

For weeks after the explosion, the smell of dynamite lingered in the Louisville air.[166] Whatever calm that the town had gotten to enjoy while Harrell was gone was immediately destroyed. Everyone was on edge again. After all, if one bomb had been set off, others could too. One resident recalled, "For weeks afterward, every porch light in town burned all night long." Special neighborhood "bomb patrols" were set up in the community as everyone kept a watchful eye for any suspicious behavior.[167]

The occurrence of the blast did at least temporarily reenergize the hunt for the missing Harrell Family. The *Decatur Daily Review* newspaper said that the FBI had to now refocus their search as the case had now taken on "extremely serious dimensions."[168]

With the aid of insurance, the Morgans were able to rebuild their store as did most of the other damaged businesses in Louisville. After the Morgans rebuilt, rumors against them sprouted up, claiming that they themselves had set off the TNT in order to secure an insurance windfall.[169]

To date, no one has ever been arrested or charged in relation to the Louisville bombing.

Many years later, Mrs. Morgan was interviewed and reported a more-or-less final chapter to this story. One day, long after the bombing, she was in the small back office of their rebuilt store when a "well-dressed" man she did not know came in. In short order, the man confessed to Mrs. Morgan that he was one who made and set off the bomb in 1963.

He explained that he believed in John Harrell at the time but had since become convinced that Harrell's organization was nothing but a money-making scheme. He apologized to Mrs. Morgan and walked away. Mrs. Morgan never saw the man again.[170]

Sadly, the destruction of their store would not be the last tragedy to befall the Morgans. Some years after the blast, in March 1978, Mr. Morgan, after years of battling depression, walked into the back office of his main street store and lifted a pistol to his temple and pulled the trigger. His body was discovered a few hours later by his wife.[171]

Though after the trial, each of the Harrell men were pleased that none of them were going to jail, they all now faced a very uncertain future. First, their home (the Harrell estate) was on the verge of foreclosure. Their money stipends (all once paid by Johnny Bob) were now gone, too. Also, their church largely vanished as quickly as their charismatic leader had. Their children, meanwhile, had to return to local schools where their notoriety got them stigmatized and often bullied.

As the court case wound up, there remained another central mystery—where was Johnny Bob and his family? Now, of course, Harrell was not just a missing person, but because of the bench warrant issued, he was also a wanted fugitive.

As such, the FBI put out a "Wanted" poster featuring Johnny Bob Harrell. Along with featuring reproductions of each of Harrell's ten fingerprints, the poster also featured two photos of Harrell—one, an undated photo, of Harrell in suit and tie and the second, from 1961, of him looking far more mug-shot-like with Harrell in a wrinkled work shirt. Harrell, the wanted man, was described as: forty-two years old; 5 feet 10 inches; 170 pounds; white with gray hair and blue eyes. The poster also noted the presence on his throat of his old lymph-cancer scar. His occupation was listed as "farmer; salesman." The poster also offered a few words of caution: "Harrell has previously surrounded himself with armed guards." The auto-signature at the bottom of the poster was that of J. Edgar Hoover.

In light of the new charges, both the FBI and the Illinois state police stepped up their efforts to find Johnny Bob. In March 1964, the FBI mailed out circulars to various southern Illinois locations in hopes of locating new leads.[172] Jim Williams, an Illinois state cop stationed one county over from Louisville, remembers being put on high alert for any cars with out-of-state license plates seen on the Louisville blacktop; authorities were convinced that Johnny Bob would eventually return to southern Illinois.[173]

Meanwhile, at the Harrell compound, CCC members kept the faith. "The Lord will see Johnny Bob home," one of them was quoted as saying. While a non-Harrell supporter said, "Watch him show up Easter Morning!"[174]

A new clue arrived in late March 1964 when Mr. and Mrs. Hancock of Success, Missouri, not far from Rolla, Missouri, received a letter from an organization called the Vigilantes for Free America.[175] The angry, typewritten letter accused the couple of breaking the lease for the building where the Kellum-managed Trading Post store was located. The letter threatened to kill Mr. Hancock and to "blow up" their building.[176] The lease in question, held by the Hancocks, had been negotiated by Johnny Bob back in February 1963, not long before the Harrells went missing.[177]

Though many—including law enforcement—believed that that letter had either been written or ghostwritten by Johnny Bob, it still did not bring them much closer to finding him or the rest of his still-missing family.[178]

Interestingly, police at the time lamented that one of the reasons the Harrells might have been difficult to trace was because they were so law-abiding. If the family was on the run, they were not committing other crimes that could have tripped them up or expose them. They never had to hold-up a gas station for cash; they had enough cash with them; unlike other fugitives, they were not depending on various other crooks who might have been willing to turn them in.[179]

Additionally, throughout their absence, there was always some question as to just how hard the police were actually looking for the Harrells and the others. Rev. Comer, for one, still feared for the family's well-being and criticized various groups for not doing more. He said about the disappearance of the three youngsters from Missouri, "No investigation was made. No fingerprints were taken. Residents of the area were not questioned."[180] Comer also said:

> Sometimes I have been visited by the FBI as many as two or three times in one week ... I gained the impression that the FBI also thought our group might have sent the three missing children to the Harrell family.
>
> ... the FBI has always taken the position that it has no jurisdiction because there was no evidence of kidnapping. There has been speculation that the Harrell family may be in Mexico, South America or Europe, but we have no reason to believe this.[181]

Comer also noted that the church membership had just mailed out 1,800 copies of a bulletin with information on the missing family in hopes that that would bring about new leads.[182] Comer also labeled any reports about Harrell's imminent return to the estate as merely "rumors."[183]

Though FBI Agent Robert Gibbons stated that his agency had been investigating all of the disappearances "as much as is necessary," outspoken Minuteman founder Robert DePugh echoed Comer's frustration about the lack of progress. He said, "I don't believe it is possible for a man and seven members of his family to hide from the FBI for this long."[184] DePugh went on to list just some of the organizations that might have wanted to abduct Harrell, including the CIA, various communist organizations, and even the FBI itself. DePugh also said he was becoming convinced that Johnny Bob and his entire family were no longer alive. DePugh told the press:

I heard from John two days before he disappeared. He said he had some extremely important information and would meet me at the Lexington, Missouri, airport, but he called later and said he had decided to drive his automobile. He said he had documentary proof of Communist membership of some highly placed people in the Government.[185]

DePugh made his statements to the press in August 1964.[186]

Like San Fidel, New Mexico, the town of Strawberry, Arkansas, is so small it does not even register on some maps. Even today, its population is less than 300. It is located in Arkansas's Lawrence County, in the northeast corner of the state; it is about 100 miles straight south of the southern border of Missouri and about 100 miles west of Tennessee. In 1964, Strawberry was known for being very transient—a lot of people came and a lot of people went from it. Hence, when a large, multi-generational family moved in, around May 1963, no one took too much notice or asked too many questions—at first.[187]

The patriarch of the expansive new family was a tall man with rather long and shaggy hair who gave his name as Thomas Taylor.[188] The family had kept mainly to themselves since they arrived in the area about a year prior. The family moved into an old house at the end of a dead-end dirt road. Yet even in Strawberry, Arkansas, such a large family coming to town and no one knowing anything about them and always keeping so to themselves made some of their neighbors wonder.[189]

It also drew the curiosity of a meter reader from the Rural Electrification Administration, who, after walking by the house several times, became concerned that someone was being held captive inside.[190] His suspicion grew more when he noted the high number of guns that seemed to be lying around the property—enough, he said, to stock a brigade.[191]

The meter reader eventually contacted Kenneth Guthrie, the local sheriff, about the family living in the farm house.[192] Arriving on the night of Friday, September 20, Sheriff Guthrie first talked with a boy who he took to be the patriarch's eldest son. The boy informed him that his father, "Tom Taylor," was away on a business trip but Guthrie became suspicious when the boy refused to divulge any other information.[193]

Before leaving the property, Guthrie looked around and discovered a tax bill that had been issued under the name "Harrell" and which further contained an address from Louisville, Illinois.[194] Back at the police station, Guthrie reached out to Deputy Bill Hiser up in Clay County, Illinois, who confirmed that they were, indeed, looking for one John Harrell, previously of Clay County.[195]

The next morning, a Saturday, armed with a search warrant, Guthrie returned to confront the older man when he returned from his business trip.[196] When the man's sedan approached Guthrie's blockade, Guthrie said he knew that the man in the car was the man who was wanted.[197] At first, the man insisted that he was Tom Taylor, but later, Johnny Bob told the officer his real name and commented, "I am the only one you want. The other people in my group are innocent."[198]

"Taylor" was then handcuffed and taken to the Pulaski County jail in Little Rock and put under a $25,000 bond.[199] At the time, authorities also wondered if Taylor may have been behind a rash of recent burglaries in the area.[200]

On September 20, 1964, the Taylor family was revealed to be the long missing family of Johnny Bob Harrell.[201] Along with Johnny Bob, his wife, and his children, also living in or near Strawberry were Mr. Harrell's mother and the two young girls reported missing from Missouri since last October. Dorothy Payne had also joined the group and was living under the alias "Dorothy Stone" while Linda Rowan was going by the name "Lynn Webster."[202]

Originally, when on the run, Harrell had adopted the name of "J.T. Smith." The family originally made their home in Williford, Arkansas. Tod Harrell later said, "We bought a place in Williford first and live there four or five months. Then we rented a place at Strawberry and later bought it."[203]

Once in Strawberry, the family resided in a four-room frame farmhouse that was later added onto, with some crudely attached rough-hewn lumber, in order to add five additional rooms. The extra space was for the expanding needs of the family; Johnny Bob's wife gave birth to their seventh child, a girl, while living in Arkansas.[204] A *St. Louis Post-Dispatch* article about the family's discovery noted that the home was "clean and well kept" and that people living nearby spoke of how quiet and well-mannered the family's children were, though they did note that the older man could prove cranky about people trespassing on or near his property.[205]

Natalia Harrell and the two non-related girls and the baby son of Mrs. Payne all resided in homes nearby. It was hoped that by dividing up family and the others, it would help diffuse suspicion.[206] From an early age, it seems the youngest of the Harrell children knew the "rules" of hiding in plain sight: if they were playing outside and a plane flew overhead, they were told to quickly run inside.[207]

The family had a considerable amount of money with them, including silver and gold coins and $7,000 that they hid in a rain barrel.[208] All funds were seized by law enforcement, including $4,000 in a bank account held by Linda Rowan.[209] Johnny Bob also earned extra cash by taking on odd jobs. The family also had in their possession various defaced license plates as well as various weapons, chain saws, and other objects.[210] In the home, officers noted the presence of three TV sets, butane gas for cooking, and two refrigerators.[211] The family had ownership of eleven different vehicles parked between their two outposts.[212] The occasional visit by various Harrell followers would bring the family new supplies of food and clothing and a growing collection of rifles, pistols, and ammunition.[213] Along with the money, Arkansas officials also seized Harrell's land, vehicles, and his large stockpile of weapons.[214]

Tod Harrell later said of the family's life in Arkansas, "Dad read a lot of history and news. He would conduct religious services for us on Sunday, when we would sing and pray and read the Bible. [In Williford], we swam in the Spring River near the house."[215]

Linda Rowan and Nancy Kellums later joined the family to assist in the care of the younger children and to tutor some of the older ones as none of the children could be enrolled in school.[216] The oldest children received their education from Harrell and the older women who, every week, assigned them to read sections from an encyclopedia or from various news magazines that they salvaged from a local junk yard. Rowan was interviewed not long after the family was exposed. She said, "I've enjoyed living here. There were some moments that were not so much fun, and of course we were not used to living like that."[217]

Johnny Bob later said about the family's extended stay in Arkansas, "[We] just lived from day to day and trusted in the Lord."[218]

Later, Tod said, "We pulled out [of Louisville] because of what the Government was trying to do to my father." Tod Harrell also said that he and his dad had purchased various pieces of furniture in various nearby towns in the hopes that they could start a used furniture store.[219]

The news of the capture of the long-missing "militant anti-communist zealot," as one newspaper described him, and his family quickly made its way back to southern Illinois and, as always, into the press.[220] A photo snapped by a UPI photographer caught Johnny Bob at the Arkansas jail. In the photo, Harrell's hair was short and mussed and his shirt was largely unbuttoned; he had grown a mustache while in hiding.

For his efforts in the capture, Deputy Hiser would later receive a personal letter of congratulations from FBI chief J. Edgar Hoover.[221]

One day after they were discovered, Tod, while still in custody, asked to speak privately with one of the police officers. To the officer, Tod revealed a detail of the family's time in the South that would add a tragic and macabre chapter to the Harrell family's story.

Six-year-old Larry Lee Payne, son of Dorothy Payne, was dead, Tod told the police. He died accidentally, on August 15, drowning in a rain barrel, and his body was buried in a grave 4 feet deep and about 300 yards from the back of the Harrells's house in Strawberry.[222] Tod related:

> Nobody saw Larry drown. It was in the afternoon, about 2 o'clock. I came out of the house and saw the bottom of his feet about even with the top of the water in the barrel.
>
> I yelled for my father. He was resting at the time, and he came out as soon as he could. We took the boy out of the barrel and into the kitchen and dried him off.[223]

Johnny Bob checked for Larry's heartbeat and found none.

> We asked his mother if she wanted to see him. But it came as such a shock that the boy was dead, she didn't want to. Then the next day we buried him.
>
> We put the body into two cloth bags and then into a plastic zipper bag. I dug a grave about four and a half feet deep. We had planned to go down six feet but we ran into rock.
>
> After the burial, Dad prayed. He was upset about the boy's death, and he didn't want to discuss it.[224]

Obviously, when the incident happened, as the Harrells and the others were in hiding from the law, they could not report it to the authorities. Instead, they performed their own hasty burial.[225]

After Tod's confession, Arkansas police officers, area coroner W. C. Bryan, and Tod immediately departed for the Harrell house. After the baby's body was exhumed, it was transported for an autopsy.[226] Autopsy findings showed no broken bones, suggesting that the child really did indeed die from drowning.[227] After the findings were reported, the body of Larry Lee Payne was sent to Illinois for a proper burial. Tod was charged with failing to report a death and burying a body in an unregistered cemetery.[228] Later, he saw those charges dropped. Tod was however later convicted of altering eight old license plates. Found in a junkyard, Tod took the old plates and repainted them in the colors of more contemporary plates. The plates were then to be affixed to some of the family's vehicles so the cars couldn't be easily traced. Tod ended up with $800 in fines and thirty days in jail for that offense.[229]

Shortly after the trial on the raid had concluded, but before the Harrells had been found, the Comer family departed again for New Mexico.

Comer's daughter, Angelyn, remembers their loaded-up their car and the U-Haul they pulled behind it stuffed with a sewing machine, a piano, and other items.[230]

As the Comers drove west, the FBI, in hot pursuit of the Harrells and believing that the Comers might be going to see them or at least knew where they were hiding, not so stealthily followed the family. Angie remembers, "It was quite obvious, really. One car behind us would peel off and then another would pull out immediately from a road by a field and begin following us."[231] The Comers also believed that their phone lines were being monitored at this time.[232]

The family made it almost to the Ozarks—complete with their FBI "tail"—when the piano and other items they were towing shifted *en route*, damaging their trailer and necessitating that the family return to Louisville.[233]

Shortly after they arrived back at the Harrell estate in Illinois, the Comers got word that the Harrells had been found. They also learned that, all this time, the family had not been kidnapped after all, but had, instead, been in hiding. Comer told the press at the time, "I'm not one to jump to any conclusions. I want to hear what everyone has to say about it before I make any conclusions."[234]

As to the three letters that had been mailed by him when he was a "hostage," Harrell, now in custody, provided an elaborate explanation that stretched his credibility to an even a greater extreme. He said he had only dreamed that he was being held hostage and that the three letters were never meant to be mailed. He had written out the dream as a way to record the details of it.[235] He said:

> Whether they were mailed by friend or foe I cannot tell but it has caused me great anguish. The Lord knows what He is doing....
>
> The Lord had me write in detail about some events in the dream and if I remember correctly it was on scratch paper ...
>
> When I heard they had been mailed it caused me much concern as they were not written to be mailed.[236]

Remarkably, despite their lack of experience and some clumsy moves (like Harrell's "hostage" letters), Johnny Bob and his family proved pretty good at "disappearing." They successfully eluded capture by law enforcement for over a year, difficult even for a single-acting long-time criminal—impressive for a novice with a large family traveling in tow.

It has long been speculated that while most of Harrell's followers were kept in the dark during the family's mysterious absence, both Lester Kellums and Flo Rowan (and possibly a few others) knew the whereabouts of the family the entire time and may have assisted them over the eighteen months they were on the run.[237]

Johnny Bob has since said that had they not been captured, it was his full intention to keep his family underground for the rest of his life, assumedly at some point coming back to reclaim Jeb who had been left behind in Louisville.[238]

In late September 1964, Harrell waived a removal hearing that was to take place in Arkansas and agreed to be taken back to East St. Louis to face charges.[239] On October 1, 1964, Johnny Bob Harrell was transported from a jail in Arkansas to the jail in East St. Louis, Illinois. He would be held there in lieu of a $40,000 bond.[240] Back in Illinois, he would face charges of harboring a deserter and of bail-jumping. If convicted, he could be ordered to pay $34,000 and could draw a prison sentence of as much as thirty-two years. Also reported in the brief article on Harrell's transfer was an update on his latest tax problems.[241] It was reported that the IRS had now slapped a lien on more of Harrell's land as he still owed back taxes totaling $257,429, all for various taxes dated between 1955 and 1961.[242]

In East St. Louis, in mid-October, once again John R. Harrell appeared in front of Judge Juergens regarding his charges. However, there would be no trial. Instead, Harrell, that day, changed his earlier plea of not guilty to guilty, telling the court, "There is no need for the court to try this case that has already been tried before."[243]

On November 4, 1964, Judge Juergens issued the court's sentence. As a suited and well-groomed Johnny Bob stood in front of the judge clutching a Bible under his arm, a group of about twenty of Harrell's followers, including his mother, sat in the courtroom.[244] They wept when the judge listed out the many penalties: three years behind bars for harboring a deserter; three years for failure to deliver a deserter after command; three years for conspiring to harbor a deserter; and six years for conspiracy to prevent a special agent from discharging his duties.[245] Additionally, Harrell got five years for bail jumping. The various sentences would be served concurrently for a total of ten years behind bars. Harrell was also levied a fine of a fine of $10,000.[246]

The entire sentencing took only fifteen minutes. After the judge delivered his orders, Harrell addressed the court, stating that he was sorry and that he knew he had made a mistake.[247] Harrell also offered to return immediately to Arkansas and never set foot in Louisville again if his sentence was commuted to probation. "We desire to return to the hills of Arkansas and live quietly, engaging ourselves in some line of productive business," Johnny Bob told the court.[248] The judge was not moved, nor did a judge agree the following December when two requests to change Harrell's guilty plea were denied.[249]

Later, Harrell's court-appointed attorney, John Cleary, criticized the sentence as being unduly harsh in light of the suspended sentences given to the other men previously tried for most of these same offenses.[250]

Though Johnny Bob's son Tod, had been arrested the day of the raid and it was reported that he would eventually stand trial, as an adult, the case against him was never pursued by the court. Tod says today, "I don't think they were, in the end, that interested in me; they were more interested in dad."[251]

After the sentencing, Johnny Bob Harrell was taken to the St. Louis city jail to wait to be transferred to a federal prison facility in Terre Haute, Indiana.[252] Later, Harrell himself said that the severity of his sentence might have been due, in part, to the general leniency shown to the other defendants.[253]

Only days after Harrell's sentencing, in another courtroom, this one in Little Rock, Arkansas, the two women who were accused of assisting in the hiding Johnny Bob and his family while they were in Strawberry were acquitted. In his ruling, Judge J. Smith Henley said fifty-seven-year-old Flora Rowan and twenty-four-year-old Dorothy Payne did not harbor or conceal the family as those terms are generally understood. He said, "There was nothing hidden or furtive about Harrell's movements in Arkansas. And he was never hidden, concealed or harbored by these defendants or anyone else."[254]

Obviously, the reason for the Harrell family's eighteen months as fugitives from the law was due to Johnny Bob's fear that he would be found guilty of the various charges related to the Dion Davis raid and that he would never be able to obtain a fair trial. Though Harrell, no doubt, suspected communism as the reason for the legal system's possible failing, his apprehension was not, perhaps, completely unfounded. He had already been convicted of violating a truancy law that was not on the books. Then his own home was the location of an overwhelming onslaught by police and military personnel carried out in the dead of night. Harrell certainly had at least a few reasons to be circumspect of how the courts would treat him.

In a 1967 interview, Johnny Bob said that before he and his family fled, the impending trial, its troubles, and frequent delays were bringing his wife and mother to near nervous collapse and that was what inspired their fleeing.[255] The family's "vanishing" was engineered quite simply: they drove up to a pre-determined location, where they were met by another car. They got in the other vehicle and abandoned theirs along the side the road.[256]

Years later, Johnny Bob reflected ruefully on his short-lived life as a fugitive from justice. He said about his flight from the law, "I shouldn't have done that. It's the one thing I regret."[257]

The Patriot

Patriotism is the last refuge....

Samuel Johnson

In Louisville and throughout parts of southern Illinois, John R. Harrell was known, to some, as being akin to Noah. In fact, Harrell once compared himself to the biblical ark-builder by stating of himself, "Remember how Noah worked on his ark for 120 years, yet none of his neighbors had the intelligence to copy him?"[1] Of course, others, no doubt, considered Johnny Bob closer to the Messiah. However, in the federal prison system, Johnny Bob Harrell was known only as "Miscellaneous 1399."[2]

Harrell obtained the moniker beginning in November 1964 when, at age forty-two, he began his ten-year prison sentence at the men's federal penitentiary in Terre Haute, Indiana.[3] First opened in 1940, the western Indiana facility, United States Penitentiary (USP Terra Haute), has the capacity to house over 1,000 inmates and is rumored to have been the model on which the U.S.'s Guantanamo Bay detention camp in Cuba was later based. Along with incarceration, the prison also practices execution by lethal injection; Oklahoma City bomber Timothy McVeigh was executed there in 2001.[4]

With their father in jail in Indiana, the Harrell family (with the exception of oldest son Tod, who was now living on his own) moved from Louisville to Marshall, Illinois. A town of approximately 3,000, Marshall sits only a few miles from the Indiana state border and only 16 miles from Terre Haute.[5] In Marshall, the Harrell family rented a large, white Victorian house to live in.[6] The family's relocation was done to make the most of the two visits per week that their father was allowed.[7] Often not making those visits was Johnny Bob's mother, who was quoted as saying, "I haven't since him since a year ago in December because of my hip ... to hear those prison doors clang, it breaks my heart."[8]

According to Harrell, not long after his arrival in Terre Haute, he was approached by prison officials about starting a prison ministry and a Bible-study group. Harrell, surprised, responded, "Don't you know what got me in here?"[9] Regardless, it was believed that Harrell's fellow inmates were greatly in need of religious instruction and education, and Johnny Bob was just the man to provide it.

While Johnny Bob started his prison ministry, outside, his son Tod (who had returned from Arkansas) announced that he had started a special fund with the goal of raising $30,000 to assist with the release of his father and, with any leftover monies, to aid other "political prisoners."[10]

In November 1964, with their founder and leader now incarcerated, Decatur newspaper reporter Michael K. Burns travelled to the Louisville estate to see how members of Harrell's devoted flock were weathering the latest chapter in the exploits of this man, Johnny Bob Harrell.[11]

First, Burns described the estate—once as pristine as a postcard—as now looking haggard and unkempt. The grass on the vast lawn had not been cut for many, many weeks, he said, and the front gate entrance was (still) in shambles. Some of the bomb shelters had even caved in. The number of people who were now calling the estate home—which once numbered almost 100—had dwindled down to just two families. One of them was the Comer family. Comer, his wife, and his daughter had assumed the living quarters over the garage, which was once the home of the Harrells.[12] The Comers had returned to Louisville after that second trip to New Mexico was canceled when Johnny Bob was discovered in Arkansas.[13] None of the followers would ever return to New Mexico.

In the article, Comer said, "Our people are becoming more scattered all the time. Most of them moved away to find work."[14] The Kellums family, for example, eventually settled in the Pinckneyville area.[15]

Burns went on to relate that both the church members' and even Mr. Comer's own attitude about Harrell were now at their lowest ebbs. He characterized Comer as a "dissolution and disappointed man." Burns seemed to think that the series of three letters written by the "hostage" Johnny Bob and then Harrell's bizarre later explanation for them were the final breaking point for Comer. In fact, Comer had recently sent a letter to Johnny Bob that read, in part, "Bob, I'll have to say frankly, I do not believe it is explanations we need, but confessions."[16]

Still, Comer had not completely given up on Johnny Bob or Harrell's overall mission. Comer was still leading a weekly CCC service on the grounds and was still mailing out the "Christian Conservative Challenge," the group's newsletter, to members nationwide.[17] Comer said, "Just because I disagree with [Harrell] doesn't mean the Lord has passed judgement."[18]

Though they resided in Marshall for a time, by early 1965, according to another press piece, Mrs. Harrell and her younger children had all returned to Louisville and were, once more, living on the estate.[19] Also returning to Louisville were Johnny Bob's mother, Natalia; Flo Rowan and her children; and Dorothy Payne and her children. Natalia Harrell had even been able to reclaim the local motel that she and her son once owned, and she was now living in some living quarters located behind it.[20] The motel would also provide housing and a livelihood for the Comers who ultimately left the compound to take it over from the older Mrs. Harrell.[21]

Around the same time that the Harrell family returned to Southern Illinois, Johnny Bob was transferred as well.[22] According to Johnny Bob, very early one morning, long before he was awake, his cell was stormed by a group of guards who seized the "political prisoner." He says, they "shackled me up and took me to Leavenworth."[23]

According to Harrell, after he was grabbed from his cell, he was restrained, blindfolded, and thrown in the back of a police vehicle with no knowledge of where he was headed until the end of the 449-mile journey, which took him to one of the United States' most infamous penitentiaries. There, according to Harrell, "I was in kept in the most dangerous section."[24]

Harrell believes he knew the reason for his abrupt transferal, which took place in November 1964. He said, "I was leading a weekly church service and they thought it was getting too big." Terrified that Harrell might mobilize and weaponize his congregation, the officials of the Terre Haute prison took the drastic action of removing Harrell completely.[25]

However, in his 1970 master's thesis on Harrell, writer-student Ronald A. Kramme lays out evidence that while in jail in Terre Haute, Harrell may have been instrumental in recruiting other inmates into the controversial Minutemen organization or other radical groups and that is what lead to his sudden move.[26]

Once they learned of Johnny Bob's transfer to Kansas (which they considered nothing more than additional persecution), the Harrell family moved once more, again to be closer to him. The family moved to a town in Missouri named St. James, a city of about 4,000 people.[27] There they rented a small farm house.[28] St. James, though not terribly close to Leavenworth, is only about 20 miles from Rolla.

As local newspapers and even the *National Enquirer* once realized, the adventures of Johnny Bob Harrell could make for "good copy" and could serve to spike readership.

In 1965, in an achievement even Johnny Bob might not have been proud of, Harrell's story made the cover of the pulp magazine *True Police Cases*.

Though now true crime tales are far more likely to be found on cable TV, for a time, quickly and cheaply produced magazines devoted to sensational crime stories loaded down America's magazine racks. One of the most successful was *True Police Cases*. In April 1965, their front cover screamed "The Cult Leader Who Defied the FBI." Along with that, the image that the magazine created to accompany it was full of spice: in the color photo, a young woman, in a flimsy white nightgown, is sitting on a brass bed, and the hand of an unseen man is shown violently grabbing her wrist while the woman, her face a study in quaking fear, looks up at her mysterious aggressor.[29]

Despite the provocative cover image, though, the article on Harrell inside the magazine was hardly exploitative. Written by Carl G. Hodges, the article covers a lengthy eleven pages and reproduces many of the photos from the Associated Press, including shots of Johnny Bob, his estate, Tod, the abandoned Sedan found near Springfield, a shot of Dion Davis at the St. Louis courthouse, and a picture of Harrell outside one of his estate's many bomb shelters. Though the author of the piece concludes it by asking of the now-imprisoned Harrell, "saint or sinner?" the write-up is surprisingly judgement free and not even very melodramatic; it is just a straight-forward account of the events as they happened, which apparently needed no greater sensationalism added.[30]

For Johnny Bob, whatever destabilization the move from one prison to another might have had on him was short-lived. In January 1967, Harrell filed an appeal to his sentence, claiming that his earlier plea was improperly acquired. Harrell said he entered the plea only after being promised by defense counsel Robert Rice that, in exchange, they would go easy on Tod. At the time, at least one judge—Walter J. Cummings—was in agreement with Johnny Bob and stated that Harrell was indeed entitled to a new hearing.[31]

However, this opinion was not supported by the U.S. Court of Appeals, who, after reviewing the case, let Harrell's conviction stand. As support, the appeals court referenced the trial's transcript. According to it, when the judge asked Harrell at his original plea hearing if he had been made any promises that would affect his plea, back then Harrell responded with a straightforward "No." Hence, in the eyes of the court, Harrell was not allowed to change his mind or recant his declaration now.[32]

It was not just (some) courts that were coming to Johnny Bob's defense at this time though. In March of that year, the *Decatur Herald* published an editorial that questioned if Harrell's sentence was appropriate for his crimes. Its headline was "Cult Leader's Worst Offense Bad Judgement."[33] The editorial also went on to note the issue of Harrell and his followers being charged with harboring a deserter when the military found Dion

Davis only as AWOL and the article also noted the wide discrepancy between the sentence Johnny Bob got compared to his other followers. The editorial concluded, "Thus it would appear the court has been as guilty of bad judgment as Harrell."[34]

The court appeal of 1967, as reported in the news, shined a light again on the Harrell Family and the 1961 raid. In March of that year, the *Decatur Herald* newspaper that had covered the Harrell situation doggedly for many years felt that enough time had passed for a retrospective and update.[35]

Denied a request to interview Harrell himself due to federal regulations, the *Herald* newsman, Jerry Parsons, instead traveled to Louisville to interview Johnny Bob's wife, Betty.[36] Parsons reported:

> Mrs. Harrell broke into tears occasionally as she spoke of the hardship that had befallen the family.
>
> She said, "I knew there'd be muddy roads ahead, but I sure didn't know there'd be so many ruts.
>
> "The little girl (Rebecca) doesn't talk. Johnny (Lance) has to go to Flora for treatment of his eyes. The family has to live on relief. There are six feet to buy shoes for, and one needs a size 12."
>
> Mrs. Harrell went on to say, "There's just got to be justice someplace...."[37]

A photo of Mrs. Harrell and four of their young children sitting around a barren kitchen table accompanied the article.[38]

In the article, Mrs. Harrell also lamented of her loneliness and separation from the citizens of Louisville. "I hardly ever see anybody," she said, "Once in a while Rev. Comer and his wife come out."[39] Mrs. Harrell also said she seldom even ventured into town these days, leaving family shopping trips to her son, Xon, who had just turned sixteen and acquired a driver's license.[40]

Johnny Bob's mother was also interviewed for the article. The elderly Mrs. Harrell, sporting graying hair and bright blue eyes, according to the article, now required the use of a walker. She said she prayed every day for her son's freedom. Also, she busied herself most days by writing "thank you" letters to her son's many followers and supporters.[41]

Then, later in 1967, it seemed like the entire Harrell family was going to become homeless. A newspaper report appeared stating that the Mt. Vernon home and the rest of the estate had just been sold—at a very reduced price—to a Mr. and Mrs. Russell D. Jameson of Raytown, Missouri. At the time of the purchase, Mr. Jameson announced his plans to turn the home and property into an electronics school (an ironic choice considering the home had never even been wired for electricity).[42]

Despite that public announcement, Jameson's plans were just smoke and mirrors. Like the earlier motel purchase by Ruth Walsh, the Jamesons were actually friends of the Harrell family and bought the home, more or less, to "hold" it until Johnny Bob's release from prison.[43]

Finally, the Harrell family received some good news in July 1968 when, after serving one-third of his ten-year sentence, Johnny Bob Harrell was to be paroled.[44] Reached for comment by a Decatur newspaper, Johnny Bob's mother, Natalia, was overcome with emotion at the news that her son was going to be free. She was quoted as saying to the reporter, "I can't talk now; I've just got to sit down and cry."[45]

The news came not only as a surprise to Mrs. Harrell, but apparently, to various bodies within the U.S. justice system as well. They said they had not been properly informed of Harrell's release before it was reported in the newspaper.[46]

Johnny Bob later related how his early release came about. He said, "[In that prison], you never saw the warden. But one day I was summoned to the Warden's office and when I sat down, he asked me, 'Johnny Bob, just who did you make mad?'"[47]

If that story of Johnny Bob's is true, it suggests that someone high up in government had played some sort of major role in Harrell's incarceration and perhaps even his move to Leavenworth.

Johnny Bob's release might also have been something of the product of the time. In 1968, many people's faith in their government was waning. The anti-establishment and anti-military attitudes of the era might very well have seen Johnny Bob recast as something of a political prisoner or, at least, a conscientious objector, one who had bravely once defied the warmongering of the establishment.

In any event, Harrell was described by the Leavenworth warden as "a model prisoner who has made an excellent adjustment and has been no trouble for the administrative staff whatsoever."[48] Harrell was released on August 22, 1968.[49] At the time of his release, Johnny Bob was forty-six years old.

Due to the restrictions of his parole, at the time of his release, Johnny Bob was prohibited from participating in interviews or in appearing in any news photos.[50] That was a major turnaround for a man who used to constantly want to speak to the press.

Though he was going to be paroled, Johnny Bob still had imposed on him some very strict mandates by the parole committee. Along with reporting regularly to a parole officer in East St. Louis (which he would have to do until November 1973), Harrell was also forbidden from engaging in any "political activities" and in preaching in any church (his own or anyone else's). He was also forbidden from associating with or contacting any of his old congregation for the next ten years.[51] The latter requirement, however, was easier to impose than act upon. Many of Harrell's old followers, if they had not remained living in Louisville, remained living in rural southern Illinois, hence, running into each other was not going to be an uncommon occurrence. Still, all parties chose to honor their requirements and their interactions usually involved little more than a wave or a quick "hello."[52]

Finally, Harrell was also ordered to find full-time employment.[53] Originally, after his sentencing back in 1964, Johnny Bob had vowed to never step foot in the Louisville town square again.[54] To the locals of Louisville, that promise and the demand that he find a full-time job— for surely no one in Louisville would ever hire him—was enough, they thought, to keep Harrell out of the town and from causing any more trouble in the county seat of Clay County, but it was not.

Quickly after his parole, Harrell—either forgetting or disclaiming his earlier vow—returned, like a prodigal son, to Louisville. Though never a "follower" of Harrell's, local businessman John ("Bud") Zink, Jr., who owned a bustling lumber and petroleum company based in Louisville, and was a longtime friend of Harrell's, offered Johnny Bob a job.[55]

Zink would later make no excuses for extending a hand to his old friend, for Harrell always had a mind worth picking, according to Zink, who said, "When I'd have a problem, I'd go out there and sit on the front porch with Johnny Bob and he'd help me puzzle through it. It was sort of like having my own think tank."[56]

Later, Harrell, ever intrepid, founded his own business—a series of resale shops, a sort of for-profit Good Will operation. He opened his first store in the Illinois town of Centralia, about 55 miles from Louisville. Others ("about half a dozen") would follow, some as far away as West Virginia and (again) New Mexico.[57]

While in prison, Harrell had gained some weight and his hair, nearly silver when he went into jail, had now turned fully white. He combed it straight-back now, and if it was on the long side, it tended to look a bit like a pompadour. Failing eyesight had caused him to wear glasses all the time now as well. The "new" Johnny Bob looked a bit like a successful Southern uncle mixed with a dash of an Elvis impersonator.

For the next few years, Harrell fully observed his parole restrictions, reconnected with his family, and continued to work for Zink. However, Johnny Bob had not mellowed. He was still vehemently worried about the state of the nation and about its future. In 1976, the year of the nation's bicentennial, Harrell resurrected the Christian Conservative Church and authored its central manifesto.[58]

Titled *Declaration and Proclamation* and dated July 4, 1976, this manifesto is seven pages long and single-spaced. It is a screed, written solely by Johnny

Bob, about the plight of America, its impending doom, and conservativism's plan to save it. In it, perhaps drawing from his own problems with the IRS, Johnny Bob rages against taxes calling them "legalized robbery" and adds that "Tax laws are used to enslave the poor and enrich the prosperous."[59]

Later, he revisits some other old wounds:

> Swarms of government agents have been sent forth to harass, harangue, investigate, agitate, and question our citizens by powerful politicians, using them and their office to silence opposition.... Such agents enter homes without search warrants—looting, pillaging, plundering, and violating the very laws they have been taken an oath to uphold.[60]

Throughout the text of the document, Harrell often utilizes long lists of words. Later, he speaks about "patriots" out to defend America from the "dangers now at our doorstep" and how they have been "censored, ridiculed, derided, defamed, demeaned, dismissed and destroyed."[61]

Still later, he lambasts the nation's "headless, heartless, irresponsive, irresponsible, monstrous, bureaucratic system" while also listing among its problems a weakened military and runaway inflation.[62]

Amid the torrid use of language, Harrell's proclamation also calls attention to the nation's constantly-climbing debt and to the need to, once again, or still, put God back in government.

Once all typed out, Harrell or people in his office made 1,000 copies and mailed them—"served" them—to every member of the U.S. Senate and every member of the U.S. House of Representatives as well as the president and vice president of the United States.[63]

After the mailing, Harrell did receive a couple of responses from officials, both quite supportive. One came from Vice President Rockefeller's office. The second came from notoriously conservative North Carolina Senator Jesse Helms.[64] The manifesto was also allegedly entered into the Congressional Record.[65]

The actions of 1976 were only a prologue. In 1977, Harrell created a new not-for-profit organization that he christened the Christian Patriots Defense League (CPDL). For it, he obtained his own Employee Identification number from the Internal Revenue Service.[66]

Harrell declared the purpose of the organization was to awaken and recruit patriots who found themselves in the wilderness contending against "humanism, modernism, communism, regionalism, Judaism, integration, taxation, gun confiscation" and other "atrocities perpetrated by evil men" among whom are the "Christ-hating International Jewish Conspiracy."[67]

The following year, 1978, Harrell formulated two unofficial companion organizations: the Citizens Emergency Defense System (CEDS), an organization to serve as a means to mobilize and train people throughout the US for personal protection from domestic, government-sanctioned terrorism; and the Paul Revere Club, the money-making arm of the organization. The Revere Club was a soliciting agency for those who could not travel to Louisville for any workshop or meeting but still wished to be part of the cause by sending in a "donation" of $5 a month in the interest of "their Country's survival and future." That fee got them not only membership and a membership card but their very own frameable 5×7 "Certificate of Recognition."[68] Interested individuals could also purchase their very own dog tags for an extra $2.[69] The group also provided its members with a phone number to a twenty-four-hour hotline.[70]

By this time, Harrell and his family were back living on the grounds of the Mt. Vernon estate, once again residing in the living quarters above the large garage.[71]

The grounds had been cleaned up, too—and they were added to. Harrell raised on the property a 20-foot tall, free-standing golden triangle made of metal. The triangle was built and prominently placed in front of the big house to represent the geographic "golden triangle" that Harrell predicted would soon become the new heart of North America. That area would stretch from the Atlantic coast of Florida and the top of Texas and up to the top of Lake Superior. Its center, of course, would be right where Johnny Bob was—Louisville or thereabouts. Harrell had long maintained that after its inevitable fall, "Our government will be moved to the Midwest and Illinois will be a key state."[72]

Harrell also had new plans for his property. This time, instead of being the home of an indefinite religious retreat, it would become a para-military training facility devoted to training "patriots" preparing for the coming Armageddon and the inevitable collapse of the United States.

Harrell was also reporting prophecy again. He said, there was "the coming crisis," which, as it is described in the Bible, would cause the land to shake to and fro "like a drunken man." He also reported that the enemies of America would "come from Cuba, from Mexico, from the Caribbean. Everywhere the cancer of Communism has taken hold."[73] He went on:

> The UN is a legitimate spy organization where countries are free to engage in espionage.
>
> Our cities will be sacked. It could easily be triggered by unemployment. People not being able to get food.
>
> We're going to have a full-scale revolution. We've got half the world's wealth and the rest of 'em are coming to take it from us. The black man's angry, the yellow man's angry. Everybody's angry but the white man and he's asleep…. We're lucky if we have two more years.[74]

Then, strongly echoing his onetime statement that "blood would flow down the streets of Louisville," Johnny Bob was now predicting that "blood and guts" would "be strewn all over this country."[75]

Beginning in the late 1970s, Johnny Bob fully embraced the newly emerging survivalist and the "Identity Church" movements. It seems that as communism faded as an overt threat to the traditional American way of life, race and religious diversity replaced it as a kind of "catch-all" enemy or target for blame. As described by the *Seattle Times* in a 1986 article, the "Identity Church" movement was a "pick-and-choose" theology that "preaches separatism and white supremacy."[76]

Starting in 1977, on the Louisville grounds, the CPL/Harrell began hosting an annual or even twice-a-year gathering of survivalists and survivalist groups. Called by one reporter, a "summer camp for freedom fighters," these "Freedom Festivals" were free and the activities of the two to three days included speeches, training exercises, education seminars and vendors selling everything from t-shirts to weapons to books (with titles like *The Origins of Jew*), as well as magazine subscriptions and "survival food."[77]

For his part, Johnny Bob began selling doomsday packages where those worried about invasion or nuclear fallout could reserve a place on the estate for that (soon to arrive) doomsday date. For a small fee, Johnny Bob would be happy to stockpile reserves for you: gasoline could be stored for $0.25 a gallon; canned goods for $1 a case per year; $5 a year to store a boat; and $24 for a car, and so on.[78] Eventually, the Mt. Vernon house became something of a warehouse, not only for the literature for Harrell's various groups but also for clothing, appliances, and other things that the survivors might need in post apocalypse America.[79]

For his new organization, Harrell was interested in recruiting as many as possible. He was especially interested in recruiting veterans of the Vietnam War and to obtaining members who, like him, were pilots and owned their own aircraft. He figured, from them, the new "Patriots" group could fashion their own air force.[80]

Despite the *New York Times* once denying his request to purchase an ad in their pages to recruit fellow "patriots," Harrell seemed to have little trouble finding members to join the CPDL.[81] By the early 1980s, Harrell claimed that he had 25,000 members and an annual budget of over $1 million.[82] As one concerned citizen not in the League put it, "Twenty-five thousand: That's not enough to make anyone jittery, but enough to get people to pay attention."[83]

For each festival, attendees were welcomed to come to the grounds and camp out on the estate—just like people did back in 1961. With the stately Mt. Vernon home serving as a magnificent and symbolic backdrop, additional large tents were then erected on the lawn and folding chairs set up under them; these would become meeting places and classrooms. If not under one of those awnings, meetings would be held in the old chapel portion of the Mt. Vernon house with its pews looking oddly like old movie theater seats and its walls once again adorned with various incarnations of the American flag.[84]

Often in those tents or in that chapel, one could find Johnny Bob himself, holding court and more-or-less preaching, just like in the old days. An account from 1982 related some of Harrell's remarks: "Governments have gotten pretty shabby these days and I'm very much afraid, my friends, that our system is going to fall of its own weight. The question is, 'WILL YOU BE READY?!'"[85]

Every year that the festivals went on, they seemed to grow in size, helped by the fact that there was no admission charge to attend it. By 1982, the twice-a-year "Freedom Festivals" were bringing in as many as 2,000 people per retreat, pulling them from nearly every state in the union.[86] The location of the festivals in Louisville was once described as being "four hours and a million rows of corn south of Chicago".[87]

A reporter who visited one of the festivals in 1980 reported it as an odd mix of country fair, religious revival, and doomsday preparedness while also making note of the rusting barbwire of the fence around the camp, the sight of volunteers putting up large tents and nailing signs to trees.[88] That author added:

> The volunteers, who came a day early from places both near and far, were getting the grounds ready for classes on how to slit a man's throat.... 37 states were represented. Although there was a sign at the front gate asking people not to bring weapons to the festival, many people brought a wide variety of guns, bows, and other less-legal weapons....[89]

Some of the classes among the fifty or so seminars offered during the festivals included: "Small Unit Defense," "Night Ambushes," and "Homemade Explosives," as well as classes on marksmanship, guard dog training, crossbow, black powder guns, "street action," and general knife fighting.[90] There was a class specifically for women on the women's role in the revolution, and children were not ignored either; they were not only welcomed to the grounds but could take training in gun safety, complete with hands-on experience.[91]

There were also sessions on how to establish a constitutional money system and how to "legally avoid paying income tax"—though, as noted by one reporter at the scene, at least two of the festival's main speakers had served time in federal prison for tax evasion and Harrell, himself, still owed the IRS over $250,000.[92] Furthermore, the IRS had removed the tax-exempt status of the CCC about ten years before.[93]

There was also a seminar on what the Bible supposedly says on the topic of race.[94] However, according to reporter Mike Billington who attended one of the events, "In many cases the classes were nothing more than hour-long political and religious harangues on topics such as Christian patriotism, the dangers of international Zionism, communism and against women's liberation."[95] Billington would go on to compare the entire scene of the festivals to "Munich in 1933."[96]

Another reporter described Johnny Bob as having "a radio preacher's voice and the affable manner of a small-town politician" who did not answer questions as much as offer short "sermonettes."[97]

Though the festivals usually only lasted three days, some members were invited to stay longer for additional "training."[98]

During the rest of the year, when the festivals were not occurring, the Harrell estate was firmly closed and its front entrance bore signs reading "KEEP OUT" and "NO TOURS." In November 1979, when a reporter showed up unannounced to the property, he was quickly approached by Harrell's then nineteen-year-old son, Lance, who fully vetted him.[99]

Finally granted entrance, the reporter, J. L. Schmidt, eventually made it into the Mt. Vernon house, which he described as having "tables piled high with league literature, illuminated by bare florescent fixtures which dangle in a maze of cords and wires."[100]

As the festivals endured, just like in the old days, Louisville found itself suddenly home to a brand-new set of unwanted attention. Once more, they had to get used to Johnny Bob's activities and his noisy airplane. Harrell, who had retained his pilot's license all these years, would, on many afternoons, fly in and out of his estate and often fly low over the town square.[101]

During this time, one of Johnny Bob's most vocal critics was an old one—June Morgan. Having stayed in town after the bombing out of her main street business and, later, the tragic suicide of her husband, Mrs. Morgan had rebuilt her life and was still running the local hardware store. And she was still critical of Harrell. She said in 1988, "Why would he buzz the town every afternoon? Except he's still trying to rattle us after all these years."[102]

Another Louisville resident, Robert Bunnell, who also ran the local drugstore, was even more blunt to an inquisitive reporter. When asked about Harrell, Bunnell replied, "Don't talk to me about that SOB. Too many folks suffered because of him."[103]

As always, Harrell remained defiant. He said, "You could say I provide a community service, since whatever goes wrong around here they blame me. I bet on judgement day, the good citizens of Louisville will beg off saying: 'None of it was my fault, Johnny Bob did it all.'"[104]

Many Louisville locals—especially those who remember back to the early and mid-1960s—were far from pleased about Johnny Bob's latest incarnation and the events taking place (again) on his property.

Due to pranksters or unwanted trespassers at the festivals, local police were often called to the grounds. Ironically, one of those cops was Priscilla Laughton Hutton's younger brother, who had spent some of his youth living in the compound.[105]

In his own way, Johnny Bob attempted to appease the citizenry of Louisville at the time of the festivals, even going so far as to place ads in the local newspaper every year to tell the locals to not be alarmed by the influx of camo- and canteen-wearing visitors often walking the streets and speaking to each other in a quasi-military-type code: "Captain! Major!"[106]

Harrell even wrote to the city and Illinois law enforcement officials that the annual visitors to his property meant no harm and describing the incoming horde as "Moral Majority-Ronald Reagan type people" who have no desire to "overthrow the government."[107]

Along with attracting the attention of Louisville residents and various Illinois and other Midwest newspapers, Harrell and his group also attracted the attention and the ire of the Jewish Anti-Defamation League and the Southern Poverty Law Center, a not-for-profit founded in 1971 and headquartered in Montgomery, Alabama.[108] Among other works, the center tracks the activities of various "hate groups" throughout the United States. Not long after it was founded, they placed the CPDL on their watch list alongside the remnants of Missouri-based Minutemen organization and such other radical groups as the Brown Berets, Aryan Nations, the Special Combat Operations Team (SCOT), and the Wisconsin-based Posse Comitatus.[109]

Regularly, as well, Harrell and his group were mentioned (and pictured) in *The Spotlight* and other newsletters and publications of the white supremacy movement. For example, in 1986, *The Spotlight* used Harrell as an example of government resistance:

> When they list good Americans such as John Harrell of the Christian-Patriots Defense League among the ranks of those being targeted by their [IRS's] Criminal Division, it is pretty evident as to how the IRS operates: like a secret police agency.[110]

Two years prior, *The Spotlight* celebrated Harrell for donating space at his next Freedom Festival to the "Populist Party," a group that was founded in 1982 in St. Louis by avowed racist Robert Weems.[111] Harrell said at the time about the times, "We are already in the tunnel and we are going to have to go through it, which will mean the collapse of our system, anarchy, and revolutions..."[112] Harrell enjoyed claiming that the CCC was the "longest continuous challenging patriotic organization in the US."[113]

Though, in the beginning, the festivals seemed to attach a wide swath of people, from various walks of life (including firefighters, police officers, veterans, and libertarians) with just an interest in survivalism, over the years, the festivals seemed to increasingly begin to attach more and more fringe groups with radical and racist agendas. One visitor to one festival reported the on-site sale of KKK-related T-shirts and the occasional flash of a swastika while the city of "New York" on the grounds was usually referred to as "Jew York" and the "United Nations" was called the "Jew-nited Nations."[114] The presence of the swastika on the Harrell property is interesting in that, years prior, it was that symbol of hate, on the bridge-hanging effigy, that terrorized so many of Johnny Bob's followers outside of Coles Chapel.

Harrell was careful to try to draw a distinction—however faint—between some other social movements and his own. He said about the KKK and its brethren, "I told them they could stay but we didn't agree with their ideas and they couldn't hand out any literature."[115]

Yet at times, Harrell sounded very much like some of those extremist groups. In 1979, he was quoted as saying, "We feel that almost 50 percent of the world's problems are caused by the mixing of races, which we believe to be totally against the natural makeup of man."[116] He allegedly told one reporter about an upcoming festival weekend, "You're welcome to join us, as long as you're white."[117] Harrell had other rules for the festivals as well, including no alcohol and no men or boys over age twelve being allowed to wear shorts.[118] In 1986, *Time* magazine quoted Harrell as saying that "Caucasians are the most proved, most capable" of all racial groups.[119] In another publication, Harrell supposedly offered to pay for blacks to return to Africa.[120]

Later Harrell added, "One reason we've got trouble around the world is that the Oriental mind, the Mongolian mind, the African mind, the Caucasian mind, they all have different values systems. They see things in a different light."[121]

Sometimes, some of the statements Harrell made seemed to echo some of the same sentiments he made in the early 1960s. He told one reporter at the time that he was planning for survival in the face of the expected communist aggression and that he foresaw a communist invasion happening soon that would leave the U.S. with only a small tract of land when it was finished. This "mid-America survival area," according to Johnny Bob, would have as its four corners—Lubbock, Texas; Scottsbluff,

Nebraska; Pittsburgh; and Atlanta.[122] Thankfully, according to Harrell at the time, this area contained the biggest collection of "patriots," a statistic he based upon CPDL membership rolls and published subscription stats from *Soldier of Fortune* magazine.[123] Due to this concentration of armed so-called patriots, this would be the area most likely to endure and to survive an enemy invasion.[124]

A 1981 article that made mention of the CPDL tried to get into the minds of these "patriots":

> They are people whose hard work has earned them only a slim piece of the American dream—but it's a piece they have no intention of giving up to any of the "enemies" that lay siege to their thoughts.[125]

An earlier observer said of those annually assembled in Louisville, "They were ripe for the plucking by Harrell and his harvesters, their ears were ready for talk of sedition and twisted race theories."[126]

By the early 1980s, Harrell was not only throwing his own very well-attended meetings of militia-type groups, he was also acting as an educator and guest speaker at other similar gatherings around the country. In January 1981, he travelled to Jackson, Michigan, to take part in the "First Michigan Survival Show," which included, besides him, martial arts demonstrations and continuous free classes on raw and wild foods, food storage, weapons, and emergency medicine. Harrell got an enthusiastic response when he attended and his picture appeared in the local Jackson newspaper. His talk, to a crowd of about 150, centered on people making themselves prepared for the forthcoming government collapse. In that same article, he also predicted an early death for President Ronald Reagan.[127]

Eventually, though, Louisville resistance to the Freedom Festivals became overt enough that Harrell moved his operation from the Louisville estate to a 232-acre spread of land near Licking, Missouri.[128] The first festival there was held in 1983.

In the festival's inaugural year, someone with a camcorder showed up and seemed to happily videotape many of the event's speakers. DVDs of some of these talks are still available for viewing—for a price—by the Christian Identity Ministries, an organization based, at this time, out of Australia.

Two of Harrell's presentations were recorded. The first is, more or less, a welcome session to those in attendance. Since the camera never shows the audience and the audio quality is rather poor, it is impossible to determine how many Harrell is speaking to. Nevertheless, the video does offer insight into Harrell as speaker and leader during this particular incarnation.

In the first of the two videos, Harrell, from behind a podium in what appears to be a simple wood and metal farm shed, speaks for a full twenty minutes. In his talk, Harrell proves characteristically funny and folksy. He is also far from rabble-rousing. Though he talks a bit about "the enemy" (assumedly, the U.S. government) and warns attendees against the possible, undercover presence of "enemy agents" there on the Missouri grounds, basically, Harrell just acts as a good host, welcoming this group of similarly-minded survivalists to the festival.

Yet if Harrell is surprisingly uncontroversial in his opening remarks, the man he brings up next is far more incendiary. The late Col. Jack Mohr, a U.S. veteran, takes to the podium and is quick in his remarks to address the enemy, the U.S. government, for their "ignoring" of various groups, specifically U.S. farmers and veterans, and to fan the flames of various conspiracy theories about immigrants and the banking industry, among other hot-button topics and issues.

A second DVD, however, is far more illustrative of Harrell at this time. In this second recording, also from Missouri, also from 1983, Harrell sits under a canvas awning supported by wooden stakes. In front of him is a group of people, all sitting in folding metal chairs. For almost an hour, Harrell, without notes of any kind present, speaks to those gathered. The question that was asked that started Harrell's discourse was not recorded but it matters little; Johnny Bob covers a wide patch of topics. He talks of his purchasing of this Missouri land more than a decade ago after being "spiritually nudged" to do so by the Lord. This area, Harrell says, is the most "survival-able" area in the US, far more plentiful with resources than many of the western mountain states where many other survivalist groups are attempting to set up a base. Harrell speaks of his plans for this area and future festivals—the buildings to be built including, he says, a 100-seat church on the property. And he touches on some of his more controversial views—his belief in race separatism, his fear of an imminent invasion from Mexico and Cuba, and his to-the-death defense of the Second Amendment.

Though there is a trace of paranoia in his speech, Harrell never loses control and remains clear and composed, quoting Abe Lincoln, George Washington, and the Bible, all with equal ease. Except for a brief mention of a stay in solitary confinement during his incarceration, Harrell makes little mention of his own personal history. Perhaps everyone there already knew the details. Even his mention of the money-raising, money-making Paul Revere Club—though he mentions that everyone can join for just a few dollars a month—is far from the hard-sell sales pitch one might expect.[129]

Though the proposed church, it seems, was never built, the Harrell site in Licking would eventually contain a set of bunkers, a mess hall and a private airstrip. Johnny Bob said that the reason for the move out of Illinois was because Louisville "got too critical" and because he also became suspicious that many federal agents were attending the Illinois Festivals under false names.[130]

Licking is about 34 miles south of Rolla, where the Harrell family hid out from the law for a time in the 1960s. The Missouri-based festivals regularly attracted as many as 3,000 people every year.[131]

In the 1980s, Harrell also held two festivals at Smithville, West Virginia (pop: 500), on about 60 acres of land that was either leased or loaned to him.[132]

In 1985, the state of Missouri started to become concerned with Harrell's annual events and the various state invaders they attracted. That year, the state congress passed a measure that would prohibit paramilitary training sessions intended for the "furtherance of civil disorder."[133] Though eventually challenged by the ACLU, the measure would stand long enough for Harrell to have to cancel his Missouri retreat that year. He and the CPDL did return the next year however but acquired a much smaller turnout; only about 500 attended.[134] That same year, the Illinois State Senate introduced a similar resolution to crack down on "hate-mongering" groups.[135]

The Missouri festivals endured until 1987, ending amid concerns about rising violence among various para-military organizations (a trend that reached a tragic crescendo in the next decade with the siege at Waco and the bombing in Oklahoma City) and amid friction over the exclusion of blacks and other minorities from the events.[136] Harrell believed that his organization was being treated unfairly and was being unjustly lumped in with far more extremist groups. He said, "They had to smear us with the same brush."[137] Harrell added, "The press has said a lot of things about me, and a few of them were even true. But most of them weren't."[138]

After the conclusion of the Missouri festivals, Johnny Bob returned to live full time in Louisville. Interestingly, from the time the Louisville/ Harrell estate began being written up as the HQ for the CPDL, the size of the estate was fully halved from how it was usually described back in the 1960s. Once always referred to as a 100-acre plot, the Harrell compound was now noted as "55 acres."[139]

If the Freedom Festivals themselves concluded in the late 1980s, Johnny Bob's cause did not. As late as 1988, Vance Comer's wife, Avelyn, was still coming regularly to the Louisville property to assist with the mailings and typing the organization's monthly newsletter.[140] The Mt. Vernon house was reinvented once again as a sorting, mailing and storage space for stacks upon stacks of brochures and form letters ready to be sent out.[141]

Since the (unofficial) end of the CCC in the 1970s when Harrell was in jail, Vance Comer had had to move and change professions several times to support himself and his family. After running the Harrell-owned motel for a time, he later worked other odd jobs including selling trailers and giving music lessons. For a time, he lived in Centralia and ran a mission there.[142]

Until the end of his life, in 1994, Mr. Comer and his family remained on good, friendly terms with Johnny Bob and his family.[143]

About a decade after Rev. Comer's passing, another major figure in the Johnny Bob-Louisville saga passed away. June Morgan died in 2005. After surviving the destruction of her main street store and then the suicide of her husband, Mrs. Morgan remained in Louisville and remained outspoken on a variety of topics; latter day issues of local newspapers contain many of her letters to the editor.[144]

Sadly, death became a regular part of Johnny Bob's life later in life as well. In April 1988, Johnny Bob's devoted mother, Natalia Harrell, passed away. She was eighty-eight years old.[145] Of Johnny Bob's seven children, two of them have passed away in adulthood. His son, Jon Lance, died in 1998 of a heart attack. His daughter, Cathy, passed away from cancer in 2007.[146] Cathy is buried in Louisville in one of the mausoleums that was built based on her father's old patent. That mausoleum is also the final resting place for Vance Comer and his wife and for some of Harrell's other one-time friends/followers, including the elder Mr. Kellums.

In 2010, after sixty-five years of marriage, Harrell's beloved, devoted wife, Betty, passed away. Her obituary, which appeared in the Effingham newspaper, was carefully worded. Though it mentioned her husband by name, it made no mention if he was still alive or dead and, if alive, where he was currently residing. It also made no mention of his church or any of the various Harrell-founded organizations or the raid or his other bits of local notoriety.[147] The names and current homes of all of Mrs. Harrell's five surviving children were however listed and the obit did trumpet Mr. and Mrs. Harrell's enduring faith:

> Also due to a series of Christian spiritual experiences she and her husband had, which began in November 1947 and continued for many years thereafter, they were most active in Christian and patriotic efforts. This including, among other things, being shown events yet to come, some of which now seem to be developing.[148]

Of Harrell's surviving children, all of them are still living in or somewhat near Louisville. They have gone on to have very "normal" careers as small business owners or even in local government. They have also provided Johnny Bob with many grandchildren and great-grandchildren. Til the end of his life, Harrell remained in contact with all of his kids except for one of his daughters, whose early 1990s marriage to an African-American man is said to have driven a deep wedge between them. About his daughter's husband, Johnny Bob was largely, surprisingly silent, saying only, "We've never met. I hear he's a nice man."[149]

At some point, Johnny Bob moved from his home on the estate (the upper part of the garage) to the Chestnut Drive building, which, in its long lifespan, has been a federal agriculture building, the schoolhouse, a construction office, the home to son Tod and his family, and finally the home for the elder Johnny Bob and his wife. Johnny Bob continued to live in the home after his wife's passing.

In 1995, it was reported that Johnny Bob currently survived mainly on his monthly Social Security checks—a deeply ironic denouement for a man who, for years, rallied against the government. Harrell was once quoted as saying, "The only thing I own now are some socks, some shirts and an old Ford."[150] Despite Harrell's statements, however, others strongly maintain that Johnny Bob is still quite wealthy.[151]

That same year, a gutsy reporter approached Johnny Bob for his thoughts on the recently occurred Oklahoma City bombing that took the lives of 168 men, women, and children. On that subject though, Johnny Bob had nothing to say.[152]

This World Is Not My Home

As mentioned earlier, Louisville is the county seat of Clay Country. That designation has helped the town immeasurably. While other nearby towns of similar size are declining, losing businesses, jobs, and people, Louisville remains prosperous with a large number of thriving businesses, both of the "mom and pop" variety and of the national franchise type. The town's downtown area—anchored still in its center by the tall, grey, stone courthouse—has not been remotely depleted.

Louisville is also an exceptionally well-kept city. Driving in past the city's "Welcome To" sign and moving toward the town square, one finds nary an abandoned storefront, a sloppy front porch or even a single up-turned trashcan. Also, every time I have been there, all the lawns have all been neatly, carefully trimmed—that is, until you get to the long-time home of Johnny Bob Harrell.

In the last thirty or so years of his life, Harrell no longer lived on his one-time Mt. Vernon-esque estate. Instead, he lived in the large and still rather-stately looking white home that at one time served as the office of his construction firm and, later, became the home of his outlaw school.

This home, on Chestnut Drive (formerly Sailor Spring Road), just down from Louisville's business district, sits back a bit on its lot. Its wide lawn is, mostly, clear of anything but grass, but that is the only part of the property that is clear of anything. Stacked up randomly against the home, all over its front porch and spilling off to the sides, as well as running along both sides of the sidewalk that stretches from the house's front door to its driveway is untold amounts of junk: an oversize cooler, a stack of mismatched folding chairs, empty paint cans, pots for plants, a rusted-out exercise bike (or two), long pieces of wood, weathered-looking Christmas wreaths, clocks, books, a microwave, a refrigerator, rugs, clothes, and frayed-looking extension cords wound up on spools.

Then, at any given time, there would also be five or six vehicles haphazardly parked in the driveway. Most of them do not look "drive-able" in the slightest. They sit out exposed in the sun as the nearby metal carport up near the house is full—of what looks like hundreds upon hundreds of empty cardboard boxes randomly stacked under its awning.

Meanwhile, stacked side to side right behind house, and perhaps piled as many as three deep and four across, is a series of abandoned trailers. None of them look remotely inhabitable, as, plainly, many are missing doors or windows, or both, and many sit rather askew having tilted and fallen into the one next to it.

For my first meeting with Mr. Harrell, it was to that house that I went. Originally, as far as a writing project was concerned, I thought I might only write something about the big Mt. Vernon house still standing there in Louisville. It was only in regard to it that I first approached the infamous Johnny Bob, but the history of that home is irrevocably connected to the story of Harrell and his one-time followers. While researching him and it, it was not difficult to become deeply intrigued by the strange events that once took place in this tiny town in southern Illinois.

Still, when I first met Mr. Harrell, though I was dying to ask a million questions about his religion, his healing, the raid, and its aftermath, I did not think it fair to "bait and switch" him, to arrive under the pretense of asking about a building only to quiz him about things that he might not want to discuss with me or anyone else.

But then, after I arrived, I had barely gotten to his house and knocked on the front screen door—yes, rickety, moth-eaten, and paint-peeled— than Johnny Bob met me with a handshake and more or less ordered me to have a seat on his slightly wobbly and quite dirty front porch swing.

The Johnny Bob Harrell that I met that day was in his nineties, but sharp of mind. Physically, though, he appeared thin and frail. The hair that was once a bright white and combed back like Elvis had receded into a thin male-pattern baldness band around his head.

No sooner had he and I sat down than Johnny Bob reached into a manila file folder he had with him and handed me a Xeroxed copy of *Persecution USA: People & Place*. "Now," he said, "Are you familiar with what happened here back in '61?" Johnny Bob was only too ready to talk to me—or it seems to anyone—about what had befallen him and his followers so many years ago.

Suddenly, I knew I was going to be writing about more than just a house. There, sitting in the sun, on the front porch, we chatted briefly. I told Mr. Harrell that I had indeed read many of the old articles about that incident but added quickly, "You know, though, I don't believe everything I read." He then began to tell me tidbits of the story of his life in Louisville.

Finally, he said, "Well, let's go over to the house." As he climbed into the passenger seat of my rental car, Mr. Harrell joked that I should leave this car with him and take back one of the others from the property. I told him that while that was a plausible idea, the nice folks at Hertz Rent-A-Car might disagree.

It took no time at all to drive over to the estate. Though many of the trees and shrubs that once faced out from the south-side of the property have since been removed, at the time, the thicket of brush was quite dense and helped to almost fully camouflage the house and other buildings during the summer months when everything was green and lush.

I pulled up to the metal gate, silver-painted and rather old-timey and Western-looking, that sealed off the front entrance of the property. At each side of the gate were two small "Checkpoint Charlies"—two tiny huts, each painted a deep red, each barely big enough for one person to stand in; these were guards stations that had been erected back in the early 1960s.

After I stopped the car in front of the gate, Johnny Bob got out of the car and went up and unlocked the gate in front of us. He swung its two arms wide open for me to drive through. He then returned to the car and we drove into the compound.

The grass and weeds on the property were tall and wild, but I could easily drive in; in preparation for my visit, Johnny Bob must have gotten someone to bushhog some of the grass, creating an *ad hoc* driveway.

Driving in, I saw the first view of the main house. Even that day, even in its aged, dilapidated state, the house was still quite impressive. The house sits at the top of a small hill. It looms there like Tara or, more obviously, like the real Mount Vernon. That said, that image is soon marred: piled in front of the home, in fact, forming a solid embankment around the entire home, is a thick, exuberant layer of junk, a hodgepodge of discards: bicycles, treadmills, paint cans, window screens, lawn chairs, old furniture, swimming pool equipment, tire rims, a wheel chair, gas containers, tarps, and lawn mowers.

Originally (and despite just seeing the condition of Harrell's current home on Chestnut), I assumed that that perimeter of junk around the house was there as a sort of barrier, a barricade against would-be trespassers, but apparently, I was giving all that debris a little too much credit. As Tod

Harrell would tell me later, "Dad's a hoarder. Every one of his buildings is just full of stuff."[1]

Later, on my second visit to see Mr. Harrell about six months later, he invited me into his current Louisville home, the building on Chestnut. The inside of that home was something straight out of an episode of *Hoarders* with stacks of vinyl albums, books, magazines, newspapers, and kitchen items piled densely everywhere. There was only a small, narrow path from the front door that leads to the kitchen. Tod was not exaggerating.

Back on the compound, as Mr. Harrell sat in the car, he allowed me (and my still camera) to freely roam the property and to take as much time as I wanted. He said that we could not go into the big house though because "they" had been doing work in there.

I walked around the entire outside of the home. Most of the house's first-floor windows had been knocked out and boarded over by that time. Those on the first floor that were still in place had so much stuff piled in front of them, it would take some serious climbing and dedication to get to them.

Finally, on the home's north side, there was one window where I could get close enough to, at least, peak into. Inside was just more junk—boxes upon boxes of what appeared to be reports, newsletters, brochures, and yellowed letters.

Then, throughout the compound, strewn across every corner of property were a wide assortment of broken down, rusted-out campers, cars, and tractor trailers. I wanted to tally them all up but continually kept losing count, they were so many and so scattered. I would estimate though that there were at least twenty-five to thirty that I could see through the tall grass. The vehicles and other discards are all apparently acquisitions of Harrell's. Ever the junk man, Harrell has obtained them and retained them as "investments."[2]

Some of the original twenty or so cabins on the property had fallen down; others are still upright (and they tended to look bigger than they did in most of the old photos). Even for those that were still standing, I did not feel brave enough to try to go into any of them.

The two-story, four-car garage—whose upper floor served for many years as the Harrell family's home—still stands. The outer solid brown brick building, the oldest building on the property and later used as the church's main office, is still standing, its borders are also ringed with a myriad of castoffs.

Back behind the house, back by the cabins and closer to the river, are other buildings and shelters. Under a metal carport are two vintage-looking tractors. Another wooden structure is sort of garage-like but its roof has caved in. Under it, peeking out from under the fallen roof is the tail of one of Johnny Bob's airplanes; I doubt it is airworthy anymore.

With all the oddly-parked old vehicles, seemingly loosely tossed around, the entire estate and grounds had an almost *Twilight Zone*-like feel to it. Looking up to the second floor of the garage through one of the windows, I could see what looked like a woman's sweater still hanging there on a hanger on a hook as if its owner had only briefly stepped out of the room or she had set it aside to be worn the next morning. Everywhere I looked it looked like when people left, they left immediately, taking nothing with them and leaving everything behind.

Just before I got back into my car, Mr. Harrell asked me, "You want a picture of me in front of the house?"

I said, "Sure," and he happily posed in front of the house's back, external staircase. I pointed and snapped my camera. Mr. Harrell could not have been a more gracious or accommodating host.

Since first learning of Johnny Bob's story and the persistent rumor that Dion Davis had been a government-sent "plant," I was most interested in exploring that aspect of his story with him. Was this true? What did he know? What did he think? I breathed a great sigh of relief—and got quite excited—when Mr. Harrell broached the topic first. After he brought it up, I asked him, "So, do you think that Davis was a plant?"

After a little considered silence, Johnny Bob replied, "There's ample evidence to suggest so." Now, having spoken extensively with Dion Davis and seen many of his military records, I do not believe Davis was anything at that time but a very young, impressionable and impulsive young man.

After that initial meeting, I would return to Louisville and visit with Johnny Bob several more times. Sometimes we spoke on the phone, me calling from my home in Virginia. In either case, we never spoke long. My in-person visits—always in his disturbingly dirty, cluttered kitchen—were usually no more than fifteen minutes or so. Yet no matter how brief, Mr. Harrell was never anything but kind and gracious.

Often—repeatedly—at visits, he would ask me about my relatives in the area and I would fill him in on my ties to Kinmundy, the town just down the road from Louisville. Often, he would gift me with things—a new pair of work gloves or a clip board.

I would ask questions, too. Mr. Harrell could be a little guarded at times. He always seemed to hesitate a bit before answering, trying to weigh just how things would sound, how they would reflect on him and his family and friends, before he offered any response. Johnny Bob has probably never been the most reliable of sources. His stories have changed over time, their progress and transmutation from one thing to another can be solidly tracked via newspaper stories and clippings.

Notably, in person, Johnny Bob was far less "fire and brimstone" than one might expect—or at least he was by the time I met him. Harrell's eldest son, Tod (who today notes with a chuckle that, believe it or not, he never spent one day or night living in his father's Mt. Vernon house), says of his dad, "Dad's cooled off a lot and he doesn't talk as much."

One big question I had for Johnny Bob back then was who owns all these buildings and all this land now. He told me, "The church. The church owns them."

Despite his statements, his constant usage of the royal "we," and some listings the church still has in various religiously-oriented national annuals, the Christian Conservative Church was, by the time of my asking, totally dormant. Even the newsletter mailings ended in 2008. Any of its one-time members who still live in the area now worship primarily at other churches even if they still consider themselves, at heart, CCC members.

That is another interesting fact about Johnny Bob Harrell—that, some fifty years on—he still has his believers. In fact, with the exception of Dion Davis, who still harbors some anger at Harrell, almost everyone else who was ever part of the CCC continues to speak very highly of Johnny Bob. Though they sometimes lament that some of the attention he got over the years maybe "went to his head," or that he sometimes got "side-tracked" on his mission, they remain quite enamored with him, praising him as an "exceptional man" and one who dared to always follow his own path.[3]

Until the end, Johnny Bob believed too. He was as devout as ever and as worried as ever. Every time I spoke to him during the last six years of his life, he always, very sincerely, inquired if I had a basement in my home, if I had canned goods and other survival necessities stored there just in case. Though he had been waiting many decades for his Armageddon, Johnny Bob still believed it was coming soon, but America, he says, will survive, especially some special parts of the Midwest. God has told him so, he always said. America is the "New Jerusalem" and, as he once noted to me, the middle letters of "Jerusalem" spell out "USA."

To a certain generation of people in Louisville and its surrounding area, the name Johnny Bob Harrell is still a firebrand, but to later generations, if they know his story at all, they just seemed to see him as a local eccentric best known for the gifts (usually dozens upon dozens of pairs of work gloves) that he donated to area churches every Christmas or for regularly showing up at the local Ace Hardware to rummage through the bargain bins there. He was also known to buy candy bars as a "thank you" gift to the Walmart pharmacists who filled his prescriptions. Sometimes he could be seen down at the local cemetery, in front of one of the mausoleums that were based on his old plans. He would pull the weeds there as this is where his daughter Cathy was buried as well as the Comers and some other friends and one-time followers of his.

Harrell was also a member of the local genealogical society which, ironically, has its offices on the town square right next to where the Morgans's store once was. According to the society's head, Jean Bailey, Johnny Bob would often come in from to regale whoever was there with stories about Louisville's very early days. Once, Bailey arranged a talk from Harrell where, surprisingly, he spoke only about his childhood in town and said nothing about politics or religion.[4]

Some things have not changed though. In the intervening years, new rumors got generated about him and his group. In the 2000s, when tattooing moved into the mainstream and many people began showcasing their faith on their flesh, a story began that those with small crosses inked between their thumb and forefinger were one-time (or current) devotees of Harrell's but that is not true; the CCC was never involved itself in any group inking.

Of course, even after whittling away all the gossip from the facts, some questions about Johnny Bob and those days in Louisville still linger. For example, there is no question that Johnny Bob Harrell was a man of great intelligence and of great faith and one of great persuasive skills, but was he always of sound mind?

Despite his great convictions, the overwhelming majority of his prophecies never came true. In 1961, he said the Lord had told him that no man would ever reach the surface of the moon, with God saying, "This is Mine for My glory."[5] Also, Ronald Reagan lived not only through his two terms as president but lived to be ninety-three years old.

Among the amateur psychologists who know of the Harrell case and history, many suggest that, at times, Johnny Bob might have been suffering from undiagnosed paranoid schizophrenia. Ironically, this was the same condition once used to label Dion Davis. Harrell's rampant, obsessive fear of communism (though somewhat culturally acceptable at that time) bespeaks of a certain paranoid element. Meanwhile, schizophrenics are known to experience voices and to sometimes have profound and very vivid hallucinations.

Another question also lingers: Was what Johnny Bob headed up in the early 1960s on his Louisville estate actually a "cult" as it has often been called? The term "cult" began being applied to Harrell and his group almost from the moment it was founded. In his excellent and thorough 2004 master's thesis on Harrell, Dain Garrett insightfully theorizes that the term "cult" was first applied to Johnny Bob's group, by locals and the press, as an insult, a prerogative, to suggest something unnatural, menacing and wrong.[6]

Regardless of what it was called, was the CCC actually a "cult"? Again, in his thesis, Garret asks that question and decides that, no, it was not.[7] While the CCC had many tenants that might make it cult-like, including a devotion to a central and charismatic leader, a shared faith, isolationism, and an "us and them" mentality, many other commonalities for "cults" were completely lacking in the Harrell group.[8]

For example, among things the Louisville group did not do they never engaged in anything resembling brainwashing and never dabbled in anything remotely occult. It is a further testament that in all the years since its founding, not one single member of this one-time "cult" has emerged with stories of abuse (physical or emotional) and no one has ever filed a lawsuit against either Harrell or his church for reparations of any kind.

Furthermore, for all his pronouncements, Johnny Bob never claimed to be the Messiah or the reincarnation of Jesus Christ, which, in and of itself, seems to set him and his group apart from such other notorious cult leaders as David Koresh, Jim Jones, and Anne Hamilton-Byrne of Australia's notorious "The Family."

Also unlike many "cult" leaders, Johnny Bob never foretold of the actual end of the world. While he did believe that great difficulties were lying ahead for America and its citizens, he never preached of total oblivion.

Then, unlike every other so-called modern "cult," including Scientology, Harrell never used his group as a money-making mechanism. In fact, despite rumors to the contrary, for Harrell, all the monies were actually flowing in the other direction—it was his personal fortune that funded the entire Louisville operation, it was he who proved the monies that all of his followers lived on.

Finally, and quite notably, especially when compared with many of the other "cults" which populate recent history, no one died in any of this long story. While the passing of little Larry Payne in Arkansas added a very sad element to the saga, everyone, including the courts and law enforcement, all agreed at the time that that was just a tragic accident.

Of course, one of the other great questions in the Harrell saga concerns the miraculous healing that he claimed to have experienced in 1959. No one seems to argue that Harrell did have some kind of cancer of the lymph system. Though he never disclosed his medical records, the doctors he has made mention of as examining him in Illinois and at the Mayo Clinic did exist at the time just as he reported. Furthermore, a biopsy scar on Harrell's neck, from where his tumor was removed, is visible in many photos; it was even noted on his 1964 FBI "Wanted" poster. Also, "proof" of his healing is in many ways substantiated by his great longevity; Johnny Bob lived to be almost 100.

Removing the possibly of divine intervention, what Johnny Bob might have experienced back in 1959 is a medical phenomenon known as "unexplained spontaneous remission." As its name suggests, this is an extraordinary medical condition where a cancer might, suddenly and inexplicitly, regress all on its own. Among documented cases of the phenomenon, it has been seen to be most prevalent in some specific types of cancers, one of them being lymphoma, the cancer Harrell had been diagnosed with.

Yet if what Johnny Bob experienced was "spontaneous remission," how does one explain his account of a great white light or of the other physical effects or of being once knocked across the room as part of his healing experience? It cannot be labeled/dismissed simply as a dream on Johnny Bob's part as he says his wife, Betty, experienced everything he did.

Again, removing the divine as a possibility, it might be possible that what Mr. and Mrs. Harrell experienced (or suffered from, depending on your point of view) is what is known as a *folie à deux,* a recognized psychological disorder in which delusional beliefs and hallucinations are transmitted from one individual to another. We know for example that Mr. Harrell could be very persuasive when sharing his beliefs to others, certainly then his powers of persuasion could extend to his wife. Notably, in her description of her husband's 1959 healing experience, Mrs. Harrell never claimed to have witnessed anything directly—she said only that she saw the evidence "spiritually."[9]

However, if Mrs. Harrell became embroiled into his extreme train of thought, do we then also say that about all the members who joined the Conservative Christian Church? If so, that could be a diagnosis of "mass hysteria" (similar, perhaps, to the reports of a "Mad Gasser" that terrorized the city of Mattoon, Illinois, in summer of 1944) and if that label were to be applied to the members of the CCC living within the estate, then it might also have to be applied to many of the people living outside of it as well, i.e. the citizens of Louisville, Illinois.

Though Johnny Bob made many mistakes and sometimes made some very bad choices, he was not always in the wrong. At its height, even the IRS recognized the CCC as a legitimate "church" and if Johnny Bob's school fight of the early 1960s were to be played out today, among today's widely-accepted practice of alternative- and home-schooling, it would be a non-issue and certainly not worthy of mention on the *Today* show.

Additionally, had Johnny Bob's retreat come about later in the 1960s or in the early 1970s, it might have been viewed less of a "cult" than as a back-to-nature sort of commune.

Certainly, some of the controversy that seemed to constantly swirl around Johnny Bob throughout his life was born out of jealousy. Angie Comer (now Angie Garcia) now sees Harrell's fall from grace as almost inevitable. She says, "Johnny Bob had a lot of money, so that made a lot of people not like him. Then he ran for office and that made more people not like him. Then, he took on the school...."[10]

In retrospect, the events of Louisville, 1959 to about 1964 was a near perfect storm of Cold War paranoia and, sadly, small town intolerance. At the height of all the "troubles," both sides—bolstered and enflamed by unbridled gossip—just reacted to a variety of threats that were real or imagined. In the end, what some saw as "cult," others simply called a "community" exercising its first amendment rights to Freedom of Religion.

What happened in Louisville (and to Louisville) in the early 1960s could just as easily happen today. Rampant fear and distrust of others and "outsiders" and the quest for religious enlightenment is as alive today as it ever was, while the recruitment of others with similar beliefs would be even easier today than it was some fifty years ago, thanks to the internet, Youtube, Facebook, and all forms of social media.

The very last time I saw Johnny Bob Harrell was in 2019, I think it was in December of that year. As usual, we sat on dusty metal chairs in the middle of his crowded kitchen. Also, per usual, we did not visit for long. Johnny Bob always claimed to be "busy," but he always seemed happy to see me. At one time, during what would become our last visit, I complimented him on how good he looked. I asked him how he explained his longevity. His answer was simple: "The Lord!"[11]

I would have visited Johnny Bob again in 2020, but the COVID pandemic grounded everyone's travel plans. Instead, I phoned Johnny Bob once during the year. He picked up the phone himself; he was still living on his own in that same house in front of his old Mt. Vernon estate. Though he remembered who I was, he seemed a little confused about the details and backstory of me, but after all, this was a man in his ninth decade of life.

Back in 2019, after leaving his house for what would turn out to be the last time, I drove over to the Mt. Vernon property. A lot of work had been done there by someone, for some reason. Huge swaths of trees that once shielded the property from the street had been removed as had the rusty barbed wire fence that once stood around the land. The old silver gate was gone as were the two small shacks at the entrance where guards once stood. Still, though mowed somewhat, the estate was still littered with old, broke down cars, rusted tractors, and lopsided trailers. Painted on some of the still standing trees up by the road were purple squares, the international sign for "No Trespassing."

Since Johnny Bob's days in Louisville as a major newsmaker, other things had changed, too. The motel that Johnny Bob owned off and on throughout the years and which the Comers helped run at one time is no longer there. It was torn down many years ago. A Dollar General stands there now. The movie theater that Harrell once owned is gone, too. Ironically, it is now a probation office. Coles Chapel, which had stood for years abandoned, boarded up but painted a deep red, eventually got torn down. The building that once housed the roller rink—a place solidly tied to the Harrell legacy in various ways—is still standing in Louisville though, but it is not a roller rink anymore.

Johnny Bob Harrell died on June 19, 2021. The last few months of his life, he had been residing in an assisted living facility in the nearby town of Altamont, Illinois, a move necessitated by a fall he experienced at his home in early 2021. At the time of his death, Johnny Bob was ninety-nine years old.[12]

His obituary, which appeared online later that day from the funeral home that was handling his burial, made note of Johnny Bob's military service, his early business, and his founding of both the CCC and the Christian Patriots Defense League. No mention was made of the raid, his jail term, or any of those other events of the late 1950s and through the 1960s. In lieu of flowers, the obit stated that memorials should be sent to the Louisville Baptist Church. It also noted that Harrell would be buried at the Orchard Hill Cemetery in Louisville.[13]

As of this writing, there is some debate regarding a final will and testament for Johnny Bob Harrell. As the sorting of his final home has gone on since his passing, various will-like documents have been found. A final will? Notes to a will? Are they legal? Do they convey his final wishes? If no will is ever, ultimately, found, his estate will be divided up in a rather straightforward fashion—it will be divided equally among his five surviving adult children.[14] How much his estate is worth, of course, is left to be seen.

In the months following Harrell's passing, the Harrell children, especially his son, Xon, have taken on the daunting task of cleaning up and clearing out his various Louisville properties. The excavation of these properties is going to take some time. None of the surviving structures— the Mt. Vernon house, the cabins, and even the house Harrell had been living in—can probably be salvaged. More than likely, they will either face a bulldozer or simply be allowed to decay and fall in on themselves.[15]

In the last couple of years before Johnny Bob's death, the U.S.A. faced a variety of extraordinary hurdles. There was the rise of Trumpism; once, on a visit with Johnny Bob just before the 2016 presidential election, he told me he would be voting and be voting for the Republican candidate, Donald Trump. Then, in 2020, there was the devastating COVID pandemic, which ultimately took over 900,000 America lives. Then, in 2021, the country saw the January 6, 2021, riot and storming of the Capitol building in D.C. by proud, angry "patriots" determined to overthrow the nation's most recent presidential election.

Are these some of the events that Johnny Bob always preached about and prepared for? Is that why he lived so long, to see his predictions come to fruition? Even then, even as extreme as these occurrences were, none of them were the work of communism nor did any of them end up destroying America. One cannot help but wonder: Did Johnny Bob end up dying disillusioned or disappointed that the enemy he spent much of his life rallying against never really showed itself?

Ultimately, the great legacy of Johnny Bob Harrell was not that these events never happened but that Johnny Bob's extraordinary faith that they would come to pass never wavered.

Endnotes

Chapter 1

1   Kramme, Ronald A. "John Robert Harrell: A Case Study of a Christian Anti-Communist, 1959-1964." Illinois State University, 1970, p. 2.
2   John R. Harrell interviews: From 2015 until his death in 2021, I personally interviewed John Harrell, in person and over the phone, several times. All quotes and other information throughout this book are drawn from those conversations.
3   Garrett, Dain. "The Johnny Bob Harrell Compound: Church, Commune or Cult?" California State University, 2004, p. 24.
4   "Johnny Bob Harrell's Mother, Natalia, dies," *Herald and Review* (April 2, 1988), p. 5.
5   Tod Harrell interviews: From 2015 onward, I personally interviewed Tod Harrell several times over the phone. All quotes and other information throughout this book are drawn from those conversations.
6   Kramme, p. 1.
7   Grossman, Ron, "Civil war," *Chicago Tribune* (Mar. 31, 1988), p. 63.
8   John R. Harrell interviews.
9   *Ibid.*
10 Grossman, p. 63.
11 John R. Harrell interviews.
12 Kramme, p. 2.
13 John R. Harrell interviews.
14 *Ibid.*
15 Kramme, p. 2.
16 Tod Harrell interviews.
17 Kramme, p. 2.
18 "Obituary: Betty Harrell," *Effingham Daily News* (July 22, 2014), unknown page number.
19 *Ibid.*
20 Kramme, p. 2.
21 Tod Harrell interviews.
22 Kramme, p. 2.
23 Tod Harrell interviews.

24 Kramme, p. 7.
25 Tod Harrell interviews.
26 findagrave.com/cgi-bin/fg.cgi?page=gr&GRid=18832677 (Cathy Harrell)
27 Tod Harrell interviews.
28 Kramme, p. 20.
29 *Ibid.*
30 *Ibid.*
31 John R. Harrell interviews.
32 *Ibid.*
33 Tod Harrell interviews.
34 "For Rent," *Kinmundy Express* (March 18, 1948), p. 6.
35 "Sells Farina Theatre," *Kinmundy Express* (June 26, 1947), p. 1.
36 John R. Harrell interviews.
37 *Ibid.*
38 *Ibid.*
39 Hancock, Samuel, "Harrell Challenges FBI to Coax AWOL Marine to Surrender After Fleeing Corps," *Daily Register* (Harrisburg, IL) (Aug. 2, 1961), p. 7.
40 John R. Harrell interviews.
41 *Ibid.*
42 Garrett, p. 1.
43 *Ibid.*
44 "Harrell's Kids Out of School," *Mt. Vernon Register-News* (Mar. 3, 1961), p. 1.
45 Kramme, p. 75.
46 Tod Harrell interviews.
47 Kramme, p. 4.
48 John R. Harrell interviews.
49 Stacey, David K. "Persecution USA: People & Place." (Louisville, IL: Christian Conservative Church, 1962), p. 1.
50 Kramme, p. 30.
51 *Ibid.*
52 *Ibid.*
53 Garrett, p. 5.
54 Stacey, p. 1.
55 "Kinmundy Methodist Men Hear John R. Harrell," *Kinmundy Express* (March 19, 1953), p. 6.
56 Hodges, Carl G., "The Cult Leader Who Defied the FBI," *True Police Cases* (April 1965), p. 34.
57 Angelyn Comer Garcia interviews: From 2015 onward, I interviewed Ms. Garcia several times over the phone and via e-mail communication; all quotes and other information in this book are drawn from those conversations.
58 Stacey, p. 2.
59 Garcia interviews.
60 Stacey, p. 2.
61 Kent O'Dell interview, June 2015.
62 Garcia interviews.
63 *Ibid.*
64 Stacey, p. 2.
65 Comer, A. Vance. *The Manifestation of God in the Healing of John R. Harrell.* (Louisville, KY: Herald Press, 1959), p. 11.
66 Tod Harrell interviews.

67 The only account of Johnny Bob Harrell's healing in 1958 is his own reportage as transcribed in *The Manifestation of God in the Healing of John R. Harrell* by A. Vance Comer (1959). It is from this volume that the following details are drawn.

68 Comer, pp. 11-13.

69 *Ibid.*, p. 12.

70 *Ibid.*, p. 13.

71 Kramme, p. 20.

72 Comer, p. 14.

73 *Ibid.*, pp. 15-16.

74 *Ibid.*, p. 16.

75 *Ibid.*, p. 17.

76 *Ibid.*, p. 6.

77 Kramme, p. 23.

78 Comer, p. 17.

79 *Ibid.*, p. 20.

80 *Ibid.*, pp. 20-22.

81 *Ibid.*, p. 22.

82 *Ibid.*, p. 24.

83 *Ibid.*

84 *Ibid.*, p. 25.

85 *Ibid.*

86 *Ibid.*, pp. 26-27.

87 *Ibid.*, p. 27.

88 *Ibid.*, p. 28.

89 *Ibid.*, pp. 28-29.

90 *Ibid.*, p. 30.

91 *Ibid.*

92 *Ibid.*, p. 31.

93 *Ibid.*, p. 93.

94 *Ibid.*

95 *Ibid.*, p. 33.

96 *Ibid.*

97 *Ibid.*, p. 34.

98 *Ibid.*, p. 33.

99 *Ibid.*, p. 34.

100 *Ibid.*

101 *Ibid.*, p. 36.

102 *Ibid.*, p. 39.

103 Stacey, p. 3.

104 Comer, p. 37.

105 *Ibid.*, p. 38.

106 *Ibid.*, p. 40.

107 *Ibid.*

108 *Ibid.*, p. 8.

109 Brinkman, Grover, "House of Fear," *National Enquirer* (June 4, 1961), p. 14.

110 Garrett, p. 15.

111 "Notice," *Mt. Vernon Register* (July 2, 1959), p. 5.

112 Stacey, p. 3.

113 "Notice," p. 5.

114 Stacey, p. 3.

115 Garrett, p. 11.
116 Comer, p. 1.
117 *Ibid.*
118 *Ibid.*
119 *Ibid.*, p. 17.
120 *Ibid.*, p. 18.
121 *Ibid.*, p. 9.
122 *Ibid.*, p. 43.
123 *Ibid.*, p. 16.
124 *Ibid.*
125 Grossman, p. 63.

Chapter 2

1 Stacey, David K. "Persecution USA: People & Place." (Louisville, IL: Christian Conservative Church, 1962), p. 3.
2 Brinkman, Grover, "House of Fear," *National Enquirer* (June 4, 1961), p. 14.
3 *Ibid.*
4 Garrett, Dain. "The Johnny Bob Harrell Compound: Church, Commune or Cult?" California State University, 2004, p. 11.
5 Kramme, Ronald A. "John Robert Harrell: A Case Study of a Christian Anti-Communist, 1959–1964." Illinois State University, 1970, p. 43.
6 Angelyn Comer Garcia interviews: From 2015 onward, I interviewed Ms. Garcia several times over the phone and via e-mail communication; all quotes and other information in this book are drawn from those conversations.
7 Stacey, p. 3.
8 *Ibid.*, p. 4.
9 *Ibid.*
10 *Ibid.*
11 *Ibid.*
12 Garrett, p. 47.
13 Priscilla Laughton Hutton interview, July 2015.
14 Garrett, p. 11.
15 Grossman, Ron, "Civil war," *Chicago Tribune* (Mar. 31, 1988), p. 63.
16 Codean Baker interview, July 2015, p. 63.
17 Grossman, p. 63.
18 Tod Harrell interviews: From 2015 onward, I personally interviewed Tod Harrell several times over the phone. All quotes and other information throughout this book are drawn from those conversations.
19 Kramme, p. 40.
20 Garrett, p. 27.
21 Hancock, Samuel D., "Harrell Says His Battle with Clay County School Officials Has Just Begun," *Daily Register* (Harrisburg, IL), (April 1, 1961), p. 3.
22 Tod Harrell interviews.
23 *Ibid.*
24 "John R. Harrell Seeks U.S. Post," *Belvidere Daily Republican* (Oct. 13, 1959), p. 8.
25 *Ibid.*
26 Kramme, p. 40.
27 "John R. Harrell Seeks....", p. 8.
28 *Ibid.*
29 Stacey, p. 5.

30   *Ibid.*
31   Doussard, Jim, "Louisville Reacts to 'The Situation,'" *Decatur Daily Review* (April 2, 1961), p. 1.
32   Kramme, p. 40.
33   *Ibid.*
34   *Ibid.*, p. 42.
35   *Ibid.*
36   Stacey, p. 5.
37   Garrett, p. 23.
38   Stacey, p. 5.
39   *Ibid.*, p. 4.
40   *Ibid.*, p. 6.
41   *Ibid.*, p. 4.
42   *Ibid.*, p. 7.
43   *Ibid.*, p. 6.
44   *Ibid.*
45   *Ibid.*, p. 4.
46   Kramme, p. 21.
47   Stacey, p. 7.
48   *Ibid.*
49   *Ibid.*
50   Garrett, p. 25.
51   Doussard, p. 1.
52   *Ibid.*
53   Kramme, p. 43.
54   Garrett, p. 26.
55   Stacey, p. 9.
56   *Ibid.*
57   Kramme, appendix.
58   "$225,000 Libel Suit Filed Here in Circuit Court," *Clay County Republican* (March, 3, 1960), unknown page number; and, "Motion Filed To Dismiss Libel Suit," *Clay County Republican* (March 10, 1960), unknown page number.
59   "Senate Candidate Charges Libel in $225,000 Suit," *Edwardsville Intelligencer* (Feb. 27, 1960), p. 2.
60   Motion Filed...," unknown page number.
61   "Harrell Loses Libel Suit in Court," *Mt. Vernon Register-News* (Nov. 15, 1961), p. 1.
62   Garrett, p. 26.
63   Stacey, p. 8.
64   Codean Baker interview.
65   Kramme, p. 42.
66   Hodges, Carl G., "The Cult Leader Who Defied the FBI," *True Police Cases* (April 1965), p. 34.
67   Stacey, p. 5.
68   Garrett, p. 12.
69   Hodges, p. 38.
70   Stacey, p. 4.
71   Hodges, p. 38.
72   *Ibid.*
73   Stacey, p. 8.
74   *Ibid.*

75   *Ibid.*

76   *Ibid.*

77   *Ibid.*

78   Stacey, p. 9.

79   *Ibid.*, p. 8.

80   Garrett, p. 13.

81   Stacey, p. 8.

82   *Ibid.*

83   Garrett, 26.

84   John R. Harrell interviews: From 2015 until his death in 2021, I personally interviewed John Harrell, in person and over the phone, several times. All quotes and other information throughout this book are drawn from those conversations.

85   Stacey, p. 89.

86   Pennington, Wilfred, "Pastor Recalls the Consternation in Louisville in 1960," unknown newspaper, unknown date, unknown page number.

87   "Harrell Says Will Continue Fight On Reds in Clay County, Nation," *Salem Times-Commoner*, unknown date [April 1961], unknown page number.

88   Stacey, p. 10.

89   Hodges, p. 34.

90   "AWOL Marine, Religious Sect Leader Arrest in Raid by FBI and Police," *Medford Mail Tribune* (Medford, OR) (Aug.7, 1961), p. 9.

91   "Alsup, Ragers, Landholt Winners; 3-Way Race for Second Demo Spot," *Decatur Herald* (April 13, 1960), p. 3.

92   *Ibid.*

93   Hodges, p. 35.

94   Stacey, p. 10.

95   *Ibid.*

96   *Ibid.*

97   "'Christian Party,'" *Decatur Daily Review* (April 29, 1960), p. 20.

98   *Ibid.*

99   *Ibid.*

100 *Ibid.*

101 Hodges, p. 31.

102 "Christian Party," p. 20.

103 John R. Harrell interviews.

104 Stacey, p. 11.

105 *Ibid.*

106 *Ibid.*, p. 12.

107 "Hecklers Absent at Anti-Red Rally," *Decatur Herald* (February 22, 1961), p. 1.

108 Stacey, p. 12.

109 Garcia interviews.

110 *Ibid.*

Chapter 3

1   John R. Harrell interviews: From 2015 until his death in 2021, I personally interviewed John Harrell, in person and over the phone, several times. All quotes and other information throughout this book are drawn from those conversations.

2   *Ibid.*

3   Stacey, David K. "Persecution USA: People & Place." (Louisville, IL: Christian Conservative Church, 1962).

4   *Ibid.*, p. 31.

5   Tod Harrell interviews: From 2015 onward, I personally interviewed Tod Harrell several times over the phone. All quotes and other information throughout this book are drawn from those conversations.

6   "Self-Styled Anti-Red Sees Atom War, Russ Invasion," *Daily Telegram* (Eau Claire, WI) (Dec. 5, 1961), p. 26.

7   John R. Harrell interviews.

8   Doussard, Jim, "Mount Vernon Replica Going Up," *Decatur Herald* (June 19, 1960), p. 4.

9   "Fire Levels 13-Room Home At Louisville," unknown newspaper, unknown date [c. 1957], unknown page number.

10   John R. Harrell interviews.

11   Angelyn Comer Garcia interviews: From 2015 onward, I interviewed Ms. Garcia several times over the phone and via e-mail communication; all quotes and other information in this book are drawn from those conversations.

12   *Ibid.*

13   Doussard, p. 4.

14   *Ibid.*

15   "Self-Styled...," p. 26.

16   Garcia interviews.

17   Kramme, Ronald A. "John Robert Harrell: A Case Study of a Christian Anti-Communist, 1959-1964." Illinois State University, 1970, p. 43.

18   Over the course of my research into John Harrell, many citizens from Louisville and nearby locations told me about the alleged mail scams that Mr. Harrell and/or his church supposedly engaged in, although, to date, no proof linking the church to these activities have been found.

19   "Harrell Now Fears Local Persecution," *Greenville News* (Greenville, SC) (Aug. 7, 1961), p. 1.

20   Over the course of my research into John Harrell, many citizens from Louisville and nearby locations told me about the alleged mail scams that Mr. Harrell and/or his church supposedly engaged in, although, to date, no proof linking the church to these activities has been found.

21   "Harrell Extends Retreat, Continues Building Log Cabins at Louisville," *Decatur Daily Review* (Mar. 12, 1961), p. 14.

22   Stacey, p. 22.

23   *Ibid.*, p. 14.

24   "Link Cross Burnings to Communists," *Journal Gazette* (Mattoon, IL), (February 22, 1961), p. 3.

25   "Soviet Flag Ripped; Minister Arrested," *Des Moines Register* (November 16, 1961), p. 13.

26   "Harrell Charges Mail Tampering; Seeks Bail for 15 Followers," *Daily Register* (Harrisburg, IL) (Aug. 7, 1961), p. 8.

27   *Ibid.*

28   Stacey, p. 13.

29   Kramme, p. 39.

30   "Burn Crosses at Louisville," *Mt. Vernon Register-News* (February 2, 1961), p. 8.

31   Garcia interviews.

32   Stacey, p. 15.

33   Garcia interviews.

34   *Ibid.*

35   Stacey, p. 17.

36 Kramme, p. 52.
37 "Clay County Official Denies Charge by Touring Speaker," *Journal Gazette* (Mattoon, IL) (Feb. 23, 1961), p. 3.
38 Kramme, p. 52.
39 "Clay County Officials Denies...," p. 3.
40 Grossman, Ron, "Civil war," *Chicago Tribune* (Mar. 31, 1988), p. 63.
41 Garcia interviews.
42 "Clay County Officials Denies...," p. 3.
43 "Fire Alarm False at Church Rally Near Louisville," *Decatur Herald* (Feb. 23, 1961), p. 1.
44 "Hecklers Absent at Anti-Red Rally," *Decatur Herald* (February 22, 1961), p. 1.
45 "Burn Crosses at Louisville," p. 8.
46 "Fire Alarm False...," p. 1.
47 Garcia interviews.
48 "Goff's Anti-Red Meeting Interrupted," *Mt. Vernon Register-News* (Feb. 23, 1961), p. 1.
49 Garcia interviews.
50 *Ibid.*
51 "Goodbye, Rev. Goff," *Decatur Daily Review* (Feb. 23, 1961), p. 28.
52 *Ibid.*
53 "Fire Alarm False...," p. 1.
54 "Clay County Officials Denies...," p. 3.
55 "Fire Alarm False...," p. 1.
56 "Goodbye, Rev. Goff," p. 28.
57 Garcia interviews.
58 *Ibid.*
59 *Ibid.*
60 "Goodbye, Rev. Goff," p. 28.
61 "Harrell, Two Followers Absent as Trial Starts in Clay County Court," *Decatur Herald* (March 21, 1961), p. 1.
62 "Goodbye, Rev. Goff," p. 28.
63 Stacey, p. 16.
64 "Louisville Man Holds Religious Retreat at Home," *Decatur Herald* (Feb. 25, 1961), p. 1.
65 *Ibid.*
66 *Ibid.*
67 *Ibid.*
68 *Ibid.*
69 "After-Class Task at Louisville," *Decatur Herald* (Mar. 24, 1961), p. 22.
70 "Harrell Extends Retreat...," p. 14.
71 "Harrell Faces New Charges in Private School Battle," unknown newspaper, unknown date [c. Feb. 1961], unknown page number.
72 Stacey, p. 30.
73 "Harrell Extends Retreat...," p. 14.
74 Tod Harrell interviews.
75 Garcia interviews.
76 "Harrell Extends Retreat...," p. 14.
77 *Ibid.*
78 Callahan, William C., "Harrell to Open Own Private School," *Decatur Herald* (Mar. 4, 1961), p. 1.

79   Malcolm Gay, "Giving Up the Memorabilia, but Not the Belief: Elvis Lives," *New York Times* (Nov. 8, 2007), unknown page number.
80   Stacey, p. 79.
81   "Peace Prevails at Louisville Anti-Red Rally; Harrell Absent," *Decatur Herald* (Mar. 7, 1961), p. 1.
82   *Ibid.*
83   Stacey, p. 22.
84   "Peace Prevails...," p. 1.
85   Stacey, p. 22.
86   Garrett, Dain. "The Johnny Bob Harrell Compound: Church, Commune or Cult?" California State University, 2004, p. 14.
87   Stacey, p. 12.
88   John R. Harrell interviews.
89   Stacey, p. 12.
90   Priscilla Laughton Hutton interview, July 2015.
91   Stacey, p. 19.
92   *Ibid.*
93   Hutton interview.
94   Stacey, p. 19.
95   "John Harrell: Is He in Southwest Missouri Area?," *Edwardsville Intelligencer* (June 18, 1963), p. 2.
96   Tod Harrell interviews.
97   John R. Harrell interviews.
98   Stacey, p. 20.
99   *Ibid.*
100   John R. Harrell interviews.
101   Garcia interviews.
102   *Ibid.*
103   *Ibid.*
104   *Ibid.*
105   John R. Harrell interviews.
106   Garcia interviews.
107   *Ibid.*
108   *Ibid.*
109   Albright, Charles E., "What Manner of Man, This Johnny Bob?" *Decatur Daily Review* (April 14, 1963), p. 10.
110   *Ibid.*
111   Stacey, p. 30.
112   Hodges, Carl G., "The Cult Leader Who Defied the FBI," *True Police Cases* (April 1965), p. 34.
113   "Harrell Says He Won't Answer Questions by IRS," *Journal Gazette* (Mattoon, IL) (Dec. 4, 1962), p. 2.
114   "Anti-Communist Builds Atomic Proof Estate in Illinois," *Medford Mail Tribune* (Medford, OR) (Dec. 7, 1961), p. 7.
115   Garcia interviews.
116   Hodges, p. 34.
117   Carr, Mike, "Harrell Plans Move to Southwest," *Decatur Daily Review* (March 3, 1963), p. 3.
118   Garrett, p. 22.
119   Stacey, p. 30.

120 "To Appeal Convictions At Louisville," *Alton Evening Telegraph* (March 28, 1961), p. 13.
121 Hutton interviews.
122 Tod Harrell interviews.
123 Stacey, p. 26.
124 Tod Harrell interviews.
125 Garcia interviews.
126 *Ibid.*
127 *Ibid.*
128 Hutton interviews.
129 John R. Harrell interviews.
130 *Ibid.*
131 Doussard, Jim, "Louisville Reacts to 'The Situation,'" *Decatur Daily Review* (April 2, 1961), p. 1.
132 Garcia interviews.
133 Stacey, p. 19.
134 Tod Harrell interviews.
135 Stacey, p. 28.
136 *Ibid.*, p. 22.
137 "Harrell Says He Won't Answer Questions by IRS," *Journal Gazette* (Mattoon, IL) (Dec. 4, 1962), p. 2.
138 Stacey, p. 28.
139 *Ibid.*, p. 22.
140 *Ibid.*
141 *Ibid.*, p. 30.
142 Garcia interviews.
143 *Ibid.*
144 *Ibid.*
145 Kramme, p. 72.
146 *Ibid.*, p. 74.
147 *Ibid.*, p. 75.
148 Stacey, p. 26.
149 Tod Harrell interviews.
150 Stacey, p. 26.
151 "Harrell's Tax Records are Being Checked," *Decatur Daily Herald* (June 4, 1961), p. 7.
152 Garcia interviews.
153 "Harrell's Kids Out of School," *Mt. Vernon Register-News* (Mar. 3, 1961), p. 1.
154 Stacey, p. 24.
155 "John Harrell's Plan Private School of 'Basic Subjects,'" *Journal Gazette* (Mattoon, IL) (Mar. 6, 1961), p. 1.
156 Stacey, p. 24.
157 *Ibid.*
158 Callahan, p. 1.
159 Burns, Michael K., "Harrell's Louisville Estate Harbors Memories," *Decatur Daily Review* (Nov. 24, 1964), p. 35.
160 Garrett, p. 22.
161 Grossman, p. 63.
162 Over the course of my research, several women in or from the Louisville area spoke to me about either the things they knew, experienced or witnessed regarding Mrs. Morgan. The women asked not to have their identities revealed.

163 Stacey, p. 23.

164 "Business Opens Own School In Plan for Anti-Red Colony," *Press and Sun-Bulletin* (Binghamton, NY) (March 6, 1961), p. 10.

165 "Louisville Man Opens Private School...," *Decatur Herald* (Mar. 3, 1961), p. 1.

166 *Ibid.*

167 "Harrell Extends Retreat...," p. 14.

168 "Man Opens His Own School to Fight Communism," *Palladium-Item* (Richmond, IN) (March 7, 1961), p. 3.

169 Albright, Charles E., "A Look Into 'Perils' of John R. Harrell," *Decatur Daily Review* (March 10, 1963), p. 6.

170 "Louisville Man Opens...," p. 1.

171 Stacey, p. 23.

172 "Harrell, Two Followers Absent...," p. 1.

173 *Ibid.*

174 Stacey, p. 24.

175 Garrett, p. 36.

176 "Clay Parents Face Charges," *Decatur Herald* (March 8, 1961), p. 1.

177 *Ibid.*

178 "Parents Deny Clay Charges," *Decatur Herald* (March 9, 1961), p. 1.

179 "Harrell Trial Starts," *Decatur Daily Review* (Mar. 20, 1961), p. 17.

180 "Stay Home 'On Divine Direction,'" *Mt. Vernon Register-News* (May 20, 1961), p. 1.

181 *Ibid.*

182 Stacey, p. 25.

183 "Stay Home...," p. 1.

184 Sadly, the transcript of these court proceedings seems to have been lost. All quotes are taken from published newspaper accounts.

185 "'Red Fighter' Hides from Law in 'Fort,'" *Lincoln Star* (Lincoln, NE) (Mar. 21, 1961, p. 13.

186 "Wealthy Communist Foe in 'Fortress' Estate," *Cincinnati Enquirer* (Mar. 21, 1961), p. 4.

187 "Stay Home...," p. 1.

188 "Jury Selected to Hear Harrell Case," *Mt. Vernon Register-News* (Mar. 21, 1961), p. 1.

189 "Physician Tells Clay Jury He Heads Harrell's Private School," *Decatur Herald* (Mar. 22, 1961), p. 1.

190 *Ibid.*

191 *Ibid.*

192 *Ibid.*

193 *Ibid.*

194 Hutton interview.

195 "Harrell Keeps His Own Private School," *Mt. Vernon Register-News* (March 23, 1961), p. 1.

196 *Ibid.*

197 *Ibid.*

198 "Harrell Faces New Charges in Private School Battle," unknown newspaper, unknown date [c. Feb. 1961], unknown page number.

199 "Six Fined on Truancy Charges at Louisville," *Decatur Herald* (Mar. 23, 1961), p. 1.

200 *Ibid.*

201 "Harrell Keeps...," p. 1.

202 *Ibid.*

203   "New Charges Face 'Truants' of Louisville," p. 15.
204   Garrett, p. 37.
205   "Sailor Springs Man Quits Harrell 'Retreat'; Son to Enter Clay School,"
      Decatur Review (March 26, 1961), p. 26.
206   *Ibid.*
207   "Harrell's Hold Weakens," *Decatur Daily Review* (March 27, 1961), p. 3.
208   *Ibid.*
209   "Harrell's Band Splits," *Southern Illinoisan* (March 27, 1961), p. 14.
210   "Harrell's Hold Weakens," p. 3.
211   "To Appeal Convictions At Louisville," p. 13.
212   "Harrell Has No Qualified Teachers," *Mt. Vernon Register-News* (March 22,
      1961), p. 1.
213   "To Appeal Convictions At Louisville," p. 13.
214   *Ibid.*
215   "Harrell To Appeal Decision," *Alton Evening Telegraph* (April 8, 1961), p. 15.
216   "Harrell Loses Bid for New Trial in Clay," *Decatur Herald* (April 8, 1961), p. 7.
217   "Physician Tells Clay Jury He Heads Harrell's Private School," p. 1.
218   "Private School Illegal," *Southern Illinoisan* (Mar. 23, 1961), p. 18.
219   Hancock, Samuel D., "Harrell Says His Battle with Clay County School
      Officials Has Just Begun," *Daily Register* (Harrisburg, IL), (April1, 1961), p. 3.
220   *Ibid.*
221   "Blames Red Vandals for House Damage," *Alton Evening Telegraph* (April 4,
      1961), p. 2.
222   "Harrell Says Reds Vandalized House," *Pantagraph* (Bloomington, IL) (April
      4, 1961), p. 16.
223   "Harrell Claims Vandals Damage Rural Building," *Decatur Herald* (April 4,
      1961), p. 1.
224   "Harrell Says Reds Vandalized House," p. 16.
225   "Harrell's Tax Records....," p. 7.
226   "This Man, John Harrell," *Decatur Daily Review* (March 24, 1961), p. 39.
227   "Harrell's Tax Records....," p. 7.
228   "Cult Leaders Freed on Bond; Says FBI, IRS Plotting Against Him," *Arizona
      Republic* (Phoenix, AZ) (Aug. 7, 1961), p. 22.
229   Stacey, p. 26.
230   "Harrell's Motel to be Sold for Bank Claim," *Decatur Daily Review* (July 27,
      1961), p. 67.
231   "Cult Leader Won't Resist Court Order," *Pantagraph* (Bloomington, IL) (July
      28, 1961), p. 5.
232   "Harrell Motel Brings $6,300," *Journal Gazette* (Mattoon, IL) (July 31,
      1961), p. 7.
233   "Harrell Motel Sold in Clay," *Decatur Review* (July 30, 1961), p. 1.
234   "Harrell Motel Brings $6,300," p. 7.
235   "Cult Leader Won't Resist Court Order," p. 5.
236   "New Flag at Louisville," *Decatur Daily Review* (June 26, 1961), p. 6.
237   *Ibid.*
238   "Hecklers Absent...," p. 1.
239   "This Man, John Harrell," p. 39.
240   *Ibid.*
241   *Ibid.*
242   Albright, Charles E., "Harrell's Troubles," *Decatur Daily Review* (Aug. 5,
      1961), p. 23.

243 Doussard, Jim, "Louisville Reacts to 'The Situation,'" p. 1.
244 *Ibid.*
245 *Ibid.*
246 *Ibid.*
247 *Ibid.*
248 *Ibid.*
249 Albright, Charles E., "Harrell's Troubles," *Decatur Daily Review* (Aug. 5, 1961), p. 23.
250 Garrett, p. 28.
251 *Ibid.*, p. 28.
252 Brinkman, Grover, "House of Fear," *National Enquirer* (June 4, 1961), p. 14.
253 *Ibid.*
254 *Ibid.*
255 *Ibid.*
256 John R. Harrell interviews.
257 Dion Davis interviews: From 2015 onward, I conducted several phone interviews with Mr. Davis; all quotes and other information herein is pulled from these conversations.

Chapter 4

1   Dion Davis interviews: From 2015 onward, I conducted several phone interviews with Mr. Davis; all quotes and other information herein is pulled from these conversations.
2   *Ibid.*
3   *Ibid.*
4   *Ibid.*
5   Copies of Dion Davis's military records were made available to the author via the National Personnel Record Center in St. Louis, Missouri, and with the permission of Mr. Davis.
6   Stacey, David K. "Persecution USA: People & Place." (Louisville, IL: Christian Conservative Church, 1962), p. 32.
7   Davis interviews.
8   Stacey, p. 32.
9   Davis interviews.
10 Stacey, p. 32.
11 Davis interviews.
12 *Ibid.*
13 Sellers, Jack. "John Harrell Says He's Fighting the Lord's Battle for 'Deserter,'" unknown newspaper, (Aug. 3, 1961), unknown page number.
14 *Ibid.*
15 Davis interviews.
16 *Ibid.*
17 *Ibid.*
18 *Ibid.*
19 *Ibid.*
20 *Ibid.*
21 Stacey, p. 31.
22 *Ibid.*
23 Davis interviews.
24 *Ibid.*

25 Stacey, p. 31.
26 *Ibid.*
27 Davis interviews.
28 "Marine Joins Harrell," *Decatur Daily Review* (Aug. 2, 1961), p. 19.
29 Davis interviews.
30 *Ibid.*
31 *Ibid.*
32 Stacey, p. 31.
33 *Ibid.*
34 *Ibid.*
35 *Ibid.*
36 Hancock, Samuel, "Harrell Challenges FBI to Coax AWOL Marine to Surrender After Fleeing Corps," *Daily Register* (Harrisburg, IL) (Aug. 2, 1961), p. 7.
37 Stacey, p. 31.
38 "FBI Captures Guarded AWOL," *Logansport Press* (Logansport Press, IN) (Aug. 5, 1961), p. 1.
39 Hancock, "Harrell Challenges...," p. 7.
40 Kramme, Ronald A. "John Robert Harrell: A Case Study of a Christian Anti-Communist, 1959-1964." Illinois State University, 1970, p. 44.
41 Stacey, p. 32.
42 Hancock, "Harrell Challenges...," p. 7.
43 "Barricades AWOL Marine Says Corps 'Flaunted Sin,'" *News Journal* (Willington, DE) (Aug. 3, 1961), p. 9.
44 "Marine Says He Won't Surrender," unknown newspaper, unknown date [c. Aug. 1961], unknown page number.
45 "Barricades AWOL...," p. 9.
46 Davis interviews.
47 "Sect Leader to Open Home to Tourists," *Kingsport Times* (Kingsport, TN) (Aug. 8, 1961), p. 10.
48 Hancock, "Harrell Challenges...," p. 7.
49 "Marine Joins Harrell," *Decatur Daily Review* (Aug. 2, 1961), p. 19.
50 Stacey, p. 34.
51 *Ibid.*
52 "Marine Joins Harrell," p. 19.
53 "Louisville's Harrell Defies FBI, Refuses To Surrender AWOL GI Seeking Sanctuary," *Edwardsville Intelligencer* (August 2, 1961), p. 1.
54 Hancock, "Harrell Challenges...," p. 7.
55 "Rich Anti-Red Crusader Defies FBI in Giving Haven to AWOL Marine," *Washington Post* (August 3, 1961), p. A3.
56 "Cult Leader Protects Marine From Camp Lejeune 'Vileness,'" *Ashville Citizen-Times* (Asheville, NC) (Aug. 3, 1961), p. 30.
57 Hancock, "Harrell Challenges...," p. 7.
58 "Barricades AWOL...," p. 9.
59 *Ibid.*
60 Stacey, p. 32.
61 Hancock, "Harrell Challenges...," p. 7.
62 *Ibid.*
63 Sellers, unknown page number.
64 *Ibid.*
65 "Harrell Balks FBI Effort to See Marine," *Decatur Daily Review* (Aug. 3, 1961), p. 68.

66　"Seize Religious Leader, Followers," *Carrol Daily Times* (Carroll, IA) (Aug. 4, 1961), p. 5.

67　Garrett, Dain. "The Johnny Bob Harrell Compound: Church, Commune or Cult?" California State University, 2004, p. 2.

68　Stacey, p. 33.

69　Kramme, p. 93.

70　Stacey, p. 33.

71　"Harrell Barks...," p. 68.

72　Stacey, p. 33.

73　Ricketts, Ruth, "Marine Keeps Refuge with Harrell," *Decatur Herald* (Aug. 4, 1961), p. 1.

74　Garrett, p. 2.

75　Grossman, Ron, "Civil war," *Chicago Tribune* (Mar. 31, 1988), p. 63.

76　Hodges, Carl G., "The Cult Leader Who Defied the FBI," *True Police Cases* (April 1965), p. 35.

77　*Ibid.*, p. 87.

78　"AWOL Marine Says He'll Stay in 'Fort,'" *Indianapolis Star* (Aug. 4, 1961), p. 10.

79　"Louisville's Harrell Defies FBI, Refuses to Surrender AWOL GI Seeking Sanctuary," *Edwardsville Intelligencer* (Aug. 2, 1962), p. 1.

80　Stacey, p. 32.

81　"AWOL Marines Says...," p. 10.

82　*Ibid.*

83　"Rich Anti-Red Crusader...," p. A3.

84　Ricketts, p. 1.

85　"Shelters Marine Deserter," *Oil City Derrick* (Oil City, PA) (Aug. 4, 1951), p. 1.

86　"Harrell Challenges FBI to Come After AWOL Marine," unknown newspaper, unknown date [*c.* Aug. 1961], unknown page number.

87　Ricketts, p. 1.

88　Davis interviews.

89　"Authorities Raid Harrell's Estate," *Belvidere Daily Republican* (Belvidere, IL) (Aug. 4, 1961), p. 1.

90　Ricketts, p. 1.

91　"Harrell Resists FBI's Attempt to Arrest Deserter at Louisville," *Decatur Herald* (Aug. 3, 1961), p. 1.

92　Stacey, p. 88.

93　Despite repeated requests and the invoking of the Freedom of Information Act, the author was never able to secure any documents from any government agency specifically pertaining to the police and military actions on the morning of August 4, 1961. This recounting of events is based upon reported news stories and interviews with various witnesses.

94　Tod Harrell interviews: From 2015 onward, I interviewed Mr. Harrell several times over the phone and via e-mail communication; all quotes and other information in this book drawn from those conversations.

95　Hedges, p. 88.

96　Garrett, p. 43.

97　Hancock, Samuel O., "Agents Capture Marine Deserter in Religious Camp," *Daily Courier* (Connellsville, PA) (Aug. 4, 1961), p. 17.

98　Garcia interviews.

99　"Harrell, AWOL Marine Captured As FBI, Troopers Storm Estate," *Edwardsville Intelligencer* (Aug. 4, 1961), p. 1.

100   "Illinois Estate Crashed by Authorities to Arrest AWOL Marine, Sect Members," *Terre Haute Star* (Aug. 5, 1961), p. 1.

101   "Harrell Cult Resistance at Raid Revealed," *Decatur Daily Review* (Nov. 18, 1963), p. 1.

102   Hodges, p. 88.

103   "Harrell Cult Resistances...," p. 1.

104   Hancock, "Agents Capture...," p. 17.

105   *Ibid.*

106   Garcia interviews.

107   "125 Peace Officers Make Arrests at Louisville (Ill.) Estate," *St. Louis Post-Dispatch* (Aug. 4, 1961), p. 1.

108   John R. Harrell interviews: From 2015 until his death in 2021, I personally interviewed John Harrell, in person and over the phone, several times. All quotes and other information throughout this book are drawn from those conversations.

109   Stacey, p. 34.

110   Davis interviews.

111   *Ibid.*

112   Mathes, Bob, "Harrell Planned to Yield Deserter, Aide Declares," *Southern Illinoisan* (Nov. 19, 1963), p. 5.

113   "FBI Lands, Has Marine Situation Under Control," *New Journal* (Wilmington, DE) (Aug. 4, 1961), p. 11.

114   Tod Harrell interviews.

115   *Ibid.*

116   *Ibid.*

117   Harold Leib interview, Aug. 2015.

118   *Ibid.*

119   Tod Harrell interviews.

120   *Ibid.*

121   "Raid Nabs AWOL Marine," *Southern Illinoisan* (Aug. 4, 1961), p. 1.

122   *Ibid.*

123   Davis interviews.

124   "Police, FBI Storm Haven of Marine Deserter," *Pittsburgh Post* (August 8, 1961), p. 1.

125   Tod Harrell interviews.

126   Garrett, p. 44.

127   "Cult Women Pray, Try to Raise Bond," *Levittown Times* (Aug. 5, 1961), p. 2.

128   Garcia interviews.

129   *Ibid.*

130   Lester Kellums interview, Sept. 2015.

131   "Harrell Balks...," p. 68.

132   Kent O'Dell interview, Aug. 2015.

133   "Police, FBI Storm....," p. 1.

134   "'Invade' Estate to Nab Marine," *Times Record* (Troy, NY) (Aug. 4, 1961), p. 1.

135   Ricketts, p. 1.

136   Garrett, p. 42.

137   Hancock, "Agents Capture...", p. 17.

138   "FBI, State Police Raid Harrell's Estate, Arrest Gun Bearers," *Alton Evening Telegraph* (Aug. 4, 1961), p. 2.

139   "Cultist Harrell, Son Go Home Under Bond," *Pantagraph* (Bloomington, IN) (Aug. 6, 1961), p. 16.

140 "Raid Nabs AWOL...," p. 1.
141 *Ibid.*
142 Despite repeated requests and the invoking of the Freedom of Information Act, the author was never able to secure any documents from any government agency specifically pertaining to the police and military actions on the morning of August 4, 1961. This recounting of events is based upon reported news stories and interviews with various witnesses.
143 "Authorities Raid...,' p. 1.
144 Seymour, Peter. "Harrell Out on Bail, Charges FBI Looted Home in Arresting Deserter," *Terre Haute Star* (Aug. 7, 1961), p. 6.
145 *Ibid.*
146 "Authorities Raid...," p. 1.
147 *Ibid.*
148 Seymour, p. 6.
149 *Ibid.*
150 Tod Harrell interviews.
151 "125 Peace Officers...," p. 1.
152 "Raid Nabs AWOL...," p. 1.
153 *Ibid.*
154 *Ibid.*
155 "Father Happy Son Now in Custody of Police," *Shamokin News-Dispatch* (Shamokin, PA) (Aug. 4, 1961), p. 1.
156 *Ibid.*
157 "Harrell Jailed in FBI Raid on Estate," *Decatur Herald* (Aug. 5, 1961), p. 1.

Chapter 5

1 "Cult Women Pray, Try to Raise Bond," *Levittown Times* (Aug. 5, 1961), p. 2.
2 "Raid Nabs AWOL Marine," *Southern Illinoisan* (Aug. 4, 1961), p. 1.
3 "Cult Women Pray...," p. 2.
4 "Cultist, Son Free on Bond," *Tennessean* (Aug. 6, 1961), p. 8.
5 Angelyn Comer Garcia interviews: From 2015 onward, I interviewed Ms. Garcia several times over the phone and via e-mail communication; all quotes and other information in this book are drawn from those conversations.
6 "Cultist Harrell, Son Go Home Under Bond," *Pantagraph* (Bloomington, IN) (Aug. 6, 1961), p. 16.
7 *Ibid.*
8 *Ibid.*
9 "Harrell Tries to Raise Bonds for Followers," *Pantagraph* (Bloomington, IN) (Aug. 7, 1961), p. 18.
10 "Cultist and Son Gain Freedom; Out on Bond," *Lakes Charles American-Press* (Aug. 6, 1961), p. 34.
11 "Cultists, Son Free After Night In Jail," *Sunday Gazette-Mail* (Charleston, WV) (Aug. 6, 1961), p. 7.
12 Seymour, Peter, "Harrell to Post Bond for Followers Today," *Decatur Herald* (Aug. 7, 1961), p. 1.
13 "Harrell Charges Mail Tampering; Seeks Bail for 15 Followers," *Daily Register* (Harrisburg, IL) (Aug. 7, 1961), p. 8.
14 "Cultist Harrell Posts Bonds for 15 Followers Seized in Raid," *St. Louis Post-Dispatch* (Aug. 7, 1961), p. 3.

15   Stacey, David K. "Persecution USA: People & Place." (Louisville, IL: Christian Conservative Church, 1962), p. 38.
16   Stacey, p. 34.
17   Seymour, p. 1.
18   "18 in Cult Remain in Jail," *Indianapolis Star* (Aug. 6, 1961), p. 11.
19   "Cultist Harrell, Son Go Home...," p. 16.
20   "Cultist Admits IRS Probing His Returns," *Palm Beach Post* (Aug. 7, 1961), p. 26.
21   "Disciples of Harrell Freed; Eccentric to Open Estate," *Journal Gazette* (Mattoon, IL) (Aug. 8, 1961), p. 1.
22   "Cult Leader Posts Bonds of $43,000 for Disciples," *Cincinnati Enquirer* (Cincinnati, OH) (Aug. 8, 1961), p. 17.
23   "Cultist Seeks to Raise Bail for Followers," *Terre Haute Tribune* (Aug. 7, 1961), p. 6.
24   "Cult Leader Post...," p. 17.
25   "Cultist Harrell Posts Bonds for 15 Followers Seized in Raid," p. 3.
26   "Harrell to Start Tours, Lectures; 15 of His Followers Free on Bond," *Decatur Herald* (Aug. 8, 1961), p. 1.
27   "Public Tours Estate of Sect Leader," *Laredo Times* (Laredo, TX) (August 14, 1961), p. 5.
28   "Harrell to Start...," p. 1.
29   Kramme, Ronald A. "John Robert Harrell: A Case Study of a Christian Anti-Communist, 1959-1964." Illinois State University, 1970, p. 51.
30   "Marine's Hideaway is 'Shrine,'" *Sandusky Register* (Sandusky, OH) (Aug. 14, 1961), p. 3.
31   *Ibid.*
32   Stacey, p. 40.
33   "Marine's Hideaway...," p. 3.
34   *Ibid.*
35   "Harrell Says No Soviet in Space," *Decatur Herald* (Aug. 9, 1961), p. 5.
36   *Ibid.*
37   Dion Davis interviews: From 2015 onward, I conducted several phone interviews with Mr. Davis; all quotes and other information herein is pulled from these conversations.
38   "Harrell's Hearing Put Off For a Week," *Hays Daily News* (Hays, Kansas) (Aug. 1, 1961), p. 2.
39   Garrett, Dain. "The Johnny Bob Harrell Compound: Church, Commune or Cult?" California State University, 2004, p. 27.
40   Kramme, p. 102.
41   *Ibid.*
42   *Ibid.*
43   *Ibid.*
44   "Cultist Waives Arraignment on Federal Charge," *Terre Haute Tribune* (Aug. 20, 1961), p. 49.
45   "Harrell Says He May Run Again for US Senate," *St. Louis Post-Dispatch* (Nov. 8, 1961), p. 3.
46   "Cultist Waives Arraignment...," p. 49.
47   Garrett, p. 42.
48   "Harrell Says He May Run Again...," p. 3.
49   "Cultist Seeks to...," p. 6.
50   "Raid Nabs AWOL Marine," p. 1.
51   *Ibid.*

52 Ricketts, Ruth, "Fast Starts at Religious Retreat," *Decatur Herald* (Aug. 5, 1961), p. 1.
53 "This Man, John Harrell," *Decatur Daily Review* (March 24, 1961), p. 39.
54 "Raid Nabs AWOL Marine," p. 1.
55 Tod Harrell interviews: From 2015 onward, I interviewed Mr. Harrell several times over the phone and via e-mail communication; all quotes and other information in this book drawn from those conversations.
56 Garrett, p. 13.
57 *Ibid.*, p. 57.
58 *Ibid.*, p. 33.
59 "Police Storm Estate Seize Marine Deserter," *Los Angeles Times* (Aug. 5, 1961), p. 8.
60 "Harrell, 12 Others Plead Not Guilty," *St. Louis Post-Dispatch* (Oct. 5, 1961), p. 3.
61 Davis interviews.
62 *Ibid.*
63 *Ibid.*
64 *Ibid.*
65 *Ibid.*
66 *Ibid.*
67 *Ibid.*
68 *Ibid.*
69 "Ex-Marine Posts Bond," *Morning Herald* (Uniontown, PA) (May 2, 1962), p. 6.
70 Davis interviews.
71 *Ibid.*
72 *Ibid.*
73 *Ibid.*
74 *Ibid.*
75 *Ibid.*
76 *Ibid.*
77 "Mob Attack Next, Cultist Predicts," *Morning News* (Wilmington, DE) (Aug. 7, 1961), p. 23.
78 Seymour, p. 1.
79 Mathes, Bob, "Harrell Planned to Yield Deserter, Aide Declares," *Southern Illinoisan* (Nov. 19, 1963), p. 5.
80 *Ibid.*
81 "AWOL Marine, Religious Sect Leader Arrest in Raid by FBI and Police," *Medford Mail Tribune* (Medford, OR) (Aug.7, 1961), p. 9.
82 "Authorities Raid Harrell's Estate," *Belvidere Daily Republican* (Belvidere, IL) (Aug. 4, 1961), p. 1.
83 "Prosecutor Ready to Sue Harrell Again," *Mt. Vernon Register-News* (March 27, 1961), p. 2.
84 Johnny Leib interview, August 2015.
85 "Private School Opens on Harrell Estate," *Decatur Herald* (Sept. 2, 1961), p. 1.
86 Hancock, Samuel D., "Harrell Says His Battle with Clay County School Officials Has Just Begun," *Daily Register* (Harrisburg, IL), (April 1, 1961), p. 3.
87 "Harrell Asks for Help," *Decatur Daily Review* (Aug. 30, 1961), p. 1.
88 Kramme, p. 85.
89 "Harrell, 12 Others Plead Not Guilty," p. 3.
90 *Ibid.*
91 Stacey, p. 39.

92   "Cultist Predicts Red Attack in 1961," *News Journal* (Wilmington, DE) (Oct. 6, 1961), p. 16.
93   *Ibid.*
94   "Cultist Predicts Red Attack...," p. 16.
95   "'Johnny Bob' Getting Set For Red Blast, Invasion," *Herald* (Jasper, IN) (Nov. 16, 1961), p. 19.
96   *Ibid.*
97   "Harrell Loses Libel Suit in Court," *Mt. Vernon Register-News* (Nov. 15, 1961), p. 1.
98   "John Harrell Posts Bond for 2 in Income Tax Cases," *St. Louis Post-Dispatch* (Jan. 9, 1962), p. 3.
99   *Ibid.*
100   *Ibid.*
101   *Ibid.*
102   "Harrell Offers Estate as Bond for Gen. Walker," *Decatur Daily Review* (Nov. 3, 1962), p. 1.
103   *Ibid.*
104   "Louisville's Harrell Defies FBI, Refuses To Surrender AWOL GI Seeking Sanctuary," *Edwardsville Intelligencer* (August 2, 1961), p. 1.
105   "Christian Conservatives Ready for Russian Bomb Blast," *Herald and News* (Klamath Falls, OR) (Feb. 4, 1962), p. 14.
106   "Anti-Communist Builds Atomic Proof Estate in Illinois," *Medford Mail Tribune* (Medford, OR) (Dec. 7, 1961), p. 7.
107   Hodges, Carl G., "The Cult Leader Who Defied the FBI," *True Police Cases* (April 1965), p. 88.
108   "Christian Conservatives Ready for Russian Bomb Blast," p. 14.
109   "Self-Styled Anti-Red Sees Atom War, Russ Invasion," *Daily Telegram* (Eau Claire, WI) (Dec. 5, 1961), p. 26.
110   Kramme, p. 45.
111   "'Red Fighter' Hides from Law in 'Fort,'" *Lincoln Star* (Lincoln, NE) (Mar. 21, 1961, p. 13.
112   "Harrell Loses Truancy Plea," *Decatur Herald* (Feb. 24, 1962), p. 2.
113   "Religious Retreat Leader Gives Up Clay County Fight," *Pantagraph* (Bloomington, IL) (April 12, 1962), p. 1.
114   "Harrell Wins Court Test Against FTC," *Daily Register* (Harrisburg, IL) (May 16, 1962), p. 10.
115   *Ibid.*
116   "Mausoleum Tycoon Teaching Survival," *Daily Herald* (Chicago, IL) (May 3, 1962), p. 21.
117   "Harrell's Mother Give 500 Acres to Son's Church," *Decatur Herald* (May 9, 1962), p. 12.
118   "John Harrell Complains of Vandalism," *Journal Gazette* (Mattoon, IL) (May 11, 1962), p. 6.
119   *Ibid.*
120   "Harrell's Tax Records are Being Checked," *Decatur Daily Herald* (June 4, 1961), p. 7.
121   "Harrell Pleads for 'Reds' to End Antagonism," *Decatur Herald* (May 12, 1962), p. 15.
122   *Ibid.*
123   *Ibid.*
124   *Ibid.*

125 "Sixth Child Born to John R. Harrell at Louisville Estate," *Decatur Herald* (August 5, 1962), p. 18.
126 "John Harrell Aids at Birth," *Decatur Daily Review* (Dec. 24, 1962), p. 2.
127 *Ibid.*
128 "Harrell Won't Talk," *Decatur Daily Review* (Dec. 3, 1962), p. 1.
129 *Ibid.*
130 "Tax Hearing For Harrell," *Decatur Daily Review* (Feb. 9, 1963), p. 8.
131 "Federal Changes Against Harrell Under Advisement," *Decatur Herald* (Dec. 8, 1962), p. 2.
132 *Ibid.*
133 Davis interviews.
134 "Federal Changes Against Harrell...," p. 2.
135 "Ex-Marine Seized in Raid on Cult Denies Charges," *St. Louis Post-Dispatch* (July 17, 1962), p. 8.
136 "Federal Changes Against Harrell...," p. 2.
137 *Ibid.*
138 Stacey, p. iv.
139 *Ibid.*, p. 1.
140 *Ibid.*, p. i.
141 *Ibid.*
142 *Ibid.*, p. ii.
143 *Ibid.*, p. 35.
144 *Ibid.*
145 Seymour, Peter, "Harrell Out on Bail, Charges FBI Looted Home in Arresting Deserter," *Terre Haute Star* (Aug. 7, 1961), p. 6.
146 "Harrell Asks for Help," p. 1.
147 Stacey, p. 40.
148 *Ibid.*, p. 37.
149 *Ibid.*, p. 42.
150 *Ibid.*, p. iii.
151 covenantpeoplesministry.org/forum/list.php?category/92-David-K-Stacey
152 *Ibid.*, p. 44.
153 John R. Harrell interviews.
154 "Harrell Has Closed Controversial School," *Mt. Vernon Register-News* (Feb. 19, 1963), p. 1.
155 "Harrell Closes His School," *Decatur Herald* (Feb. 20, 1963), p 12.
156 *Ibid.*
157 Carr, Mike, "Harrell Plans Move to Southwest," *Decatur Daily Review* (March 3, 1963), p. 3.
158 *Ibid.*
159 "Father Objecting To Girls on Sect Area, Wins Custody," *Daily Register* (Harrisburg, IL) (March 2, 1963), p. 1.
160 *Ibid.*
161 Carr, p. 3.
162 Garrett, p. 37.
163 Carr, p. 3.
164 *Ibid.*
165 *Ibid.*
166 *Ibid.*
167 "Harrell Leaving State Next Week," *Mt. Vernon Register-News* (March 29, 1963), p. 1.

168   *Ibid.*
169   *Ibid.*
170   "Harrell Set To Go West," *Southern Illinoisan* (March 29, 1963), p. 1.
171   Carr, p. 3.
172   "Harrell's Followers To Start Trek," unknown newspaper, unknown date [c. April 1963], unknown page number.
173   *Ibid.*
174   "Anti-Red Harrell Plans to Move to New Mexico," *Edwardsville Intelligencer* (March 2, 1963), p. 3.
175   *Ibid.*
176   Garcia interviews.
177   Carr, p. 3.
178   *Ibid.*
179   "Harrell Leaving State Next Week," p. 1.
180   *Ibid.*
181   "John Harrell Missing; Car Found Abandoned South of Springfield," *Decatur Daily Review* (April 6, 1963), p. 1.
182   *Ibid.*
183   Albright, Charles E., "Harrell Mystery Worries Followers," *Decatur Herald* (April 10, 1983), p, 1.

Chapter 6

1   Garrett, Dain. "The Johnny Bob Harrell Compound: Church, Commune or Cult?" California State University, 2004, p. 7.
2   "John Harrell Missing; Car Found Abandoned South of Springfield," *Decatur Daily Review* (April 6, 1963), p. 1.
3   "Cultist John R. Harrell Missing; Auto Found," *Decatur Daily Review* (April 7, 1963), p. 1.
4   "John Harrell Missing…," p. 1.
5   *Ibid.*
6   "Cult Leader Harrell and Family Disappear," *Southern Illinoisan* (April 7, 1963), p. 2.
7   *Ibid.*
8   John Harrell Missing…," p. 1.
9   "Cultist John R. Harrell Missing…," p. 1.
10   Kramme, Ronald A. "John Robert Harrell: A Case Study of a Christian Anti-Communist, 1959-1964." Illinois State University, 1970, p. 132.
11   "Cultist John R. Harrell Missing…," p. 1.
12   "Cult Leader Harrell and Family Disappear," p. 2.
13   Garrett, p. 6.
14   "Cultist John R. Harrell Missing…," p. 1.
15   *Ibid.*
16   *Ibid.*
17   Hodges, Carl G., "The Cult Leader Who Defied the FBI," *True Police Cases* (April 1965), p. 89.
18   "Harrell Plane Vanishes Too; State in Hunt," *Decatur Herald* (April 9, 1963), p. 1.
19   "Zealot and 7 in Family Disappear," *Mt. Vernon Register-News* (April 8, 1963), p. 1.
20   "Cult Leader Harrell and Family Disappear," p. 2.

21 "Zealot and 7 in Family Disappear," *Mt. Vernon Register-News* (April 8, 1963), p. 1.

22 Hodges, p. 90.

23 "Search for Anti-Communist Harrell Centers on Locating Private Plane," *Edwardsville Intelligencer* (April 8, 1963), p. 1.

24 Hodges, p. 90.

25 "Search for Anti-Communist Harrell...," p. 1.

26 Stewart, Charles O., "FBI Suspects Threatening Letter Was Written By Harrell," *Southern Illinoisan* (March 20, 1964), p. 9.

27 "Search for Anti-Communist Harrell...," p. 1.

28 Albright, Charles E., "What Manner of Man, This Johnny Bob?," *Decatur Daily Review* (April 14, 1963), p. 10.

29 *Ibid.*

30 *Ibid.*

31 "Minutemen Offer $5,000 for Info on Harrell," *Dixon Evening Telegraph* (April 15, 1963), p. 5.

32 *Ibid.*

33 "200 Louisville Residents Gets Harrell Inquiry Letters," *Decatur Herald* (April 16, 1963), p. 5.

34 "Minutemen Offer...," p. 5.

35 "200 Louisville Residents Gets...," p. 5.

36 "Offers $5,000 Reward If Harrell Is Away 7 Years," *Mt. Vernon Register-News* (April 23, 1963), p. 6.

37 *Ibid.*

38 "Fail to Find Harrell in Search Here Wednesday," unknown newspaper, unknown date [c. April 1963], unknown page number.

39 "Large Gold Purchases By Missing Harrell Reported," *Decatur Herald* (April 18, 1963), p. 1.

40 "Offers $5,000 Reward...," p. 6.

41 "Will of Missing Harrell Found," *Decatur Herald* (May 1, 1963), p. 5.

42 Hodges, p. 89.

43 Garrett, p. 8.

44 Harold Leib interview.

45 "Start Cutting Weeds—Harrell May Return," *Mt. Vernon Register-News* (August 2, 1963), p. 1.

46 Harold Leib interview.

47 "Start Cutting Weeds...," p. 1.

48 "Last of Harrell's Flock Leaving Illinois," *Mt. Vernon Register-News* (April 26, 1963), p. 3.

49 Garcia interviews.

50 "Last of Harrell's Flock Leaving Illinois," p. 3.

51 "Author Reigns at Harrell's New Colony," *Decatur Herald* (April 24, 1963), p. 5.

52 "Start Cutting Weeds...," p. 1.

53 "John Harrell: Is He in Southwest Missouri Area?," *Edwardsville Intelligencer* (June 18, 1963), p. 2.

54 Younkin, Lou, and Jim Doussard, "Ozarks Stirred by Searchers for Missing J.R. Harrell," *Decatur Daily Review* (August 4, 1963), p. 1.

55 "John Harrell: Is He in Southwest Missouri Area?," p. 2.

56 *Ibid.*

57 "Police Adopt Wait-See Stand on Harrell," *Decatur Herald* (June 17, 1963), p. 2.

58 Younkin and Doussard, p. 1.
59 *Ibid.*
60 *Ibid.*
61 Becherer, Thomas P., "Anti-Communist Leader Harrell Still Missing," *Las Vegas Daily Optic* (July 26, 1963), p. 4.
62 *Ibid.*
63 Younkin and Doussard, p. 1.
64 *Ibid.*
65 Becherer, Thomas, "Harrell Aids in Ozarks," unknown newspaper (Jun 26, 1963), unknown page number.
66 *Ibid.*
67 *Ibid.*
68 "Start Cutting Weeds...," p. 1.
69 *Ibid.*
70 "Harrell Missing As Sect Gathers," *Mt. Vernon Register-News* (Oct. 15, 1963), p. 7.
71 "Harrell Fails to Return for Son as Planned," *Decatur Herald* (April 22, 1963), p. 1.
72 Becherer, "Anti-Communist...," p. 4.
73 "Harrell Still Missing Trial Scheduled Nov. 4," *Southern Illinoisan* (Sept. 24, 1963), p. 6.
74 "Lawyer Says Harrell Writes He's Captive," *Decatur Herald* (Oct. 14, 1963), p. 1.
75 *Ibid.*
76 "United Press Bureau at Marion Receives Lengthy Letter from Missing J.R. Harrell," *Daily Register* (Harrisburg, Illinois) (Oct. 14, 1963), p. 1.
77 "Reveals 2nd Letter from Missing Harrell," *Pantagraph* (Bloomington, Illinois) (Oct. 15, 1963), p. 10.
78 *Ibid.*
79 *Ibid.*
80 "United Press Bureau at Marion Receives Lengthy Letter from Missing J.R. Harrell," *Daily Register* (Harrisburg, Illinois) (Oct. 14, 1963), p. 1.
81 *Ibid.*
82 *Ibid.*
83 *Ibid.*
84 *Ibid.*
85 *Ibid.*
86 *Ibid.*
87 *Ibid.*
88 *Ibid.*
89 *Ibid.*
90 *Ibid.*
91 "Harrell Writes from 'Prison,'" *Decatur Herald* (Oct. 15, 1963), p. 1.
92 Albright, Charles E., "Aide Denies Knowing Where Johnny Bob Is," *Decatur Daily Review* (Oct. 20, 1963), p. 1.
93 *Ibid.*
94 *Ibid.*
95 "12 Pupils in School at Harrell's Colony," *Southern Illinoisan* (Oct. 22, 1963), p. 14.
96 *Ibid.*
97 *Ibid.*
98 "Land Sold for Taxes," *Decatur Daily Review* (Nov. 14, 1963), p. 36.

99   "Harrell Estate Sold for 1961 and 1962 Taxes," *Mt. Vernon Register-News* (Nov. 14, 1963), p. 1.
100 "Three Children of Harrell's Followers Reported Missing," *Edwardsville Intelligencer* (Oct. 30, 1963), p. 1.
101 "Cult Children Still Missing," *Journal Gazette* (Mattoon, IL) (Oct. 31, 1963), p. 1.
102 "Three Children...," p. 1.
103 "Bullet Holes Found in Door of Farm House," *Decatur Herald* (Oct. 31, 1963), p. 1.
104 Albright, Charles E., "FBI Begins Search for Harrell as Trial for Cultists Opens," *Decatur Herald* (Nov. 13, 1963), p. 1.
105 "Jury Selected in Trial of Harrell's Followers," *Southern Illinoisan* (Nov. 13, 1963), p. 1.
106 "Harrell Had Been Warned," *Daily Chronicle* (DeKalb, Illinois) (Nov. 15, 1952), p. 12.
107 Albright, p. 1.
108 *Ibid.*
109 "Harrell Not Expected to Appear on New Trial Date," *Decatur Herald* (Nov. 5, 1963), p. 5.
110 *Ibid.*
111 Albright, p. 1.
112 *Ibid.*
113 The official court transcript to this trial has, seemingly, been lost. These accounts and quotations are from newspaper reports on the trial.
114 Mathes, Bob, "FBI Agent Relates Raid on Harrell," *Decatur Daily Review* (Nov. 14, 1963), p. 1.
115 "Sobriety of Harrell's Raiders Questioned," *Decatur Daily Review* (Nov. 16, 1963), p. 2.
116 "FBI Agent Relates Raid on Harrell," p. 1.
117 *Ibid.*
118 *Ibid.*
119 *Ibid.*
120 Albright, p. 1.
121 "Prison is 'God's Will'?," *Decatur Daily Review* (Nov. 13, 1963), p. 1.
122 *Ibid.*
123 Albright, p. 1.
124 *Ibid.*
125 "FBI Agent Tells of Threat By Religious Sect Leader," *Chicago Tribune* (Nov. 15, 1963), p. 36.
126 Mathes, "Sobriety of Harrell's Raiders Questioned," p. 2.
127 *Ibid.*
128 *Ibid.*
129 "Sect Member Tells Jury of Fight with FBI," *Chicago Tribune* (Nov. 20, 1963), p. 32.
130 *Ibid.*
131 "Harrell Cult Resistance at Raid Revealed," *Decatur Daily Review* (Nov. 18, 1963), p. 1.
132 Mathes, "Sobriety of Harrell's Raiders Questioned," p. 2.
133 *Ibid.*
134 *Ibid.*
135 *Ibid.*
136 *Ibid.*

137 "Sect Member Tells Jury of Fight with FBI," *Chicago Tribune* (Nov. 20, 1963), p. 32.

138 Mathes, "Harrell Planned to Yield Deserter, Aide Declares," *Southern Illinoisan* (Nov. 19, 1963), p. 5.

139 "Harrell Followers on Trial In U.S. District Court," unknown newspaper, unknown date [c. Nov. 1963], unknown page number.

140 Mathes, "Harrell Planned to Yield Deserter, Aide Declares," *Southern Illinoisan* (Nov. 19, 1963), p. 5.

141 "Jury Finds 11 Harrell Members Guilty," *Jacksonville Daily Journal* (Jacksonville, IL) (Nov. 11, 1963), p. 4.

142 "12 Harrell Followers Placed on Probation," *Decatur Herald* (March 4, 1964), p.12.

143 *Ibid.*

144 "Louisville Folks Feel Harrell About to Return," *Decatur Daily Review* (March 29, 1964), p. 10.

145 *Ibid.*

146 Grossman, Ron, "Civil war," *Chicago Tribune* (Mar. 31, 1988), p. 63.

147 "Explosion Set Off at Harrell Foe's Store," *Decatur Daily Review* (December 6, 1963), p. 1.

148 "Blast Shatters 200 Windows," unknown newspaper, unknown date [c. Dec. 1963], unknown page number.

149 "Explosion Sets Off...," p. 1.

150 "Blast Rocks Louisville," unknown newspaper, unknown date [c. Dec. 1963], unknown page number.

151 "Explosion Rips Square," *Southern Illinoisan* (Dec. 5, 1963). p. 4.

152 *Ibid.*

153 *Ibid.*

154 "Explosion Set Off...," p. 1.

155 *Ibid.*

156 "Blast Shatters 200 Windows," unknown page number.

157 "Blast Rocks...," unknown page number.

158 "Explosion Set Of...," p. 1.

159 "Explosion Rips Square," p. 4.

160 "Explosion Set Of...," p. 1.

161 *Ibid.*

162 "Explosion Rips Square," p. 4.

163 "Louisville Citizens Except Results," *Clay Country Republican* (Dec. 12, 1963), unknown page number.

164 "Explosion Rips Square," p. 4.

165 "Explosion Set Of...," p. 1.

166 "New Dimension on Harrell Case," *Decatur Daily Review* (December 12, 1963), p. 6.

167 Grossman, p. 63.

168 "New Dimension...," p. 6.

169 Kramme, p. 50.

170 Grossman, p. 63.

171 Garrrett, p. 26.

172 "FBI Circulars Ask Police Aid in Harrell Search," *Decatur Daily Review* (March 12, 1964), p. 1.

173 Jim Williams interview with author.

174 "Louisville Folks Feel Harrell About to Return," *Decatur Daily Review* (March 29, 1964), p. 10.

175 Stewart, Charles O., "FBI Suspects Threatening Letter Was Written By Harrell," *Southern Illinoisan* (March 20, 1964), p. 9.

176 *Ibid.*

177 *Ibid.*

178 *Ibid.*

179 *Ibid.*

180 Collins, Robert H., "Three Children of Harrell Sect Gone 10 Months," *St. Louis Post-Dispatch* (August 23, 1964), p. 3.

181 *Ibid.*

182 *Ibid.*

183 "Harrell Fools Louisville Spectators," unknown newspaper, unknown date [c. March 1964], unknown page number.

184 Collins, Robert H., "FBI Frustrated in Long Search for Anti-Red Leader Harrell," *St. Louis Post-Dispatch* (August 16, 1964), p. 3.

185 *Ibid.*

186 *Ibid.*

187 "Harrell Found with Family, Missing Girls in Arkansas," *St. Louis Post-Dispatch* (Sept. 20, 1964), p. 1.

188 *Ibid.*

189 *Ibid.*

190 Garrett, p. 9.

191 "Harrell Family Found...," p. 1.

192 *Ibid.*

193 *Ibid.*

194 Garrett, p. 9.

195 "Harrell Family Found...," p. 1.

196 Hodges, p. 92.

197 *Ibid.*

198 "Harrell Family Found...," p. 1.

199 "Body of Boy Found In Grave On Farm Hideout of Harrell," unknown newspaper, unknown date [c. Sept. 1963], unknown page number.

200 *Ibid.*

201 *Ibid.*

202 Kramme, p. 132.

203 Collins, Robert H., "Harrell Family Lived Quietly, Self-Sufficiently in Arkansas," *St. Louis Post-Dispatch* (Sept. 24, 1964), p. 39.

204 *Ibid.*

205 *Ibid.*

206 *Ibid.*

207 Angelyn Comer Garcia interviews: From 2015 onward, I interviewed Ms. Garcia several times over the phone and via e-mail communication; all quotes and other information in this book are drawn from those conversations.

208 Collins, "Harrell Family Lived Quietly,...," p. 39.

209 *Ibid.*

210 Garrett, p. 10.

211 Collins, "Harrell Family Lived Quietly,...," p. 39.

212 *Ibid.*

213 *Ibid.*

214 "US Agents Seize Harrell's Property," *Southern Illinoisan* (Sept. 23, 1964), p. 21.

215 Collins, "Harrell Family Lived Quietly,...," p. 39.

216   John R. Harrell interviews: From 2015 until his death in 2021, I personally interviewed John Harrell, in person and over the phone, several times. All quotes and other information throughout this book are drawn from those conversations.

217   Collins, "Harrell Family Lived Quietly,...," p. 39.

218   *Ibid.*

219   *Ibid.*

220   Grossman, p. 63.

221   *Ibid.*

222   Collins, "Harrell Family Lived Quietly,...," p. 39.

223   *Ibid.*

224   *Ibid.*

225   Kramme, p. 134.

226   "Cult Leader Returned to East St. Louis," *Chicago Tribune* (Oct. 1, 1964), unknown page number.

227   Garrett, p. 9.

228   "Body of Boy Found In Grave On Farm Hideout of Harrell," unknown newspaper, unknown date [c. Sept. 1963], unknown page number.

229   Tod Harrell interviews.

230   Garcia interviews.

231   *Ibid.*

232   *Ibid.*

233   *Ibid.*

234   "Body of Boy Found In Grave On Farm Hideout of Harrell," unknown page number.

235   Garrett, p. 7.

236   Garcia interviews.

237   John R. Harrell interviews.

238   "Harrell Transferred to East St. Louis," *Decatur Herald* (Oct. 1, 1964), p. 1.

239   "Harrell To Face Trial in E. St. Louis," *Mt. Vernon Register* (Sept. 25, 1964), p. 1.

240   *Ibid.*

241   *Ibid.*

242   "US Agents Seize Harrell's Property," *Southern Illinoisan* (Sept. 23, 1964), p. 21.

243   "Harrell Pleads Guilty to Federal Charges," *Decatur Herald* (Oct. 1, 1964), p. 4.

244   "John R. Harrell Gets 10 Year Prison Term," *Decatur Herald* (Nov. 5, 1964), p. 1.

245   "Harrell Starts Serving 10-Year Prison Term," *Pantagraph* (Bloomington, IL) (Nov. 5, 1964), p. 22.

246   "Harrell Gets 10-Year Term, Is Fined $10,000," *St. Louis Post-Dispatch* (November 4, 1964), p. 1.

247   Kramme, p. 135.

248   "Harrell Gets 10-Year Term,...," p. 1.

249   "Harrell Plea Changed Denied," *Decatur Herald* (Dec. 24, 1964), p. 8.

250   Kramme, p. 138.

251   Tod Harrell interviews: From 2015 onward, I interviewed Mr. Harrell several times over the phone and via e-mail communication; all quotes and other information in this book drawn from those conversations.

252   "Harrell Begins Prison Sentence," *News-Herald* (Franklin, PA) (Nov. 6, 1964), p. 14.

253   John R. Harrell interviews.

254   "2 Acquitted for Hiding John Harrell," *Freeport Journal-Standard* (Freeport, IL) (Nov. 18, 1964), p. 13.

255 Parsons, Jerry, "Cult Leader Wages Battle for Freedom," *Decatur Herald* (March 19, 1967), p. 14.

256 Tod Harrell interviews.

257 Bray, Bob, "Afraid government 'is going to fall,' Patriots ready to put it back together," *Birmingham News* (Aug. 30, 1981), unknown page number.

Chapter 7

1 Garrett, Dain. "The Johnny Bob Harrell Compound: Church, Commune or Cult?" California State University, 2004, p. 29.

2 Parsons, Jerry, "Cult Leader Wages Battle for Freedom," *Decatur Herald* (March 19, 1967), p. 14.

3 "Harrell Starts Serving 10-Year Prison Term," *Pantagraph* (Bloomington, IL) (Nov. 5, 1964), p. 22.

4 Townsend, Catherine, "Federal Death Row" (January 1, 2017), crimefeed. com/2017/01/dylann-roofs-long-strange-trip-to-the-gas-chamber-on-federal-death-row/

5 Garrett, p. 33.

6 Angelyn Comer Garcia interviews: From 2015 onward, I interviewed Ms. Garcia several times over the phone and via e-mail communication; all quotes and other information in this book are drawn from those conversations.

7 Burns, Michael K., "Harrell's Louisville Estate Harbors Memories," *Decatur Daily Review* (Nov. 24, 1964), p. 35.

8 Parsons, p. 14.

9 John R. Harrell interviews: From 2015 until his death in 2021, I personally interviewed John Harrell, in person and over the phone, several times. All quotes and other information throughout this book are drawn from those conversations.

10 "Fund Planned for Harrell," *Decatur Herald* (Feb. 13, 1965), p. 6.

11 Burns, Michael K., "Harrell's Louisville Estate Harbors Memories," *Decatur Daily Review* (Nov. 24, 1964), p. 35.

12 Garcia interviews.

13 *Ibid.*

14 Burns, p. 35.

15 Parsons, p. 14.

16 Burns, p. 35.

17 *Ibid.*

18 *Ibid.*

19 "Harrell's Family Back on Estate," *Journal Gazette* (Mattoon, IL) (Feb. 6, 1965), p. 3.

20 *Ibid.*

21 Garcia interviews.

22 Garrett, p. 33.

23 John R. Harrell interviews.

24 *Ibid.*

25 *Ibid.*

26 Kramme, Ronald A. "John Robert Harrell: A Case Study of a Christian Anti-Communist, 1959-1964." Illinois State University, 1970, p. 138.

27 Tod Harrell interviews: From 2015 onward, I interviewed Mr. Harrell several times over the phone and via e-mail communication; all quotes and other information in this book drawn from those conversations.

28 Garcia interviews.
29 Hodges, Carl G., "The Cult Leader Who Defied the FBI," *True Police Cases* (April 1965), p. 34.
30 *Ibid.*
31 "Judge Says Harrell Should Get Hearing," *Decatur Herald* (Jan. 12, 1967), p. 37.
32 "Conviction Of Harrell Upheld," *Edwardsville Intelligencer* (Jan. 9, 1967), p. 1.
33 "Cult Leader's Worst Offense Bad Judgement," *Decatur Herald* (March 19, 1967), p. 48.
34 *Ibid.*
35 Parsons, p. 14.
36 *Ibid.*
37 *Ibid.*
38 *Ibid.*
39 *Ibid.*
40 *Ibid.*
41 *Ibid.*
42 Geiger, Kay, "Cult Leader to Be Paroled," *Decatur Daily Review* (July 31, 1968), p. 2.
43 Garcia interviews.
44 Geiger, p. 2.
45 *Ibid.*
46 *Ibid.*
47 John R. Harrell interviews.
48 "Parolee Harrell Returns Home to Louisville," *Decatur Herald* (August 31, 1968), p. 10.
49 *Ibid.*
50 *Ibid.*
51 Grossman, Ron, "Civil war," *Chicago Tribune* (Mar. 31, 1988), p. 63.
52 Harold Leib interview.
53 Grossman, p. 63.
54 Garrett, p. 23.
55 "Parolee Harrell Returns...," p. 10.
56 Grossman, p. 63.
57 John R. Harrell interviews.
58 Garrett, p. 51.
59 Harrell, John R. *Declaration and Proclamation: Christian Conservative Church* (July 19, 1976).
60 *Ibid.*
61 *Ibid.*
62 *Ibid.*, p. 4.
63 Garrrett, p. 63.
64 Helms, Jesse. Letter to John Harrell, August 20, 1976; *and* Canfield, H. Spofford (Office of the Vice President). Letter to John Harrell, July 19, 1976.
65 *Ibid.*
66 Notice of New Employer Identification Number Assigned, Internal Revenue Service, March 14, 1977.
67 *Identity Churches: A Theology of Hate.* New York: Anti-Defamation League of B'nai B'rith, 1983).
68 Garrett, p. 78.

69 *Ibid.*, p. 78.
70 *Ibid.*
71 Tod Harrell interviews.
72 Carr, Mike, "Johnny Bob is Back and Willing to Talk," *Decatur Herald* (June 25, 1977), p. 11.
73 Schmidt, J.L., "Johnny Bob Harrell still recruits 'patriots,'" *Southern Illinoisan* (Nov. 13, 1979), p. 20.
74 *Ibid.*
75 *Ibid.*
76 Duncan, Don, "A pick-and-choose theology," *Seattle Times* (April 21, 1986), unknown page number.
77 Grossman, p. 77.
78 "ADL Shows Active," *Wisconsin Jewish Chronicle* (Nov. 7, 1980), p. 9.
79 "Survivalist tones down message," *Herald and Review* (Decatur, IL) (June 1, 1987), p. 46.
80 "Violence on the Right," *Newsweek* (March 4, 1985), p. 23.
81 Garrett, p. 17.
82 Gauen, Patrick M., "'Christian Patriot' Caught by Time," *St. Louis Post-Dispatch* (July 2, 1995), p. 1.
83 Garrett, p. 15.
84 Carr, Mike, "Johnny Bob is Back and Willing to Talk," *Decatur Herald* (June 25, 1977), p. 11.
85 Bray, Bob, "Afraid government 'is going to fall,' Patriots ready to put it back together." *Birmingham News* (Aug. 30, 1981), unknown page number.
86 Chandler, Russell, "'New Age' Religious Groups Abandon Cities, Head for the Hills," *Washington Post* (Nov. 13, 1981), p. C5.
87 *Ibid.*
88 Billington, Mike, "'Freedom Fest' Hatred Recalls Munich of 1933," *Courier-Express* (Buffalo, NY) (Oct. 13, 1980), unknown page number.
89 *Ibid.*
90 "ADL Shows...," p. 9.
91 *Ibid.*
92 Schmidt, p. 20.
93 Garrett, p. 51.
94 Billington, unknown page number.
95 *Ibid.*
96 *Ibid.*
97 Carr, Mike, "Johnny Bob is Back and Willing to Talk," p. 11.
98 Schmidt, p. 20.
99 *Ibid.*
100 *Ibid.*
101 Grossman, p. 63.
102 *Ibid.*
103 *Ibid.*
104 *Ibid.*
105 Priscilla Laughton Hutton interview.
106 Garrett, p. 106.
107 "Survivalist tones down...," p. 46.
108 Sprayregen, Joel. J., "Extremist Centers in Illinois," *Chicago Tribune* (June 2, 1985), unknown page number.
109 *Ibid.*

110   Francis, William, "Secret IRS 'Hit List' Found: Document to Be Destroyed," *Spotlight* (Sept. 22, 1986), p. 5.

111   "Site is Donated for Party Caucus," *Spotlight* (April 23, 1984), p. 16.

112   "John Harrell, followers worried about survival," *Journal Gazette* (Mattoon, IL) (July 1, 1980), p. 3.

113   Garrett, p. 51.

114   Billington, unknown page number.

115   Bray, unknown page number.

116   "Quote/Unquote," *Chillicothe Constitution-Tribune* (Chillicothe, MO) (Nov. 5, 1979), p. 4.

117   Morrison, Donald, "In Illinois: Festival of the Fed-Up," *Time* (Nov. 5, 1979), unknown page number.

118   Saponar, R.C. "Survivalists to converge on Louisville next month," unknown newspaper, unknown date [c. 1982], unknown page number.

119   Morrison, unknown page number.

120   Press, Robert M., "They play war games in US countryside," *Christian Science Monitor* (March 23, 1981), unknown page number.

121   Ludwick, Jim, "When US is invaded, they'll be ready," *Herald and Review* (July 2, 1980), p. 9.

122   Press, unknown page number.

123   *Ibid.*

124   *Ibid.*

125   *Ibid.*

126   Billington, unknown page number.

127   Kolb, David J., "'Survival show,'" *Citizen-Patriot* (Jackson, MI) (Jan. 26, 1981), p. A-1.

128   Garrett, p. 52.

129   *Ibid.*

130   *Ibid.*

131   Hahn, Steve, "Paramilitary group ban OK'd by Senate panel," *Evening Journal-Register* (Springfield, IL) (April 26, 1985), p. 1.

132   John R. Harrell interviews.

133   Hahn, p. 1.

134   *Ibid.*

135   *Ibid.*

136   Gauen, p. 1.

137   Hoogesteger, John, "Ready, waiting," *News-Leader* (Springfield, MO) (Aug. 31, 1986, p. 1A.

138   Gauen, p. 1.

139   Morrison, unknown page number.

140   Grossman, p. 63.

141   Garrett, p. 15.

142   Grossman, p. 63.

143   Garcia interviews.

144   Jean Bailey interview, August 18, 2017.

145   "Johnny Bob Harrell's Mother, Natalia, dies," *Herald and Review* (April 2, 1988), p. 5.

146   "Obituary: Betty Harrell," *Effingham Daily News* (July 22, 2014), unknown page number.

147   *Ibid.*

148   *Ibid.*

149 Gauen, p. 1.
150 *Ibid.*
151 Various people I spoke to throughout the researching and writing of this shared their belief that, along with his various land and property ownings, John Harrell still retained considerable bank funds at this time.
152 Gauen, p. 1.

Chapter 8

1 Tod Harrell interviews: From 2015 onward, I interviewed Mr. Harrell several times over the phone and via e-mail communication; all quotes and other information in this book drawn from those conversations.
2 *Ibid.*
3 *Ibid.*; and, Jean Bailey interview, August 18, 2017.
4 Bailey interview.
5 "Harrell Says No Soviet in Space," *Decatur Herald* (Aug. 9, 1961), p. 5.
6 Garrett, Dain. "The Johnny Bob Harrell Compound: Church, Commune or Cult?" California State University, 2004, p. 39.
7 *Ibid.*, p. 55.
8 *Ibid.*, p. 20.
9 Comer, A. Vance. *The Manifestation of God in the Healing of John R. Harrell.* (Louisville, KY: Herald Press, 1959), p. 20.
10 Angelyn Comer Garcia interviews: From 2015 onward, I interviewed Ms. Garcia several times over the phone and via e-mail communication; all quotes and other information in this book are drawn from those conversations.
11 John R. Harrell interviews: From 2015 until his death in 2021, I personally interviewed John Harrell, in person and over the phone, several times. All quotes and other information throughout this book are drawn from those conversations.
12 "John Robert Harrell" (obituary), *Clay Country Republican* (June 23, 2021).
13 *Ibid.*
14 Xon Harrell interview, Sept. 1, 2021.
15 *Ibid.*

Bibliography

"2 Acquitted for Hiding John Harrell," *Freeport Journal-Standard* (Freeport, IL) (Nov. 18, 1964), p. 13.

"12 Harrell Followers Placed on Probation," *Decatur Herald* (Mar. 4, 1964), p. 12.

"12 Pupils in School at Harrell's Colony," *Southern Illinoisan* (Oct. 22, 1963), p. 14.

"18 in Cult Remain in Jail," *Indianapolis Star* (Aug. 6, 1961), p. 11.

"125 Peace Officers Make Arrests at Louisville (Ill.) Estate," *St. Louis Post-Dispatch* (Aug. 4, 1961), p. 1.

"200 Louisville Residents Gets Harrell Inquiry Letters," *Decatur Herald* (April 16, 1963), p. 5.

"$225,000 Libel Suit Filed Here in Circuit Court," *Clay County Republican* (Mar. 3, 1960), unknown page number.

"ADL Shows Active," *Wisconsin Jewish Chronicle* (Nov. 7, 1980), p. 9.

"After-Class Task at Louisville," *Decatur Herald* (Mar. 24, 1961), p. 22.

Albright, C., "Aide Denies Knowing Where Johnny Bob Is," *Decatur Daily Review* (Oct. 20, 1963), p. 1; "FBI Begins Search for Harrell as Trial for Cultists Opens," *Decatur Herald* (Nov. 13, 1963), p. 1; "Harrell Mystery Worries Followers," *Decatur Herald* (April 10, 1983), p. 1; "Harrell's Troubles," *Decatur Daily Review* (Aug. 5, 1961), p. 23; "A Look Into 'Perils' of John R. Harrell," *Decatur Daily Review* (Mar. 10, 1963), p. 6; "What Manner of Man, This Johnny Bob?" *Decatur Daily Review* (April 14, 1963), p. 10.

"Alsup, Ragers, Landholt Winners; 3-Way Race for Second Demo Spot," *Decatur Herald* (April 13, 1960), p. 3.

"Anti-Communist Builds Atomic Proof Estate in Illinois," *Medford Mail Tribune* (Medford, OR) (Dec. 7, 1961), p. 7.

"Anti-Red Harrell Plans to Move to New Mexico," *Edwardsville Intelligencer* (Mar. 2, 1963), p. 3.

"Authorities Raid Harrell's Estate," *Belvidere Daily Republican* (Belvidere, IL) (Aug. 4, 1961), p. 1.

"Author Reigns at Harrell's New Colony," *Decatur Herald* (April 24, 1963), p. 5.

"AWOL Marine, Religious Sect Leader Arrest in Raid by FBI and Police," *Medford Mail Tribune* (Medford, OR) (Aug. 7, 1961), p. 9.

Bailey, J., interview with author, Aug. 2017.

Baker, C., interview with author, July 2015.

"Barricades AWOL Marine Says Corps 'Flaunted Sin,'" *News Journal* (Willington, DE) (Aug. 3, 1961), p. 9.

Becherer, T., "Anti-Communist Leader Harrell Still Missing," *Las Vegas Daily Optic* (July 26, 1963), p. 4; "Harrell Aids in Ozarks," unknown newspaper (June 26, 1963), unknown page number.

Billington, M., "'Freedom Fest' Hatred Recalls Munich of 1933," *Courier-Express* (Buffalo, NY) (Oct. 13, 1980), unknown page number.

"Blames Red Vandals for House Damage," *Alton Evening Telegraph* (April 4, 1961), p. 2.

"Blast Rocks Louisville," unknown newspaper, unknown date [c. Dec. 1963], unknown page number.

"Blast Shatters 200 Windows," unknown newspaper, unknown date [c. Dec. 1963], unknown page number.

"Body of Boy Found In Grave On Farm Hideout of Harrell," unknown newspaper, unknown date [c. Sept. 1963], unknown page number.

Bray, B., "Afraid government 'is going to fall,' Patriots ready to put it back together," *Birmingham News* (Aug. 30, 1981), unknown page number.

Brinkman, G., "House of Fear," *National Enquirer* (June 4, 1961), p. 14.

"Bullet Holes Found in Door of Farm House," *Decatur Herald* (Oct. 31, 1963), p. 1.

"Burn Crosses at Louisville," *Mt. Vernon Register-News* (Feb. 2, 1961), p. 8.

Burns, M., "Harrell's Louisville Estate Harbors Memories," *Decatur Daily Review* (Nov. 24, 1964), p. 35.

"Business Opens Own School In Plan for Anti-Red Colony," *Press and Sun-Bulletin* (Binghamton, NY) (Mar. 6, 1961), p. 10.

Callahan, W., "Harrell to Open Own Private School," *Decatur Herald* (Mar. 4, 1961), p. 1.

Canfield, H. (Office of the Vice President), letter to John Harrell, July 19, 1976.

Carr, M., "Harrell Plans Move to Southwest," *Decatur Daily Review* (Mar. 3, 1963), p. 3; "Johnny Bob is Back and Willing to Talk," *Decatur Herald* (June 25, 1977), p. 11.

Chandler, R., "'New Age' Religious Groups Abandon Cities, Head for the Hills," *Washington Post* (Nov. 13, 1981), p. C5.

"Christian Conservatives Ready for Russian Bomb Blast," *Herald and News* (Klamath Falls, OR) (Feb. 4, 1962), p. 14.

"'Christian Party,'" *Decatur Daily Review* (April 29, 1960), p. 20.

"Clay County Official Denies Charge by Touring Speaker," *Journal Gazette* (Mattoon, IL) (Feb. 23, 1961), p. 3.

"Clay Parents Face Charges," *Decatur Herald* (Mar. 8, 1961), p. 1.

Collins, R., "FBI Frustrated in Long Search for Anti-Red Leader Harrell," *St. Louis Post-Dispatch* (Aug. 16, 1964), p. 3; "Harrell Family Lived Quietly, Self-Sufficiently in Arkansas," *St. Louis Post-Dispatch* (Sept. 24, 1964), p. 39; "Three Children of Harrell Sect Gone 10 Months," *St. Louis Post-Dispatch* (Aug. 23, 1964), p. 3.

Comer, A. *The Manifestation of God in the Healing of John R. Harrell.* (Louisville, KY: Herald Press, 1959), p. 11+.

"Conviction Of Harrell Upheld," *Edwardsville Intelligencer* (Jan. 9, 1967), p. 1.

"Cult Children Still Missing," *Journal Gazette* (Mattoon, IL) (Oct. 31, 1963), p. 1.

"Cultist Admits IRS Probing His Returns," *Palm Beach Post* (Aug. 7, 1961), p. 26.

"Cultist and Son Gain Freedom; Out on Bond," *Lakes Charles American-Press* (Aug. 6, 1961), p. 34.

"Cultist Harrell Posts Bonds for 15 Followers Seized in Raid," *St. Louis Post-Dispatch* (Aug. 7, 1961), p. 3.

"Cultist Harrell, Son Go Home Under Bond," *Pantagraph* (Bloomington, IN) (Aug. 6, 1961), p. 16.

"Cultist John R. Harrell Missing; Auto Found," *Decatur Daily Review* (April 7, 1963), p. 1.

"Cultist Predicts Red Attack in 1961," *News Journal* (Wilmington, DE) (Oct. 6, 1961), p. 16.

"Cultist Seeks to Raise Bail for Followers," *Terre Haute Tribune* (Aug. 7, 1961), p. 6.

"Cultists, Son Free After Night In Jail," *Sunday Gazette-Mail* (Charleston, WV) (Aug. 6, 1961), p. 7.

"Cultist, Son Free on Bond," *Tennessean* (Aug. 6, 1961), p. 8.

"Cultist Waives Arraignment on Federal Charge," *Terre Haute Tribune* (Aug. 20, 1961), p. 49.

"Cult Leader Posts Bonds of $43,000 for Disciples," *Cincinnati Enquirer* (Cincinnati, OH) (Aug. 8, 1961), p. 17.

"Cult Leader Protects Marine From Camp Lejeune 'Vileness,'" *Ashville Citizen-Times* (Asheville, NC) (Aug. 3, 1961), p. 30.

"Cult Leader Returned to East St. Louis," *Chicago Tribune* (Oct. 1, 1964), unknown page number.

"Cult Leader Won't Resist Court Order," *Pantagraph* (Bloomington, IL) (July 28, 1961), p. 5.

"Cult Leaders Freed on Bond; Says FBI, IRS Plotting Against Him," *Arizona Republic* (Phoenix, AZ) (Aug. 7, 1961), p. 22.

"Cult Leader's Worst Offense Bad Judgement," *Decatur Herald* (Mar. 19, 1967), p. 48.

"Cult Women Pray, Try to Raise Bond," *Levittown Times* (Aug. 5, 1961), p. 2.

Davis, D., interviews with author, 2015-2021.

"Disciples of Harrell Freed; Eccentric to Open Estate," *Journal Gazette* (Mattoon, IL) (Aug. 8, 1961), p. 1.

Doussard, J., "Louisville Reacts to 'The Situation,'" *Decatur Daily Review* (April 2, 1961), p. 1; "Mount Vernon Replica Going Up," *Decatur Herald* (June 19, 1960), p. 4.

Duncan, D., "A pick-and-choose theology," *Seattle Times* (April 21, 1986), unknown page number.

"Ex-Marine Posts Bond," *Morning Herald* (Uniontown, PA) (May 2, 1962), p. 6.

"Ex-Marine Seized in Raid on Cult Denies Charges," *St. Louis Post-Dispatch* (July 17, 1962), p. 8.

"Explosion Rips Square," *Southern Illinoisan* (Dec. 5, 1963). p. 4.

"Explosion Set Off at Harrell Foe's Store," *Decatur Daily Review* (Dec. 6, 1963), p. 1.

"Fail to Find Harrell in Search Here Wednesday," unknown newspaper, unknown date [c. April 1963], unknown page number.

"Father Happy Son Now in Custody of Police," *Shamokin News-Dispatch* (Shamokin, PA) (Aug. 4, 1961), p. 1.

"Father Objecting To Girls on Sect Area, Wins Custody," *Daily Register* (Harrisburg, IL) (Mar. 2, 1963), p. 1.

"FBI Agent Tells of Threat By Religious Sect Leader," *Chicago Tribune* (Nov. 15, 1963), p. 36.

"FBI Captures Guarded AWOL," *Logansport Press* (Logansport Press, IN) (Aug. 5, 1961), p. 1.

"FBI Circulars Ask Police Aid in Harrell Search," *Decatur Daily Review* (Mar. 12, 1964), p. 1.

"FBI Lands, Has Marine Situation Under Control," *New Journal* (Wilmington, DE) (Aug. 4, 1961), p. 11.

"FBI, State Police Raid Harrell's Estate, Arrest Gun Bearers," *Alton Evening Telegraph* (Aug. 4, 1961), p. 2.

"Federal Changes Against Harrell Under Advisement," *Decatur Herald* (Dec. 8, 1962), p. 2.

"Fire Alarm False at Church Rally Near Louisville," *Decatur Herald* (Feb. 23, 1961), p. 1.

"Fire Levels 13-Room Home At Louisville," unknown newspaper, unknown date [c. 1958], unknown page number.

"For Rent," *Kinmundy Express* (Mar. 18, 1948), p. 6.

Francis, W., "Secret IRS 'Hit List' Found: Document to Be Destroyed," *Spotlight* (Sept. 22, 1986), p. 5.

"Fund Planned for Harrell," *Decatur Herald* (Feb. 13, 1965), p. 6.

Garcia, A., interviews with author, 2015-2021.

Garrett, D., "The Johnny Bob Harrell Compound: Church, Commune or Cult?" California State University, 2004, p. 24+.

Gauen, P., "'Christian Patriot' Caught by Time," *St. Louis Post-Dispatch* (July 2, 1995), p. 1.

Gay, M., "Giving Up the Memorabilia, but Not the Belief: Elvis Lives," *New York Times* (Nov. 8, 2007), unknown page number.

Geiger, K., "Cult Leader to Be Paroled," *Decatur Daily Review* (July 31, 1968), p. 2.

"Goff's Anti-Red Meeting Interrupted," *Mt. Vernon Register-News* (Feb. 23, 1961), p. 1.

"Goodbye, Rev. Goff," *Decatur Daily Review* (Feb. 23, 1961), p. 28.

Grossman, R., "Civil war," *Chicago Tribune* (Mar. 31, 1988), p. 63.

Hahn, S., "Paramilitary group ban OK'd by Senate panel," *Evening Journal-Register* (Springfield, IL) (April 26, 1985), p. 1.

Hancock, S., "Agents Capture Marine Deserter in Religious Camp," *Daily Courier* (Connellsville, PA) (Aug. 4, 1961), p. 17; "Harrell Challenges FBI to Coax AWOL Marine to Surrender After Fleeing Corps," *Daily Register* (Harrisburg, IL) (Aug. 2, 1961), p. 7; "Harrell Says His Battle with Clay County School Officials Has Just Begun," *Daily Register* (Harrisburg, IL), (April 1, 1961), p. 3.

"Harrell, 12 Others Plead Not Guilty," *St. Louis Post-Dispatch* (Oct. 5, 1961), p. 3.

"Harrell Asks for Help," *Decatur Daily Review* (Aug. 30, 1961), p. 1.

"Harrell, AWOL Marine Captured As FBI, Troopers Storm Estate," *Edwardsville Intelligencer* (Aug. 4, 1961), p. 1.

"Harrell Balks FBI Effort to See Marine," *Decatur Daily Review* (Aug. 3, 1961), p. 68.

"Harrell Begins Prison Sentence," *News-Herald* (Franklin, PA) (Nov. 6, 1964), p. 14.

"Harrell Challenges FBI to Come After AWOL Marine," unknown newspaper, unknown date [c. Aug. 1961], unknown page number.

"Harrell Charges Mail Tampering; Seeks Bail for 15 Followers," *Daily Register* (Harrisburg, IL) (Aug. 7, 1961), p. 8.

"Harrell Claims Vandals Damage Rural Building," *Decatur Herald* (April 4, 1961), p. 1.

"Harrell Closes His School," *Decatur Herald* (Feb. 20, 1963), p. 12.

"Harrell Cult Resistance at Raid Revealed," *Decatur Daily Review* (Nov. 18, 1963), p. 1.

"Harrell Estate Sold for 1961 and 1962 Taxes," *Mt. Vernon Register-News* (Nov. 14, 1963), p. 1.

"Harrell Extends Retreat, Continues Building Log Cabins at Louisville," *Decatur Daily Review* (Mar. 12, 1961), p. 14.

"Harrell Faces New Charges in Private School Battle," unknown newspaper, unknown date [c. Feb. 1961], unknown page number.

"Harrell Fails to Return for Son as Planned," *Decatur Herald* (April 22, 1963), p. 1.

"Harrell Fools Louisville Spectators," unknown newspaper, unknown date [c. Mar. 1964], unknown page number.

"Harrell Found with Family, Missing Girls in Arkansas," *St. Louis Post-Dispatch* (Sept. 20, 1964), p. 1.

"Harrell Followers on Trial In U.S. District Court," unknown newspaper, unknown date [c. Nov. 1963], unknown page number.

"Harrell Gets 10-Year Term, Is Fined $10,000," *St. Louis Post-Dispatch* (Nov. 4, 1964), p. 1.

"Harrell Had Been Warned," *Daily Chronicle* (DeKalb, Illinois) (Nov. 15, 1952), p. 12.

"Harrell Has Closed Controversial School," *Mt. Vernon Register-News* (Feb. 19, 1963), p. 1.

"Harrell Has No Qualified Teachers," *Mt. Vernon Register-News* (Mar. 22, 1961), p. 1.

"Harrell Jailed in FBI Raid on Estate," *Decatur Herald* (Aug. 5, 1961), p. 1.

Harrell, J., interviews with author, 2015–2020; *Declaration and Proclamation: Christian Conservative Church* (July 19, 1976).

"Harrell Keeps His Own Private School," *Mt. Vernon Register-News* (Mar. 23, 1961), p. 1.

"Harrell Leaving State Next Week," *Mt. Vernon Register-News* (Mar. 29, 1963), p. 1.

"Harrell Loses Bid for New Trial in Clay," *Decatur Herald* (April 8, 1961), p. 7.

"Harrell Loses Libel Suit in Court," *Mt. Vernon Register-News* (Nov. 15, 1961), p. 1.

"Harrell Loses Truancy Plea," *Decatur Herald* (Feb. 24, 1962), p. 2.

"Harrell Missing As Sect Gathers," *Mt. Vernon Register-News* (Oct. 15, 1963), p. 7.

"Harrell Motel Brings $6,300," *Journal Gazette* (Mattoon, IL) (July 31, 1961), p. 7.

"Harrell Motel Sold in Clay," *Decatur Review* (July 30, 1961), p. 1.

"Harrell Not Expected to Appear on New Trial Date," *Decatur Herald* (Nov. 5, 1963), p. 5.

"Harrell Now Fears Local Persecution," *Greenville News* (Greenville, SC) (Aug. 7, 1961), p. 1.

"Harrell Offers Estate as Bond for Gen. Walker," *Decatur Daily Review* (Nov. 3, 1962), p. 1.

"Harrell Plane Vanishes Too; State in Hunt," *Decatur Herald* (April 9, 1963), p. 1.

"Harrell Plea Changed Denied," *Decatur Herald* (Dec. 24, 1964), p. 8.

"Harrell Pleads for 'Reds' to End Antagonism," *Decatur Herald* (May 12, 1962), p. 15.

"Harrell Pleads Guilty to Federal Charges," *Decatur Herald* (Oct. 1, 1964), p. 4.

"Harrell Resists FBI's Attempt to Arrest Deserter at Louisville," *Decatur Herald* (Aug. 3, 1961), p. 1.

"Harrell Says He May Run Again for US Senate," *St. Louis Post-Dispatch* (Nov. 8, 1961), p. 3.

"Harrell Says He Won't Answer Questions by IRS," *Journal Gazette* (Mattoon, IL) (Dec. 4, 1962), p. 2.

"Harrell Says No Soviet in Space," *Decatur Herald* (Aug. 9, 1961), p. 5.

"Harrell Says Reds Vandalized House," *Pantagraph* (Bloomington, IL) (April 4, 1961), p. 16.

"Harrell Says Will Continue Fight On Reds in Clay County, Nation," *Salem Times-Commoner*, unknown date, unknown page number.

"Harrell Set To Go West," *Southern Illinoisan* (Mar. 29, 1963), p. 1.

"Harrell Starts Serving 10-Year Prison Term," *Pantagraph* (Bloomington, IL) (Nov. 5, 1964), p. 22.

"Harrell Still Missing Trial Scheduled Nov. 4," *Southern Illinoisan* (Sept. 24, 1963), p. 6.

"Harrell Transferred to East St. Louis," *Decatur Herald* (Oct. 1, 1964), p. 1.

"Harrell To Appeal Decision," *Alton Evening Telegraph* (April 8, 1961), p. 15.

"Harrell To Face Trial in E. St. Louis," *Mt. Vernon Register* (Sept. 25, 1964), p. 1.

"Harrell to Start Tours, Lectures; 15 of His Followers Free on Bond," *Decatur Herald* (Aug. 8, 1961), p. 1.

"Harrell Trial Starts," *Decatur Daily Review* (Mar. 20, 1961), p. 17.

"Harrell Tries to Raise Bonds for Followers," *Pantagraph* (Bloomington, IN) (Aug. 7, 1961), p. 18.

"Harrell, Two Followers Absent as Trial Starts in Clay County Court," *Decatur Herald* (Mar. 21, 1961), p. 1.

"Harrell Wins Court Test Against FTC," *Daily Register* (Harrisburg, IL) (May 16, 1962), p. 10.

"Harrell Won't Talk," *Decatur Daily Review* (Dec. 3, 1962), p. 1.

"Harrell Writes from 'Prison,'" *Decatur Herald* (Oct. 15, 1963), p. 1.

"Harrell's Band Splits," *Southern Illinoisan* (Mar. 27, 1961), p. 14.

"Harrell's Family Back on Estate," *Journal Gazette* (Mattoon, IL) (Feb. 6, 1965), p. 3.

"Harrell's Followers To Start Trek," unknown newspaper, unknown date [c. April 1963], unknown page number.

"Harrell's Hearing Put Off For a Week," *Hays Daily News* (Hays, KS) (Aug. 1, 1961), p. 2.

"Harrell's Hold Weakens," *Decatur Daily Review* (Mar. 27, 1961), p. 3.

"Harrell's Kids Out of School," *Mt. Vernon Register-News* (Mar. 3, 1961), p. 1.

"Harrell's Motel to be Sold for Bank Claim," *Decatur Daily Review* (July 27, 1961), p. 67.

"Harrell's Mother Give 500 Acres to Son's Church," *Decatur Herald* (May 9, 1962), p. 12.

"Harrell's Tax Records are Being Checked," *Decatur Daily Herald* (June 4, 1961), p. 7.

Harrell, T., interviews with author, 2015-2021.

Harrell, X., interview with author, Sept. 2021.

"Hecklers Absent at Anti-Red Rally," *Decatur Herald* (Feb. 22, 1961), p. 1.

Helms, J., letter to John Harrell, Aug. 20, 1976.

Hodges, C., "The Cult Leader Who Defied the FBI," *True Police Cases* (April 1965), p. 88.

Hoogesteger, J., "Ready, waiting," *News-Leader* (Springfield, MO) (Aug. 31, 1986), p. 1A.

Hutton, P., interview with author, July 2015.

"Identity Churches: A Theology of Hate." (New York: Anti-Defamation League of B'nai B'rith, 1983).

"Illinois Estate Crashed by Authorities to Arrest AWOL Marine, Sect Members," *Terre Haute Star* (Aug. 5, 1961), p. 1.

"'Invade' Estate to Nab Marine," *Times Record* (Troy, NY) (Aug. 4, 1961), p. 1.

"John Harrell Aids at Birth," *Decatur Daily Review* (Dec. 24, 1962), p. 2.

"John Harrell Complains of Vandalism," *Journal Gazette* (Mattoon, IL) (May 11, 1962), p. 6.

"John Harrell, followers worried about survival," *Journal Gazette* (Mattoon, IL) (July 1, 1980), p. 3.

"John Harrell: Is He in Southwest Missouri Area?," *Edwardsville Intelligencer* (June 18, 1963), p. 2.

"John Harrell Missing; Car Found Abandoned South of Springfield," *Decatur Daily Review* (April 6, 1963), p. 1.

"John Harrell Posts Bond for 2 in Income Tax Cases," *St. Louis Post-Dispatch* (Jan. 9, 1962), p. 3.

"John Harrell's Plan Private School of 'Basic Subjects,'" *Journal Gazette* (Mattoon, IL) (Mar. 6, 1961), p. 1.

"John R. Harrell Gets 10 Year Prison Term," *Decatur Herald* (Nov. 5, 1964), p. 1.

"John R. Harrell Seeks U.S. Post," *Belvidere Daily Republican* (Oct. 13, 1959), p. 8.

"'Johnny Bob' Getting Set For Red Blast, Invasion," *Herald* (Jasper, IN) (Nov. 16, 1961), p. 19.

"Johnny Bob Harrell's Mother, Natalia, dies," *Herald and Review* (April 2, 1988), p. 5.

"John Robert Harrell" (obituary) *Clay Country Republican* (June 23, 2021).

"Judge Says Harrell Should Get Hearing," *Decatur Herald* (Jan. 12, 1967), p. 37.

"Jury Finds 11 Harrell Members Guilty," *Jacksonville Daily Journal* (Jacksonville, IL) (Nov. 11, 1963), p. 4.

"Jury Selected in Trial of Harrell's Followers," *Southern Illinoisan* (Nov. 13, 1963), p. 1.

"Jury Selected to Hear Harrell Case," *Mt. Vernon Register-News* (Mar. 21, 1961), p. 1.

Kellums, L., interview with author, Sept. 2015.

"Kinmundy Methodist Men Hear John R. Harrell," *Kinmundy Express* (Mar. 19, 1953), p. 6.

Kolb, D., "'Survival show,'" *Citizen-Patriot* (Jackson, MI) (Jan. 26, 1981), p. A-1.

Kramme, R. "John Robert Harrell: A Case Study of a Christian Anti-Communist, 1959-1964." Illinois State University, 1970, p. 2+.

"Land Sold for Taxes," *Decatur Daily Review* (Nov. 14, 1963), p. 36.

"Large Gold Purchases By Missing Harrell Reported," *Decatur Herald* (April 18, 1963), p. 1.

"Last of Harrell's Flock Leaving Illinois," *Mt. Vernon Register-News* (April 26, 1963), p. 3.

"Lawyer Says Harrell Writes He's Captive," *Decatur Herald* (Oct. 14, 1963), p. 1.

"Link Cross Burnings to Communists," *Journal Gazette* (Mattoon, IL) (Feb. 22, 1961), p. 3.

Leib, H., interview with author, Aug. 2015.

"Louisville Citizens Except Results," *Clay Country Republican* (Dec. 12, 1963), unknown page number.

"Louisville Folks Feel Harrell About to Return," *Decatur Daily Review* (Mar. 29, 1964), p. 10.

"Louisville Man Holds Religious Retreat at Home," *Decatur Herald* (Feb. 25, 1961), p. 1.

"Louisville Man Opens Private School...," *Decatur Herald* (Mar. 3, 1961), p. 1.

"Louisville's Harrell Defies FBI, Refuses To Surrender AWOL GI Seeking Sanctuary," *Edwardsville Intelligencer* (Aug. 2, 1961), p. 1.

Ludwick, J., "When US is invaded, they'll be ready," *Herald and Review* (July 2, 1980), p. 9.

"Man Opens His Own School to Fight Communism," *Palladium-Item* (Richmond, IN) (Mar. 7, 1961), p. 3.

"Marine Joins Harrell," *Decatur Daily Review* (Aug. 2, 1961), p. 19.

"Marine Says He Won't Surrender," unknown newspaper, unknown date [c. Aug. 1961], unknown page number.

"Marine's Hideaway is 'Shrine,'" *Sandusky Register* (Sandusky, OH) (Aug. 14, 1961), p. 3.

Mathes, B., "FBI Agent Relates Raid on Harrell," *Decatur Daily Review* (Nov. 14, 1963), p. 1; "Harrell Planned to Yield Deserter, Aide Declares," *Southern Illinoisan* (Nov. 19, 1963), p. 5; "Sobriety of Harrell's Raiders Questioned," *Decatur Daily Review* (Nov. 16, 1963), p. 2.

"Mausoleum Tycoon Teaching Survival," *Daily Herald* (Chicago, IL) (May 3, 1962), p. 21.

"Minutemen Offer $5,000 for Info on Harrell," *Dixon Evening Telegraph* (April 15, 1963), p. 5.

"Mob Attack Next, Cultist Predicts," *Morning News* (Wilmington, DE) (Aug. 7, 1961), p. 23.

Morrison, D., "In Illinois: Festival of the Fed-Up," *Time* (Nov. 5, 1979), unknown page number.

"Motion Filed To Dismiss Libel Suit," *Clay County Republican* (Mar. 10, 1960), unknown page number.

"New Dimension on Harrell Case," *Decatur Daily Review* (Dec. 12, 1963), p. 6.

"New Flag at Louisville," *Decatur Daily Review* (June 26, 1961), p. 6.

"Notice," *Mt. Vernon Register* (July 2, 1959), p. 5.

"Obituary: Betty Harrell," *Effingham Daily News* (July 22, 2014), unknown page number.

O'Dell, K., interview with author, June 2015.

"Offers $5,000 Reward If Harrell Is Away 7 Years," *Mt. Vernon Register-News* (April 23, 1963), p. 6.

"Parents Deny Clay Charges," *Decatur Herald* (Mar. 9, 1961), p. 1.

"Parolee Harrell Returns Home to Louisville," *Decatur Herald* (Aug. 31, 1968), p. 10.

Parsons, J., "Cult Leader Wages Battle for Freedom," *Decatur Herald* (Mar. 19, 1967), p. 14.

"Peace Prevails at Louisville Anti-Red Rally; Harrell Absent," *Decatur Herald* (Mar. 7, 1961), p. 1.

Pennington, W., "Pastor Recalls the Consternation in Louisville in 1960," unknown newspaper, unknown date, unknown page number.

"Physician Tells Clay Jury He Heads Harrell's Private School," *Decatur Herald* (Mar. 22, 1961), p. 1.

"Police Adopt Wait-See Stand on Harrell," *Decatur Herald* (June 17, 1963), p. 2.

"Police, FBI Storm Haven of Marine Deserter," *Pittsburgh Post* (Aug. 8, 1961), p 1.

"Police Storm Estate Seize Marine Deserter," *Los Angeles Times* (Aug. 5, 1961), p. 8.

Press, R., "They play war games in US countryside," *Christian Science Monitor* (Mar. 23, 1981), unknown page number.

"Prison is 'God's Will'?," *Decatur Daily Review* (Nov. 13, 1963), p. 1.

"Private School Illegal," *Southern Illinoisan* (Mar. 23, 1961), p. 18.

"Private School Opens on Harrell Estate," *Decatur Herald* (Sept. 2, 1961), p. 1.

"Prosecutor Ready to Sue Harrell Again," *Mt. Vernon Register-News* (Mar. 27, 1961), p. 2.

"Public Tours Estate of Sect Leader," *Laredo Times* (Laredo, TX) (Aug. 14, 1961), p. 5.

"Quote/Unquote," *Chillicothe Constitution-Tribune* (Chillicothe, MO) (Nov. 5, 1979), p. 4.

"Raid Nabs AWOL Marine," *Southern Illinoisan* (Aug. 4, 1961), p. 1.

"'Red Fighter' Hides from Law in 'Fort,'" *Lincoln Star* (Lincoln, NE) (Mar. 21, 1961), p. 13.

"Religious Retreat Leader Gives Up Clay County Fight," *Pantagraph* (Bloomington, IL) (April 12, 1962), p. 1.

"Reveals 2nd Letter from Missing Harrell," *Pantagraph* (Bloomington, Illinois) (Oct. 15, 1963), p. 10.

"Rich Anti-Red Crusader Defies FBI in Giving Haven to AWOL Marine," *Washington Post* (Aug. 3, 1961), p. A3.

Ricketts, R., "Fast Starts at Religious Retreat," *Decatur Herald* (Aug. 5, 1961), p. 1; "Marine Keeps Refuge with Harrell," *Decatur Herald* (Aug. 4, 1961), p. 1.

"Sailor Springs Man Quits Harrell 'Retreat'; Son to Enter Clay School," *Decatur Review* (Mar. 26, 1961), p. 26.

Saponar, R.C., "Survivalists to converge on Louisville next month," unknown newspaper, unknown date [c. 1982], unknown page number.

Schmidt, J.L., "Johnny Bob Harrell still recruits 'patriots,'" *Southern Illinoisan* (Nov. 13, 1979), p. 20.

"Search for Anti-Communist Harrell Centers on Locating Private Plane," *Edwardsville Intelligencer* (April 8, 1963), p. 1.

"Sect Leader to Open Home to Tourists," *Kingsport Times* (Kingsport, TN) (Aug. 8, 1961), p. 10.

"Sect Member Tells Jury of Fight with FBI," *Chicago Tribune* (Nov. 20, 1963), p. 32.

"Seize Religious Leader, Followers," *Carrol Daily Times* (Carroll, IA) (Aug. 4, 1961), p. 5.

"Self-Styled Anti-Red Sees Atom War, Russ Invasion," *Daily Telegram* (Eau Claire, WI) (Dec. 5, 1961), p. 26.

Sellers, J., "John Harrell Says He's Fighting the Lord's Battle for 'Deserter,'" unknown newspaper (Aug. 3, 1961), unknown page number.

"Sells Farina Theatre," *Kinmundy Express* (June 26, 1947), p. 1.

"Senate Candidate Charges Libel in $225,000 Suit," *Edwardsville Intelligencer* (Feb. 27, 1960), p. 2.

Seymour, P., "Harrell Out on Bail, Charges FBI Looted Home in Arresting Deserter," *Terre Haute Star* (Aug. 7, 1961), p. 6; "Harrell to Post Bond for Followers Today," *Decatur Herald* (Aug. 7, 1961), p. 1.

"Shelters Marine Deserter," *Oil City Derrick* (Oil City, PA) (Aug. 4, 1951), p. 1.

"Site is Donated for Party Caucus," *Spotlight* (April 23, 1984), p. 16.

"Six Fined on Truancy Charges at Louisville," *Decatur Herald* (Mar. 23, 1961), p. 1.

"Sixth Child Born to John R. Harrell at Louisville Estate," *Decatur Herald* (Aug. 5, 1962), p. 18.

Stacey, D., *Persecution USA: People & Place.* (Louisville, IL: Christian Conservative Church, 1962), p. 32+.

"Start Cutting Weeds--Harrell May Return," *Mt. Vernon Register-News* (Aug. 2, 1963), p. 1.

"Stay Home 'On Divine Direction,'" *Mt. Vernon Register-News* (May 20, 1961), p. 1.

Stewart, C., "FBI Suspects Threatening Letter Was Written By Harrell," *Southern Illinoisan* (Mar. 20, 1964), p. 9.

"Soviet Flag Ripped; Minister Arrested," *Des Moines Register* (Nov. 16, 1961), p. 13.

Sprayregen, J., "Extremist Centers in Illinois," *Chicago Tribune* (June 2, 1985), unknown page number.

"Survivalist tones down message," *Herald and Review* (Decatur, IL) (June 1, 1987), p. 46.

"Tax Hearing For Harrell," *Decatur Daily Review* (Feb. 9, 1963), p. 8.

"This Man, John Harrell," *Decatur Daily Review* (Mar. 24, 1961), p. 39.

"Three Children of Harrell's Followers Reported Missing," *Edwardsville Intelligencer* (Oct. 30, 1963), p. 1.

"To Appeal Convictions At Louisville," *Alton Evening Telegraph* (Mar. 28, 1961), p. 13.

Townsend, C., "Federal Death Row," (Jan. 1, 2017). (Online posting.)

"United Press Bureau at Marion Receives Lengthy Letter from Missing J.R. Harrell," *Daily Register* (Harrisburg, IL) (Oct. 14, 1963), p. 1.

"US Agents Seize Harrell's Property," *Southern Illinoisan* (Sept. 23, 1964), p. 21.

"Violence on the Right," *Newsweek* (Mar. 4, 1985), p. 23.

"Wealthy Communist Foe in 'Fortress' Estate," *Cincinnati Enquirer* (Mar. 21, 1961), p. 4.

Williams, J., interview with author, Nov. 2015.

"Will of Missing Harrell Found," *Decatur Herald* (May 1, 1963), p. 5.

Younkin, L., and J. Doussard, "Ozarks Stirred by Searchers for Missing J.R. Harrell," *Decatur Daily Review* (Aug. 4, 1963), p. 1.

"Zealot and 7 in Family Disappear," *Mt. Vernon Register-News* (April 8, 1963), p. 1.